NINO RICCI
Essays on His Works

ESSENTIAL WRITERS SERIES 43

**Canada Council   Conseil des Arts
for the Arts   du Canada**

**ONTARIO ARTS COUNCIL
CONSEIL DES ARTS DE L'ONTARIO**

an Ontario government agency
un organisme du gouvernement de l'Ontario

Canadä

Guernica Editions Inc. acknowledges the support of the Canada Council
for the Arts and the Ontario Arts Council. The Ontario Arts Council
is an agency of the Government of Ontario.

We acknowledge the financial support of the Government of Canada.
Nous reconnaissons l'appui financier du gouvernement du Canada.

NINO RICCI
Essays on His Works

Edited by
Marino Tuzi

**GUERNICA
EDITIONS**
TORONTO • BUFFALO • LANCASTER (U.K.)
2016

Marino Tuzi, editor
Michael Mirolla, general editor
Joseph Pivato, series editor
Cover and interior design: David Moratto
Front cover photo: Rafy
Guernica Editions Inc.
1569 Heritage Way, Oakville, (ON), Canada L6M 2Z7
2250 Military Road, Tonawanda, N.Y. 14150-6000 U.S.A.
www.guernicaeditions.com

Distributors:
University of Toronto Press Distribution,
5201 Dufferin Street, Toronto (ON), Canada M3H 5T8
Gazelle Book Services, White Cross Mills, High Town,
Lancaster LA1 4XS U.K.

First edition.
Printed in Canada.

Legal Deposit — First Quarter
Library of Congress Catalog Card Number: 2015952390
Library and Archives Canada Cataloguing in Publication
Nino Ricci : essays on his work / edited by Marino
Tuzi. -- First edition.

(Essential writers series ; 43)
Issued in print and electronic formats.
ISBN 978-1-55071-951-2 (paperback).--ISBN 978-1-55071-952-9
(epub).--ISBN 978-1-55071-953-6 (mobi)

1. Ricci, Nino, 1959- --Criticism and interpretation.
I. Tuzi, Marino, 1952-, editor II. Series: Writers series
(Toronto, Ont.) ; 43

PS8585.I126Z85 2016   C813'.54   C2015-906642-5   C2015-906643-3

Contents

Marino Tuzi

Foreword

THE FICTIONAL TEXTS examined in this book, *Nino Ricci: Essays on His Works*, are presented chronologically in terms of publication, starting with *Lives of the Saints* and the other two novels that comprise the *Lives of the Saints* trilogy (*In A Glass House* and *Where She Has Gone*). The novels in this trilogy are examined individually and then the trilogy itself is explored as a whole. Following the essays on the *Lives of the Saints* trilogy, there are individual essays devoted to each subsequent novel that Ricci has published to the present day, respectively *Testament*, *The Origin of Species*, and *Sleep*. This chronological organization of the study of the novels written by Ricci gives the reader a sense of continuity involving the range of ideas and narrative techniques that encompass his work as a writer of literary fiction.

The essays in this book analyze Ricci's novels from a variety of critical perspectives. These perspectives include concepts about literature, culture, identity, politics, and society in relation to Canada and the modern world. Each contributor examines a specific novel in its own terms or as a part of the trilogy, focusing on the prevailing themes and literary elements used by Ricci to construct his work of fiction. This analytical study allows the reader to enhance one's understanding of Ricci's particular style and vision as a writer. It also provides an understanding of his contribution to contemporary Canadian fiction and world literature.

Marino Tuzi

Disjunction, Paradox, and the Deromanticization of the Old World in *Lives of the Saints*

AS HE TELLS the story of his childhood in Italy, Vittorio Innocente evokes a world in which actions and events transmit multiple and opposed meanings. Speaking of his Aunt Marta, Innocente observes that "her comments [were] like riddles or oracles that refused to give up their meaning, that slipped away as soon as you tried to grab hold of them."[1] Nino Ricci's *Lives of the Saints*, underlines the precariousness of a tradition-based peasant culture in Valle de Sole. The author develops an "Italianness" — as a set of identifiable cultural qualities — which is not unitary and is constantly being reshaped by an evolving social environment.

Innocente's various interpretations of the peasantry suggest a complex and unclosed reading of the old world. The villagers are represented as the descendants of a glorious pre-Christian civilization, as vital, fanciful, and indomitable, as technologically backward, stultifying, and narrow-minded, as the victims of regional politics, and as part of a community on the brink of radical change. The ambiguity is further supported by the narrator's own inconsistent personal attitudes, which are constantly filtered through the consciousness of his younger self. These attitudes are often characterized by such emotional responses as sentimentality, bitterness, empathy, disillusionment, yearning, and detachment.

Francesco Loriggio states that to "reorganize the spatiotemporal coordinates [of the past] and bring into play the notion of belonging to and being away from" is "to originate [a] discourse"[2] about the multi-centred nature of ethnic identity. Such a discourse proclaims itself in "tensional strategies"[3] which invoke the problematic of a diffused and evolving ethnic identity. In minority texts, the "tensional totality" of ethnicity "call[s] for paradigms that assert both stability and instability."[4]

Innocente's troubled retrospective, focusing on a brief period of his life (a seven-year-old boy in an isolated mountain village along the Apennines), resonates with ambivalence and irony. The discontinuities of agrarianism and immigration underpin the destabilizing of the narrator-character's self-image. Irony is at the core of the text's exploration of ethnicity, encompassing many formal strategies. Irony is embedded in the narrative voice that continually oscillates between the "Remembering I" of the adult narrator and the "Remembered I" of the boyhood self. As Ricci himself has admitted: "There is a sense of distance and irony that comes precisely from the distance between the narrator and the child."[5] This textual ambiguity is built into the narrative structure of the novel. The "Remembering I" and the "Remembered I" manifest the multiple self of the narrator-character. The Italian-Canadian self simultaneously reconstructs and deconstructs the story of the Italian other.

The presence of long sentences serves numerous functions. Protracted sentences evoke the overflow of memories and nostalgia for a time and place that appear to be irrecoverable. They initiate an onslaught of details that reveal the multiple gradations of experience. Long sentences provide numerous motivations for a particular action, and examine the contradictory responses of young Vittorio (a.k.a. Vitto) to a specific individual or event.

The use of juxtaposition both advances conflicting images of the native country, and sets images of the old against those of the new. Juxtaposition ruptures the text's realism: the ordinary meets the fantastic, enabling the textures of society to hover between oncoming modernity and lingering medievalism. The text relies on sociohistorical description to present a specific ethno-cultural context and expose the disjunctions of agrarianism. The narrator makes reference to folklore and local myths, and uses hagiography as an ironic commentary on the lives of the characters. In moving between various modes of representation, the text problematizes the narrator-character's position and underscores the relativity of competing cultural models. The textual fabric of the novel reveals the social construction of Innocente's identity by pinpointing the multifarious and often contradictory elements that compose it. According to Nino Ricci: "I wanted to play with the construction of morality — of acceptable behaviour. And the values that go beyond those moral systems that society has constructed."[6]

Lives of the Saints covers a nine-month period, from July 1960 to March 1961, and takes place during a period of significant social and economic change in post-war Italy. The eventual push towards greater industrialization and urbanization mirrors the general trends that began in Canada as well as in the rest of the industrial world. The pressures of modernity and the declining rural economy form an important part of the narrative's background and are apparent in the villagers' constant emigration. The recurrent picture of ruin and desolation, expressed through images of old, dilapidated and deserted homes and of an over-cultivated and shrinking land base, reflects southern Italy's socioeconomic crisis. The mother's [Cristina] revolt against the patriarchal-matrifocal arrangements of Valle del Sole and Vitto's accompanying dislocation are also dramatic reenactments of the clash between agrarianism and modernity.

The novel is typified by some of the distinguishing features of Italian-Canadian writing; historical references and Italian words are interwoven with pre-Christian and Catholic mythology. These various non-fictional, "extraliterary"[7] modes play a critical part in the social reconstruction of the old world and have been revised to suit the text's ironic depiction of the narrator's childhood in Valle del Sole.

In *Lives of the Saints*, Italian identity is primarily a metaphorical and symbolic construct and only at its most basic level is it a product of historical forces. For Ricci, the rendering of peasant life and the process of immigration entails the reworking of mythological structures: "The fact that there is a mythology attached to the experience of immigration ... connects itself to the whole history of Western mythology ... That ... is very much operative in the immigrant mind ... I wanted to tie into that larger mythology."[8]

The text represents Vittorio Innocente's ambivalence in the way his consciousness simultaneously fuses with and diverges from the perspective of his younger self. Vittorio demonstrates the link to his Italianness by interpreting for the reader the meaning of what he felt and experienced as a boy in Valle del Sole. What supports this connection is a sympathetic portrayal of his mother and the arresting tableaux of the hilly landscape. The narrator is dissociated from his other self, openly debating young Vitto's words or actions: "'It tastes like shit,' I said. I had got it out now, spit out, my resentment like something that had stuck in my throat. But an instant later my face was burning: my mother slapped me, hard, against the cheek" (71). Vittorio's sophistication is opposed to his younger self's naiveté. The narration underlines this detachment from the native culture. When Vitto is awakened "by a muffled shout" which "sounded like a man's" voice (10), the implication is that, unbeknownst to him, Cristina and her male companion are making love in the barn. The text exploits this irony later as Vitto, obsessed with the idea that Cristina's woes are the result of the evil eye incarnated in the poisonous snake, ritualistically burns a dead chicken to lift the curse placed on her. The use of irony exposes Cristina's contradictory position, for she appears to be hemmed in by the village patriarchy and responsible for abdicating her maternal duties. This double movement strengthens the villagers' opprobrium. The play between the omniscient voice of the narrator and the limited consciousness of his younger self leads to an ironic view of this parochial world.

The narrator's distance from his Italian heritage is shown in the portrayal of the severe socioeconomic conditions of the Apennine region in south-central Italy. The allusions to a golden age of economic, social and cultural achievement, evident in the references to the Samnite civilization, only serve to highlight the bleakness of the present. Such deprivation has instilled in the peasantry a sense of fatalism and forced large numbers to emigrate elsewhere, resulting in the dramatic depopulation of local villages. In deromanticizing peasant culture,

Innocente tacitly reassesses his relationship to his Italian origins, imprinting his contradictory attitude towards Valle del Sole onto the story of his younger self. Villa del Sole's natural beauty — "the world seemed encased in glass, trees and rocks and circling sparrows cut against a background of sky and slope like essences of themselves" (32) — often is overtaken by an undertone of malevolence, as in his depiction of Cristina: "my mother's quiet sobbing mingling with the sigh of the wind like something inhuman, as if the air could no longer carry any human sounds, all of them smothered into the earth by the silence" (77).

Flooded with intense images of the past, the narrator presents his story in long, elaborate sentences. He piles up physical details, as is exemplified in the opening description of Valle del Sole, and he itemizes the subtleties of a particular action: for example, Vitto's fight with Vincenzo Maiale. He also describes states of mind: as in the scene of Vitto's delirium, found near the end of the novel. Images of peasant life crowd the mind, but they quickly evaporate at the moment of apprehension: "the world, for all its seeming stability, was actually spinning around at a tremendous speed" (76).

The complexities of lived experience and the tentativeness of the social order prevent the narrator from having a unified and solid picture of the past. Vittorio cannot sort out from a surfeit of information what is important and what is incidental. The sensory and intellectual overload underlines the various and conflicting perspectives of the narrator and those of the other characters. Often a specific event elicits differing responses, such as the light and sound show during the village festival that produces shock, pleasure, and indignation. The presence of others also induces contradictory and fluctuating perceptions. Vitto sees his teacher as friend, tormentor, victim, and stranger. The presentation of competing impulses, of a multiplicity of reasons for particular actions, and of a variety of responses to a given situation implies the absence of a singular purpose.

The constant barrage of information disorients the reader and makes the familiar appear to be alien and inaccessible, and, as such, magnifies the text's depiction of the discontinuities that characterize both Vitto's personal life and his relation to external reality.

The recurrence of lengthy sentences transmits the image of a self-conscious narrator-character who examines in painstaking detail the factors that constituted a specific experience. For example, Vittorio Innocente reconstructs in several winding sentences an incident in which his father throws an object at his mother. Searching for a motivation behind this violent act, he describes from the point of view of his younger self his father's physical characteristics, the location and particular social context of the event, and his mother's physical and emotional response to the attack. After he vividly recreates this memory of his father, he immediately questions its veracity: "The memory was so dim and insubstantial that I could not say if it had actually happened" (37). The "tiny scar" (37) that he observes on his mother's cheek provides the proof that he needs to verify his memory. Similarly, the narrator thickens his descriptions of the physical and natural environment of Vale del Sole and of the appearance and behaviour of its inhabitants. These vivid passages, which are composed of extended sentences, are at odds with Vitto's revelation that he lives in a world in which people and things are at times indecipherable: "some secret village seemed to be lurking there in the darkness, one that could not be seen in

the light of day" (113). This form of observation and ostensible analysis raises more questions than it answers,
also constantly fails to arrive at a final meaning. The
formal trait in the novel shows a lack of certainty in the
way one distinguishes the concrete from the imagined,
and tends to subvert the depiction of reality. All of this
underscores the provisional subjectivity of the narrator-
character.

The abundance of details forges a heightened picture of the past in which the old world is shrouded in
mythic qualities. We are given a vivid description of the
disparity and harshness of agrarian life: "why the lot of
the *contadini* now was such a hard one, their plots of
land scattered piecemeal across the countryside, often
miles from the village; why the soil offered up yearly only
the same closed fist, though the farmers cursed and ca-
joled it in the way they did a stubborn mule" (52). Against
this tableau, the narrator juxtaposes allusions to re-
splendent, fecund, and legendary time: "Once, my grandfather had told me, long before the time of Christ, the
land around Valle del Sole had all been flat, unpeopled
jungle, rich and fertile, the trees a mile high and the
river a mile wide" (52). In this background is set the splen-
dour of an ancient and indigenous civilization: "The Samnites, a fierce mountain people, had been first to settle
the region ... Their imposing cities ... carved it was said
right out of the bare rock of the mountains, had been
leveled by Romans, only a few odd ruins remaining
now — roadside markers of forgotten import, the mossy
foundations of a temple or shrine, the curved stone seats
of an amphitheatre" (59-60).

Whether in decline or in a state of prosperity, the old
world of myth and history is presented as a consistent
force in the novel; yet it is continually steeped in ambigu-

ity. The stirring power of memory delivers a world awash in nostalgia. This acute rendering of the past injects historical events with an aura of the fantastic or the unreal, and makes the customs and behaviour of the villagers extraordinary, not part of conventional society.

Storytelling is itself a way out of such instability since, from the tumultuous vortex of past events, it locates the critical moment which sets into motion an inexorable movement towards tragedy. The recovery of a particular instant — "that beginning occurred on a hot July day in the year 1960, in the village of Valle del Sole, when my mother was bitten by a snake" (7) — echoes the fall from Eden, but does not arrest time and revive one's innocence. Instead, it makes plain one's deep and inexpressible disillusionment with the original culture. Sifting through the detritus of lost innocence, the narrator-character tries to recompose his peasant heritage. His yearning for a coherent self finds its expression in young Vitto's vision of Santa Cristina's spiritual ascension: "At last [the archangel] reached out his hand to her and he led up into the heavens, while on the earth a great storm was finally unleashed, and the Roman ship and all aboard it were swallowed into the sea" (136).

The text's invocation of hagiography signifies Vitto's desire to relieve Cristina's suffering and to reassume a tranquil and pure state of being. It is highly ironic since it foreshadows the mother's death at sea, which is a tragic inversion of the myth of Santa Cristina. The structural irony entrenches the text's assertion that what has been lost cannot ever fully be recuperated. This view is connected to the narrator's mourning for a time before family problems destroyed his idyllic childhood. Elegy, however, is undermined by an awareness on the narrator's part that the peasantry has always been disunified and disenfranchised because of a hierarchical social structure and debilitating socioeconomic conditions.

Juxtaposition constructs a picture of the old world in which abundance is contrasted to deprivation. Idyllic images of Valle del Sole emanate from several sources: references to the natural environment and festive occasions, as well as allusions to hagiography, folk tales, and local mythology. The surrounding landscape frequently is adorned with sunlight, inferring a kind of spiritual ascendancy: "[T]he sun was shining and the whole world seemed wrapped in a warm, yellow dream ... The sun was rising over Colle di Papa, round and scarlet, sucking in dawn's darkness like God's forgiveness" (9, 58). Land is represented as being fertile and bountiful: "The wheat in our region ripened in a slow wave which started in the valleys and gradually worked its way up the slopes through summer ... the greening of the slopes in the spring" (58, 88). Nature's powerful presence is endowed with a luminous quality: "[the wheat was] like sunlight emerging behind a cloud" (58).

The use of light imagery is evident in the description of the Feast of the Madonna, especially in the reference made to the stage show in which the ordinary fuses with the spiritual: "It seemed as if we had been transported into one of la maestra's stories of the saints, the world suddenly filled with light, and all possibilities open again" (99). Light recurs in the allusions made to the purity of the saints: "A golden halo hovered above [San Francesco's] head ... Santa Cristina ... dressed in flowing white ... a soft shaft of light trained on [her]" (133, 136). Images of fecundity are pervasive in the genesis myth: the villagers grow out of a giant's body parts: "In the spring, a strange thing happened — the fingers on Gambelunghe's severed hands began to grow, those on the left growing into five women, those on the right to five men ... one couple for each field" (53).

Countervailing images, however, contest such lyricism and sentimentality. The fertility of the natural environment is undermined by allusions to its meager resources and the arduousness of agrarian life. Light imagery is continually offset by images of darkness. Ubiquitous rainstorms and immovable clouds blot out the sun. An impenetrable shadowy world is often associated with the depths of night. Images of growth are embodied by Cristina who "stood out like a flower in a bleak landscape" (31) and Aunt Marta, "in whom knowledge seemed to be ... burgeoning ... like a plant in rocky soil" (130). In contrast, we are given static and concrete images, in which the villagers are indistinguishable from the mountainscape: "[they] stood still like stone, seemed to have merged with the rock of the houses and pavement, become finally themselves simply crags and swells in the hard mountain face of the village" (184). Social decay and dire poverty abound: the deserted Giardini estate in Rocca Secca, once emblematic of prosperity and cultural sophistication, is as much a ruin as the ramshackle, crumbling houses in Valle del Sole.

Although the Feast of La Madonna provides temporary respite from daily hardship, it cannot ultimately lift the villagers out of their despair. Their celebrations reveal "a kind of joyless intensity that bordered on violence" (102). Such emotional deprivation substantiates earlier descriptions of callous and belligerent village women and school children who cruelly chastise Cristina and Vitto for Cristina's infidelity and illicit pregnancy. The allusions to tortured saints, the ever-present evil eye, and the decapitated chicken dramatize the bleakness and severity of parochialism: "the ... air of desolation [of] the village square" (144). In contrast to Cristina's nudity in the cave, invoking a kind of purity, Vitto's erotic and disturbing vision of la maestra's heavy-set body inspires mixed feelings of "excitement and horror" (42). This fantasy is a product of a confused state of mind. The ambivalent image of the teacher mirrors the ambiguity of the cave scene, which not only marks Vitto's idealization of Cristina, but also implies his sexual attraction towards her. There is an almost incestuous quality to both scenes. These two instances allude to the repressiveness of peasant society, in which sexual desire is perceived as sinful.

The retelling of the creation myth focuses on the inbred malevolence of the villagers whose antediluvian ancestors are presented as being avaricious, jealous, and deserving of God's pitiless retribution. We are told that "He caused mountains and rocks to grow out of the ground, and made the soil tired and weak" (53).

The ambivalence of the old world is recapitulated through Cristina's contradictory position. She signifies the nurturing side of the feminine principle in both the Great Goddess mythology and Catholicism. The caves of Valle del Sole, where she bathes in the hot spring and meets her lover, provide a womb-like environment in which she enacts her fertility rite and releases her sexual energy. This erotic image of Cristina is contrasted to descriptions of the flaccid, distorted and unattractive bodies of the village women. Cristina's creativity is also shown as she works in the garden and becomes part of its lush growth. The snake symbolizes the locus of her powers, for it not only moves through the ripening garden, but the snake is present when she makes love in the stable. Vitto's mother is delineated as having a snake-like appearance: "[she is] ... standing above me for a moment utterly naked, smooth and slick as she had just peeled back an old layer of skin" (33). The snake stands as an icon of fertility and sexuality.

Cristina's life-giving attributes also resemble those of the Madonna, who appears to be an imperious goddess figure, "seated atop her litter like an ancient queen" (82-83). She is associated with fecundity when she receives such offerings as "fruits and eggs" or "garlands" (84). The Madonna's connection to spring, Easter, rebirth and resurrection underlines a Catholic view of womanhood. The Virgin Mary is an embodiment of both ancient and Christian feminine values. In *Lives of the Saints*, Cristina is closely linked to the Madonna. Yet, the use of Catholic and pagan mythology intones Cristina's dark side. This is conveyed in the scene of the Madonna being removed from the church and taken to the chapel cemetery in wintertime, as well as in the allusions to the snake's stealthy movements and venomous bite. The snake is given Christian meaning; the snake meanders through the garden and descends into the ravine, where the lower elevation, duskiness and wild growth are opposed to the serenity, orderliness, and copiousness of the garden. This juxtaposition of conflicting images of Eden and the fallen world is present in Vitto's mind. This is why Cristina appears both as a nurturing and protective figure and as a reckless, self-absorbed, and neglectful parent.

The binary of negative and positive femininity is countered by Cristina's victimization. The prohibition against sexual freedom is mirrored in the fact that Cristina almost dies from the snake's bite. The cave imagery highlights Cristina's imprisonment. In sharp contrast to the caves, which allowed Cristina to revel in her physicality, her family home is a stony cage. It is at home where she leads a silent and shadowy existence. Her cabin in the bowels of the ship is claustrophobic. Again "home" is the place of birth, physical suffering, and eventual death. Unlike the water imagery symbolizing fertility and life, the sea is the site of her burial.

Often Cristina is part of the narrator-character's sexual objectification of women. The scene in the cave foregrounds Cristina's sensuality and sexuality, and intimates Vitto's sexual urges towards his mother. The sight of Cristina's sinuous body leads to a graphic detailing of Vitto's erotic fantasy of his teacher. Vitto's awareness of Cristina's sexuality is stressed by references to his mother's breasts, hidden under her dress but which constantly hover over him. Vitto is jealous of the attention other men give his mother: Vitto refuses to eat his meal at the restaurant after his mother has had an intimate conversation with Luciano.

Ricci's uncertain depiction of Valle del Sole grows directly from Cristina. Here is a peasant woman who has modern ideas about a woman's role, but who is imprisoned in a peasant community that promotes social conformity. Cristina's striving for independence is contrasted to patriarchal coercion: her father's autocracy and her husband's violence towards her. The latter's abusiveness is a repetition of his own father's mistreatment of his wife. Patriarchy is legitimized by the other women's support of male authority. The women attempt to force Cristina to confess her transgressions before the village congregation. This ideological-gender conflict is depicted through a set of opposing images. While Cristina's pregnancy instills in her a sense of mission, expressed by her defiant demeanour, her father undergoes a process of slow disintegration: "[his] face had grown pale and gaunt ... loose skin draped over sharp, thin bones" (174).

Cristina's vitality is transmitted by scenes that highlight the attractiveness of her sleek, smooth body and upright posture. She stands out in the village where women lead a deadened existence. The deformed bodies of the other village women are marked by "ruddy, swollen hands ... round bellies ... slow elephantine gait" (48-49). The portrait of Cristina opposes the stereotypical depiction of the other peasant women. Her childhood friends accept stoically patriarchy: "both had married local farmers and borne several children, had long ago completed the rite of passage from the small freedoms of adolescence to the daily toils of peasant motherhood" (49).

The registering of ideological-gender conflict is problematized by an implied set of ironies. Cristina's father has cooperated with the powers that be, the Fascist regime and the post-war governments, in order to defend his fellow villagers and maintain his socio-political status. He is himself overtaken by circumstances which appear to be beyond his control. The impoverishment of Valle del Sole and the pressures of modernization have compelled a sizable segment of the village population to emigrate abroad. The community is not stable or unified. Rather, it is one that is assailed by a series of internal and external difficulties. When Cristina's extra-marital affair besmirches her father's reputation and forces him to resign as mayor, the villagers not only abandon him but gloat over his misfortune. As Cristina and her son prepare to leave the village, he voices his profound disillusionment at the old world: "this country ... [i]s a place of Judases and cowards" (175). The grandfather personifies the problem of peasant life: its maltreatment of women, class antagonisms, and economic deprivations. He is destroyed by modernity, embodied in the form of his daughter, which he has tried to forestall and which has inspired his son-in-law to emigrate to Canada in search of economic betterment for himself and his family. Yet, the old man is as much a victim as he is a victimizer: "he had always seemed a man who loomed large, who commanded respect; but now suddenly he seemed shrunken and small, as if some aura around him had faded or died" (74).

While the village women denounce Cristina's infidelity because it threatens the fabric of traditional family life and reminds them of their own failure in throwing off the fetters of patriarchy, they feel exploited by the village's patriarchal structure. Cristina's attitude towards other women hurt by patriarchy seems to be inconsistent. Not only is Cristina indifferent to their plight, she also is repelled by their acceptance and promotion of traditional womanhood. At one point in the novel, she expresses her sympathy for the Captain's wife, whose husband has taken on a mistress. Nevertheless, as the text implies, the Captain's wife's social and economic state is markedly less restrictive than that of the village women. Cristina's relatively privileged position as the daughter of a village patriarch, which is also the focus of the peasant women's resentment, has allowed her more freedom and to some extent has facilitated her subversion of patriarchy. In her inability to transcend her own self-interest and objectively acknowledge the misery of the village women, Cristina remains tied to patriarchy. The account of Cristina's contradictory behaviour, which is part of a story about intergenerational and communal strife, indicates the narrator's [Vittorio Innocente] ambivalence towards his ethnic origins.

In emphasizing the difference between the peasants' and young Vitto's perception of Valle del Sole, the text further develops the conflicting character of the old country. In the villagers' world view, the everyday world co-exists with the supernatural: "goats were common animals and yet the locus of strange spirits ... la strega of Belmonte was both a decrepit old woman and a witch, a sorceress" (162). The severity of a parochial, agrarian life has bred a sense of fatalism among the peasants. They believe that "beneath every simple event there lurked some dark scandal" (21). Fatalism infuses all aspects of experience with a deep meaning. As Luciano tells Cristina, "peasants like that everything is a sign" (66-67).

Several sections in the novel exemplify this particular interpretation of reality. We are given an explanation of the reasons for the villagers' indigence, which reads like a morality play organized around the theme of invidia. In reconstructing this tale of woe, the narrator interweaves realism with mythology. He begins the tale with an overview of the villagers' current privation and then shifts into mythological time. The narrator presents both a pre-Christian genesis and a Christian vision of retribution, in which God punishes the villagers for their jealousy and greed. The mixing together of the two modes of representation recurs later in the narrative. There, a historical synopsis of the progressive subdivision and over-cultivation of the village's land merges with an invocation of the supernatural, of the evil eye. We are told of attempts to ward off the evil eye's harmful effects: Dagnello sprinkles his fields with a potion from "la strega di Belmonte" (54) and the villagers avoid Fiorina Girasole's doorway after the death of her twin baby boys. The narrator concludes with a ruined town, named Belmonte, devastated by war and which now is filled "with moss and weeds and wildflowers and overrun with lizards" (55). The town's sole inhabitant is la strega, "an ancient woman with tough, darkened skin and long grey hair" (55). This passage alludes to the savage militarism of modernity: "Belmonte … had been destroyed by the Germans in the second war, and out of superstition the residents refused to rebuild there" (54). The peasants' belief that the present is merely a repetition of the failures of a mythical past indicates the harshness of their living conditions.

The disparity of peasant life is perfectly embodied in the villagers' duplicitous perception of snakes. Snakes represent fertility — "to improve their harvest, they would buy a powder made of ground snake skins" (11) — good fortune and, at the same time, ill will since they are "agents of the evil eye" (11). Snakes commonly associated with pride: "where pride is the snake goes" (11). In Catholic hagiography, monstrous "venomous" (135) serpents engage in deadly combat with saints. The defeat of the forces of good emblematizes the peasants' inability to overcome adversity. The villagers invest every action or event with prophetic meaning: "people saw now an oracle, the prediction of their town's declining fortunes" (61). Cristina's snakebite symbolizes her threat to the equilibrium of the village. The downfall of the Giardini estate signifies a kind of collective degeneration.

Immersed in a primitive ethos, the *contadini* believe the world is governed by a malevolence, in the form of the evil eye, which "stood outside the normal categories of good and evil, subsumed them, striking both the righteous and the depraved" (54). Peasant culture is contradictory since the prescribed Christian order is at odds with ancient ways of seeing the world: "[t]he eye was the locus of all the powers which could not be explained under the usual religion, the religion of the churches" (54). According to Ricci: "The everyday world [of the peasant] verged on the miraculous and on [the] underworld of spirituality which the religion itself didn't give people directly. It imposed laws and codes of behaviour but tended not to incorporate this more magical, imaginative level which had been a way of organizing the world before Christianity was imposed."[9]

Through Vitto's unstable perspective, the text repeats and contests the peasants' world view. The narrator shows that his younger self is at once part of and distanced from his cultural environment. Vitto endows his mother with mythic qualities, apparent in her snake-like form while she is in the cave and in the link made between her "indifference to pain" (17) and the invincibility of Santa Cristina, who "emerged from [a large tub of boiling water] as if she had merely taken a warm bath" (135). The merging of the real with the mythic echoes the priest's depiction of Mary as both a saintly figure and a peasant woman: "the wife of a simple labourer, such ... as you might see walking down the streets of the village" (81). In describing his elderly aunt Marta, Vitto not only notes her agelessness but also refers to the villagers' belief that she is at once "simple and yet possessed of mystical powers, a witch" (47).

The joining of polarities attains its apotheosis in a brightly lit stage show in which modern technology is used to facilitate a religious ritual during the village festa. Vitto sees the workaday world as a façade. This is hinted at in the references made to Di Lucci's mask-like face and the "surface smiles" (62) of the Rocca Seccans. Underneath such posturing is a sinister and inscrutable reality, proffered in images of "some secret village [which] seemed to be lurking in the darkness" (113), and of its inhabitants, "the crowd [which was] suddenly disembodied ... voices around us only so many ghosts" (103), as well as in Cristina herself, who is shrouded in "a shadowy silence" (74). Yet, the nether side of experience is often as ephemeral as the textures of daily life.

Vittorio Innocente's narrative of his youth exposes the fissures in peasant culture. The primary signifier of this disunity is Cristina's revolt against the village patriarchy. Such incoherence is epitomized by Vitto's splintered perception of la maestra: "[she] seemed a stranger to me, as if she had split before my eyes into two separate people: one who had babies that died, the other who appeared as if from nowhere every morning in our classroom, and who faded into some shadowy limbo when school was over" (172). Details of everyday life are situated next to a bodiless world, usually called forth through ghostly figures who loom menacingly from out of thick shadows. These images in turn are supported by a veil that prevents contact between the inner and outer realms of experience. Accompanying this imagery are recurrent references to depredation: deteriorating ancient monuments and structures, and an unremittingly barren landscape.

The tentativeness of the protagonist's perceptions is conjoined to the evanescence of daily life. Often the external world either is imbued with a hallucinatory quality—"a stole of white shimmering so richly around his neck and down the front of his vestments it seemed on the verge of bursting into colour" (79)—or defamiliarized: "the world had abruptly changed into its opposite, been completely overturned" (121).

The defamiliarization of external reality is strengthened by the superimposition of exotic or fantastic images onto descriptions of ruin and decay, evident in the eerie and exaggerated representation of the Giardini estate. This disorientation is induced by the use of jarring analogies, such as Cristina's father's withdrawal from village life: "Over [his] face a film had formed, tangible as stone, which he retreated behind like a snail into its shell" (57). There is an instability to existence which makes any form of human endeavour appear superficial and inconsequential: "you had only to turn your back and the glitter would fade" (62). Reality can be apprehended only as flux, as impermanence: "the market in Rocca Secca seemed real, at least honest in its transience" (62). The ephemerality of the market place stands as a metaphor for the construction of social reality: "[the market] had been carted in ... and by afternoon it would be faded and finished ... the stalls boarded up until the following day" (62). This view is revisited later in the novel when Vitto becomes startled by the incongruity between technology and medievalism: "the ... equipment ... looked strange and unreal, like something that had no connection to the square or the people gathered there, that might have descended suddenly from the sky to impose itself among us" (93). In juxtaposing images of modernization to those of pre-industrial society, the text suggests the constant reframing of reality. The act of electrical wizardry temporarily transforms Villa del Sole's stony and ancient square "into a pocket of rich modernity" (99).

The slipperiness of Vitto's apprehension of reality — experience is fleeting and rarefied — communicates the inconstancies of peasant culture and, thus, the impossibility of reconstituting an essential Italianness. The intangibility of human action is recapitulated in the villagers' subjective interpretation of Cristina's social defiance: "It was as if my mother had simply written a character in the air, a cipher, and those who looked on it were happy enough to give it the meaning that suited them" (142). As Innocente reinhabits his other self, his mind fills with contorted images of peasant life: "the world

looked oddly warped and unstable, like something seen
through a piece of curved glass ... all the events of the
afternoon beginning to distort and skew like objects in
a curved mirror" (47, 127). These glass and mirror images
not only express Vitto's confusion and displacement but
also, and more importantly, evoke a fragmented Italian
identity. Like aunt Marta, who wavers "between nonsense and lucidity" (131), Innocente reconfigures from
out of the disparate materials of memory a sometimes
revelatory but relentlessly unsteady picture of the immigrant past.

In joining dream to lived experience, the text deep-
ens its study of the uncertainties of Italian-Canadian
subject. Not only do dreams reenact actual moments in
time — "strange images troubled me ... Father Nick standing solemnly before a coffin in the church, reciting a
mass for Mr. Mario Gallino" (116) — but so does reality
manifest itself through reverie: "remembering that I was
in my bare feet and undershirt I felt suddenly ashamed,
like in dreams I had where I found myself inexplicably
naked in school or in church" (22). There appears to be
no firm ground that forms reality. Daily activity is repeatedly indistinguishable from Vitto's unconscious.
The fusing of dream and reality mirrors the peasants'
sense of the world and reveals Vitto's troubled relations
with his fellow villagers and family, as well as his subsequent trauma of immigration. Disturbing images of past
events infiltrate Vitto's unconscious. The bloody corpse
of a chicken implies an incapacity to protect his mother
from the malice of the village. Vitto's terror over Cristina's pregnancy arises from his fear that she will give
birth to a snake-headed child, "some new demon took
possession of her" (110), and from a haunting dream of
her hatching a "large blue egg" (119).

Vitto's journey is presented as a kind of mirage, signifying the marvel and strangeness of immigration. Features of his trip — the shoreline, "a dusty sun-drenched town of white adobe" (202), the sea, which stretched "away in every direction, it seemed, to the very ends of the earth" (204), and the bowels of the ship, where "everything seemed larger than life, as if made by giants" (203) — are suffused with an intensity and vivacity which dramatize Vitto's whimsical and child-like view of the world. The journey itself proves to be nightmarish. Vitto's frightening encounter with the sea is framed in fantastical terms: "for a moment it seemed the world had obeyed me ... [and had] give[n] me time to crawl into the sea's belly and find whatever spoils of storms and tempests lay half-digested there" (219). The force of the waves knocks him against a stairwell, rendering him unconscious: "Then as if in a dream the wave finally closed over me, and the world went black" (219). The brutality of the storm foreshadows Vitto's tragic and final break from Valle del Sole. Relieved by the birth of his baby sister, whose human shape erases his dread of the evil eye, Vitto sees a wondrous world, disclosed in the image of the evening sky: "a thousand stars glinting overhead" (22). Yet, his victory over the powers of darkness (embodied by the storm) is short-lived. Vitto moves between wakefulness and dream as his mother bleeds profusely. The eeriness of the scene invokes Vitto's incredulity and terror.

Cristina's death throws him into a state of delirium. Confusion, incoherence and hallucination mark his psychological separation from the old world (represented by the ship) and the new (signalled by the presence of his father). Vitto's delirium symbolically calls attention to the provisionality of Italian-Canadian identity. It is made obvious by the sense of dreadfulness that pervades the depictions of both the old and new world. Images of Canada's forbidding natural environment reproduce the narrator's rendering of the rocky and arid landscape of Valle del Sole.

The overlayering of the real on the numinous and irrational, and the affiliation of dream with reality sabotage any notion that there exists a solid referential universe outside human consciousness. Vittorio Innocente's contradictory reexploration of his Italian childhood destabilizes "the fixity of origins."[10] Italian-Canadian writers, such as Ricci, Paci and Minni, deconstruct "images of fixity"[11] by continually focusing on the discontinuities within and between two separate and often adverse cultural perspectives. *Lives of the Saints*, *Black Madonna* and *Other Selves* invoke the conflicted nature of the culture of origin and present an precarious reading of ethnicity. This instability is evident in the way the three texts describe the protagonists' ambivalent view of (and their difficult experiences in) Canadian industrial-urban society.

In *Lives of the Saints*, the new world imparts a sense of disjunction: "America. How many dreams and fears and contradictions were tied up in that single word ... some said [Canada] was a vast cold place with rickety wooden houses and great expanses of bush and snow, others a land of flat green fields that stretched for miles and of lakes as wide as the sea, an unfallen world without mountains or rocky earth" (160, 162). This passage seethes with irony, for while it harks back to the privations in the old country, its countervailing images of fertility and bountifulness betray the immigrant's attempt to regain a lost paradise which "shimmered just beneath the surface of the seen" (162).

Immigration to North America is perceived to be a

way out of the ferment and incoherence of southern Italy. The act of mythification, in which "America ... [was] more a state of mind than a place" (162), is quickly undermined by allusions to unrelenting hardship: "sooty factories and back-breaking work and poor wages and tiny bug-infested shacks" (162). The wasteland imagery of industrial society evokes the dark side of the Sun Parlour, a shadowy world not unlike that of Valle del Sole. The interchangeability of the two places is ironically underlined by the similarity of their names. The new world perpetuates the injustices and miseries of the old: "America ... continued merely the mundane life which the peasants accepted as their lot, their fate, the daily grind of toil without respite" (162).

The fragmented story of Vitto's father restates the contradictions of both Canada and rural Italy. References to his indecipherable letters and mysterious life in the new world elicit a disembodied figure, whom Vitto "sometimes imagined ... had no face at all, merely a shadowy blank that hid him from the world like a veil" (36). Mario Innocente personifies the inadequacies of a male-centred peasant society. He is depicted as a tyrannical and violent man who physically abused his wife, Cristina, and who still controls the lives of his family from afar. He tells his wife that she and her son should no longer sleep in the same bed. The indictment of the father is mitigated by the sending of a part of his earnings to Cristina so that she and Vitto can be economically stable. The text's account of Innocente's immigration to Canada, nevertheless, is highly ambivalent. After being laid off from his factory job, Innocente is compelled to do menial work on a farm in order to make ends meet. He lives in a refurbished room next to the barn, which Cristina sarcastically refers to as "a chicken coop" (94).

Although Mario Innocente can always find some form of employment in Canada, the working conditions there are as burdensome as those in Valle del Sole.

There is an ambiguity to the narrator-character's representation of Canadian and Italian society. The trauma of emigration, in which "it seemed [mother and son] were being ripped untimely from our womb" (164), is as hurtful as Vitto's social ostracism in the village. The reference to the womb is doubly ironic since it recalls Vitto's moment of joy and unity with his mother in the cave. Immigration, then, signifies not only that the new world is fundamentally undefined terrain — "a kind of limitless space" (165). The old country remains ingrained in the consciousness of the immigrant. According to the narrator, Vitto was on "a journey ... that took direction not from its destination but from its point of departure, Valle del Sole, which somehow could not help but remain always visible on the receding shore" (165).

The conclusion of the novel centres on Cristina's death. Here is invoked the demise of the old way of life: "The words of a song were floating into my head, surfacing like sunken relics from a place that was no longer visible on the horizon, that had been swallowed into the sea" (237). Such nullification is in marked contrast to earlier images of the liberating journey. The narrative is drenched in allusions to the natural elements: "the air and sun seemed to bring back to my mother a warm radiance, as if the crisp blue of the sky and sea had seeped inside of her ... around us the sea lay bright blue and placid" (202, 204). Instead of symbolically acting as a bridge to the new land, the ocean metaphorically entombs the old culture as Cristina is buried at sea. As Ricci has observed, "'[w]hile immigration is providing this escape, it is also destroying a certain way of life.'"[12]

When Vitto finally arrives in Canada, he finds an inhospitable place — "we rolled across a desolate landscape, bleak and snow-covered" (234) — totally at odds with the mythic America promised by the peasants. The old world lingers on. It persists as ethnic identity in the new. But it soon becomes Vitto's final, dark view of Valle del Sole: "the villagers — some of them had begun to move now, drifting like wraiths towards the edge of town" (184). This picture of ruin will finally reinforce Vitto's avowed desire to break from his Italian culture. His relationship with a fellow village boy, Fabrizio, now is transmitted through images of entrapment and self-mutilation: "I hated him ... as if he were something shackled to me that I must cut away at all costs, the way animals gnawed off their own limbs when caught in a hunter's trap" (127). Fabrizio is socially and economically marginalized and he reminds Vitto of the imperfections of the old world.

The interweaving of the stories of Cristina and Santa Cristina discloses the ironies and contradictions of village life in Abruzzi. Cristina's opposition to a conformist and patriarchal social system is linked to her saintly counterpart's scorning of the materialism and idolatry of Roman civilization. (In both stories, the paternal figure is characterized as oppressive and spiritually sterile.) As a result of their iconoclasm, the two women are made to undergo "a long series of chastisements" (135), typified by brutal torture or social ostracism.

The interrelation between the mythic and the "real" further manifests itself through references to physical endurance. The menacing presence of a snake/serpent and the light imagery respectively suggest purity, salvation, and blessedness. The text's reworking of hagiography — of the veneration of the Roman Cristina — privileges an emancipated womanhood. The sheer force of

Santa Cristina's presence evokes a selfless but powerful femininity. This evocation reinforces the image of Cristina as a sexually and emotionally liberated woman who defies the dictates of patriarchy. The use of the story of Santa Cristina underlines the gap between myth and reality. Despite the extremity of her predicament and the wickedness of Roman civilization, Santa Cristina achieves spiritual transcendence and immortality. In contrast, Cristina's life appears to be empty of such redemption, for even the birth of a daughter, which signifies feminine continuity, does not alleviate the tragedy of her death.

For Cristina, America connotes a place where individuality takes precedence over collective duty and she appears to act out the villagers' hidden desires. On the eve of her departure for Canada, Cristina berates her fellow villagers for their lack of independence: "not one of you knows what it means to be free and make a choice" (184). Vitto innocently accepts his mother's criticism of Valle del Sole and sees the journey to the new world as an act of liberation: "all that could ever cause pain and harm was being left behind on the receding shore, and my mother and I would melt now into an endless freedom as broad and as blue as the sea" (201). This statement is ironic, for Cristina's decision to emigrate is based on the belief that the new world will provide a better nurturing environment for her son and soon-to-be-born child.

Immigration reasserts the importance of family in Cristina's life. However, as her death attests, the immigrant is not immune to the damaging effects of the ancestral culture, organized around an inflexible patriarchal social order. Ultimately, the story of Santa Cristina's altruism and salvation is out of step with Vitto's experiences in the Apennines and his traumatic immigration to Canada. Cristina's tragic death at sea functions as an ironic inversion of Santa Cristina's ascension. The sea swallows up Cristina, not her tormentors. Santa Cristina's self-abnegation allows her entry into paradise, yet Cristina Innocente is punished for affirming her individuality. Unlike the angels in the Christian fable, Darcangelo, the captain's assistant, who attends to Cristina's needs on the ship, does not rescue her from impending doom.

The conclusion of *Lives of the Saints* confirms the ironic and ambivalent character of Vittorio Innocente's narrative. As Vitto's lucky lira slips out of his hand and tumbles into the sea, the text repeats the opening image in the novel in which the reenactment of the past is presented in metaphorical terms, through the evocation of water imagery: "If this story has a beginning, a moment at which a single gesture broke the surface of events like a stone thrown into the sea ... " (7). The use of the qualifier "If", indicates that the narrator implicitly questions his attempt to reduce the details of personal history to a specific incident. In doing so, he emphasizes not just the arbitrariness of his tale but an inability to fashion from the dynamic of lived experience a whole picture of the past. He perceives personal history to be essentially unclosed, without final resolution or resting point: "the ripples cresting endlessly" (7).

The lira sinks into the swirling vortex of the sea as a stone puncturing the water's surface and symbolically brings the ending and the beginning of the story together. This intimating of a circular movement highlights the narrator's act of remembering. The two images respectively initiate and conclude his storytelling. The text problematizes such closure by constructing an ambiguous and, ultimately, grim picture of immigration. The lira (a talisman of the old world) is unable to protect Vitto from misfortune and cannot provide him with any sign that will redeem his tragic journey to Canada. While he looks intently at the rolling coin, searching for "some final secret message, some magic consolation" (238), it "tilt[s] fatally towards the rails ... tumbling out to the sea" (238). The image both symbolically re-dramatizes Cristina's burial and reiterates the passage of the old way of life.

The text's ironic and elegiac representation of the old world is magnified by the terrible uncertainty of Vitto's existence. In the final moments of the narrative, he remains suspended between two worlds, one that has disappeared from view but which still haunts his consciousness and another which, while it is near, is beyond his reach. *Lives of the Saints* portrays Vitto's cultural dislocation in the way that it moves from Cristina's burial to glimpses of his father and the Canadian landscape and back to the Saturnia where Vitto is recovering from his delirium.

This circular movement recapitulates the overall narrative thrust of the novel whose gaze is turned backward. In focusing on the act of crossing over, rather than on embarkation or settlement in the new world, the text calls attention to the transience and indeterminacy of the immigrant and, by implication, to cultural transformation. Unlike the ending of the story of Santa Cristina, which evokes victory over evil and human suffering, the conclusion of the novel is suffused with a sense of loss that preempts any form of redemption. It also ironically reminds us of the peasants' amoral vision of life: evil strikes both the wicked and the righteous. This remembering of Vitto's Italian past is characterized by unrelenting ambiguity and irony. The text's ironic use of point of view and mythology, whether pre-Christian or Catholic, breaks open the cultural-ideological contradictions of the old world and signals to us the disjunctions within the consciousness and narrative of Vittorio Innocente.

Notes

1. Nino Ricci, *Lives Of The Saints* (Dunvegan, Ontario: Cormorant Books, 1990) 131. Further page references are in this essay.

2. Francesco Loriggio, "The Question of Corpus: Ethnicity and Canadian Literature." *Future Indicative: Literary Theory and Canadian Literature*, ed. John Moss (Ottawa: University of Ottawa Press, 1987) 61.

3. Loriggio, 61.

4. Loriggio, 63, 60.

5. Nino Ricci, "Recreating Paradise: An Interview with Nino Ricci by Jeffrey Canton," 6. *Paragraph* Vol. 13 (1991): 6.

6. Ricci, *Paragraph* 5.

7. Loriggio, "Italian-Canadian Literature: Basic Critical Issues," *Writers in Transition: The Proceedings of the First Annual Conference of Italian Canadian Writers*, eds. C. Dino Minni and Anna Foschi Ciampolini (Montreal: Guernica Editions, 1990) 92.

8. Ricci, *Paragraph* 4.

9. Ricci, *Paragraph* 5.

10. Stephen Slemon, "Magic Realism: A Post-Colonial Discourse," *Canadian Literature* No. 116 (Spring 1988): 17.

11. Slemon, 16.

12. Ricci, *Paragraph* 5.

Lise Hogan

Modernity and the Problem of Cultural Identity: A Critical Analysis of *In A Glass House*

AT THE BEGINNING of Nino Ricci's *In A Glass House*, the second novel in the trilogy, the Italian locality of Valle del Sole, a tiny village in Abruzzo, is the point of reference for the central character's cultural identity. As the reader discovered in *Lives of the Saints*, this is a localized 'Italian identity', since the previous narrative compared peasant culture and postwar industrial society in Italy. *Lives of The Saints* gave the impression that the village of Valle Del Sole was emerging from a "peasant" tradition that remained bound to feudalism. Feudal or neo-feudal forms of exploitation of the south were in place until the 1950s. When Vittorio moves to Canada, his relationship with his father opens up a conflict between the peasant past and the modern world, represented by Canadian society. This state of cultural conflict undermines almost at every turn the establishment of social stability. The central character's doubts with respect to his new surrounding is expressed throughout the second book with such recurrent phrases as "I had the sense," "it seemed," "somehow," and "as if." Vittorio's constant feeling of uncertainty demonstrates his difficulty in dealing with the fluid nature of his ethnic identity. As the novel indicates, immigration introduces in the life of Vittorio the problem of contrasting, and even contradictory, cultural perspectives. The uncertainties created by cultural and social displacement force him to change his expectations and perceptions towards the people in his new social context: his immediate family (his father, his aunt, and half-sister), the members of the immigrant Italian community and members of mainstream English Canadian society.

In the early part of *In A Glass House*, the radical change of physical environment causes emotional distress for the young Vittorio. The openness of Canadian space, especially the agricultural community where his father has established himself, in Mersea, is a dramatic contrast to the enclosed village in the mountainous terrain of central Italy. For Vittorio, the "tidy arrangements" of buildings in the Canadian landscape "made it seem like something in a picture, without dimension, unreal" (In A Glass House, 5).[1] This semblance of order in the Canadian landscape differed from Italy where the buildings, which appeared in a random, superimposed manner over many centuries, imparted a sense of continuity. The notion of space makes the two countries distinct from each other since every aspect of life in Italy depended on physical proximity and a sense of long-shared community whereas Canadian space signifies physical distance and social unfamiliarity.[2] For Vittorio, the translocation to Canada has led to the fragmentation of community: "Here they're just in their own little groups" (163). In Mersea, the Italian immigrants cannot automatically reestablish their community. Also, immigration to Canada has altered the relationship among members of the extended family As Vittorio/Victor notes, "[it was] as if we could no longer be the same people we'd been once, now that we were in Canada" (163). Therefore, Vittorio experiences the terrible sensation of 'being thrown' into a completely unfamiliar world. He does not feel that he fits in anywhere in his new surroundings: "both home and school now merely two limbos I moved between, each a waiting for an ending, for an opening into some truer other life" (140). This social disorientation is emphasized in the narrative with the shifting back and forth in the use of the central character's Italian and English names, Vittorio and Victor, as he moves in and out of his Italian and English Canadian contexts both physically and psychologically. The constant change in name from Vittorio to Victor, or the reverse, mirrors the central character's confusion and ambivalence about each cultural context. This linguistic situation underscores Vittorio/Victor's lack of control over his existence that produces a state of alienation from people. In reaction to this feeling of dispossession, with its loss of a comfort zone and with its impending sense of chaos, Vittorio is determined to find a kind of order to overcome his alienation. His pursuit of a Canadian identity and social integration makes him reject his perceived "crude" immigrant background. In the story, his aspiration to modernity is juxtaposed with a disdain towards a backward ethnic tradition. Ironically, it is his immigrant upbringing that supports his belief in hard work and social conformity as the means to achieve academic success and social stability.

As exemplified by the situation of the central character, the cultural tension in the narrative is between tradition, represented by the Italian past, and modernity, in the form of urban life in Canada. The narrative maintains an Italian socio-cultural background in the development of Vittorio's personal outlook. Yet this Italian heritage produces a sense of fear and shame, supported by such words as the "threat of ... humiliation" and "disgrace." In the novel, the glass metaphor is symbolic of his view that "[people] could see the humiliation already inside me, as if I were made of glass" (50). His fear of being considered a rough immigrant, "[a] disgraziat just off the boat" (111), who is unfamiliar with the customs of Canadians (111), is the basis for his constant anxiety. Vittorio's negative view of himself makes him reject his Italian culture in order to fit into his new social context. However, he is unable to turn his back on his ethnic past and repress his emotional ties, especially his bond with his dead mother and half-sister, Rita. But when his little sister is adopted by the Amherst family, the reaction of his father and his aunt as well as his own to this dramatic situation is a kind of resignation which reinforces an inherent peasant fatalism: "we'd merely given ourselves over to what had happened as to an act of fate, never daring, in our immigrant helplessness, to question what rules such matters were governed by here" (121).

Vittorio attempts to repress his Italian side but Canadian society reminds him that he is different culturally. The desire to be someone else to replace his Italian identity and his unremitting self-consciousness about not fitting into the new social environment make him vulnerable to the external expectations of the host society. As an adolescent in high school, Vittorio tries to fit in socially by attending both Catholic and Protestant church services. This participation seems to be essentially passive; it is a kind of "silent acquiescence" and he feels that he did not have "the right to reject the redemption being offered" (134). Vittorio recognizes the necessity to comply with a different set of rules, but he feels he is betraying his true self and he is unable to succeed in making new relationships. This inability to find a stable set of beliefs and to develop strong personal bonds with individuals at school and in social circles, especially in terms of religious institutions, sustains his feelings of anger and humiliation. This shame leads him to a form of psychological erasure, expressed in his "desire to vanish into thin air" with "all history silently shifting like water to efface every memory of me": his shame can only be overcome by a complete disengagement from his ethnic background.

The television images of the 1950s and early 1960s, mostly American, dominated the young imagination of many Italian immigrant children with false impressions of domestic bliss. For the protagonist, his father's purchase of a television set realizes a tangible measure for bringing the family through the looking glass, so to speak, into modernity: "he bought a television, at long last bringing us into modernity. ... It seemed to shift the house's whole centre of gravity ... holding more life in its tiny screen than all the empty rooms it ruled over. ... the new window it provided on the world ... as if nothing else was real. (88) The hypnotic medium, with its soothing and neutralizing flow of images, is thus offered overtly as a window into modernity and as the deceptive mirror of a modernity imbued with the American Dream. The fascination with television images impairs a vision of the real world, by creating new sets of mythologies at the cultural level. The television shows transmit the ideals of modernity connected to consumerism, social refinement and the nuclear family, which are in opposition to tradition, hard work, roughness of manner and the obligations in the extended family. Generational tensions begin to increase when Vittorio evaluates every aspect of his father's outlook and behaviour according to the criteria of modern 'refinement' and in contrast to their "make-shift immigrant crudeness" (140). Since the Inno-cente family cannot fit into conventional television im-ages of the family, the traditional aspect takes on an image of backwardness that must be replaced by ways of the modern order. The family farm designates a fixed order in which Vittorio finds himself misplaced because of his identification with modern Canadian society: "My own role in this order defined exactly by my exclusion" (188).

The unsteady relationship with his father marks his deflection from a past considered to be a "liability to be gotten beyond" (228) and his life on the farm seems to have merely reinstated the order that the family had sought to escape: "[we were] living our lives with the same frugality, the same sense of threat, as the peasants in Italy who'd wondered from one year to the next if their harvest would last the winter ... feeling not so much of having moved forward as of having struggled to remain the same, forever stranded as on an island within the tight logic and rules of what was acceptable, how far we could reach" (190). For Vittorio, modernity, represented by mainstream urban society with its idea of progress, provides the alternative to a culturally and socially back-ward and deprived life for his Italian family in a rural setting. Modernity thus provides the opportunities for individualism and social independence.

The completion of a university degree in English Lit-erature extends the separation between Vittorio and his cultural heritage. However, the university comes to rep-resent another exclusionary world revolving around its own 'natural orbit': "But in my first months there I felt as if I had stepped out suddenly into empty space: I had nothing, finally, that defined me, not even the dull routines that had made up my life in Mersea ... there seemed some rhythm I couldn't quite catch, some crucial moment I'd missed when a decisive action or word could have brought me suddenly inside of things. Everything about the university gave the impression of a fixed but impenetrable order, everywhere taken for granted & nowhere explained ... groups... had an air of exclusion about them, of enclaves already complete and fully-formed" (200, 201).

At home, his academic achievement, basically, is not recognized by his family, whose peasant way of life and cultural insularity do not allow them to see the value of a formal and advanced education.[3] Generally, an advanced education should set him apart from the 'other' immigrants and bring him a kind of social status, especially in the eyes of mainstream Canadians.[4] Caught between his repressed Italian identity and his uncertain Canadian self, his high level education doesn't allow him to transcend his ethnic past and integrate him fully into English Canadian society.

Still seeking his 'proper' identity, Vittorio undertakes a research project for the Italian Historical Committee, where he conducts a series of interviews with the three Italian immigrant groups in the region, comprised of the (as Vittorio puts it) "molisani, (aka abruzzesi), ciociari and Sicilians" (276). The project requires him to find out "[e]verything. ... Not just about here, but what it was like over there, how they lived, what they ate, who ruled over them, the padroni, the government, Mussolini" (269). Through his gathering of oral histories of the particular Italian regional groups, Vittorio is made aware of the wide sense of distrust of the status quo among the subjects of these interviews, not only because of their 'shameful,' deprived social and economic beginnings, but especially, because of the fear that they would be misunderstood and this would threaten their peaceful existence in the new country.[5] The project of documenting the immigrant experience leads to the view that the Italian immigrants do not share a common culture: "What culture? ... There's no culture, they're all farmers" (270). As Vittorio gathers the interviews for the Italian Historical Society, he remarks that "perhaps they would merely sit gathering dust in some office of multi-culturalism having no value beyond their official one, simply a proof that the government had given its sanction to an ethnic community" (285). This statement is joined to many other references to "the gap between the rhetoric of how things should be and the reality of how they were" (304).

Given that Vittorio's mother has passed away and his father is unable to provide emotional and social security, Vittorio cannot find a means to reinforce his personal ethnic history. This lack of support system impedes his attempts at building a bond with his father. But the problems of communication with his father are not merely linguistic and cultural. Vittorio's father, like many other Italian immigrants, was forced to abandon his country of origin because the severe economic challenges no longer made it possible to make sense of his existence in the homeland. The need to find his own form of social stability—since Vittorio does not want to be a farmer like his father in Mersea—compels Vittorio to undergo a second displacement. This internal migration, from the town to the city, permits him to take charge of his life and to choose his own particular cultural values. The movement into the academic world sets up a subsequent and significant displacement into another cultural context when he relocates to Africa as a son leaving the household, "like an immigrant, accepting that humiliation when no logic compelled it" (250). The shared experiences of father and son, which derived from a common sense of estrangement from the culture of origin, makes it impossible for them to ever come together: "there seemed no language between us that wasn't infected with misunderstanding" (250). Yet, Vittorio believes that his father perceives his son's behaviour as an embodiment of his own unfulfilled desires as a young man in Italy: " [he] seemed almost ready to take pride in me, to admit whatever unrealized part of himself, his own lost freedom, he saw taking vicarious shape in me now" (251).

Vittorio must first escape from an immigrant identity with all its negative connotations and the accompanying, perceived sense of shame. (In the novel, he is referred to as Vittorio to emphasize his Italian identity and as Victor to emphasize his English-Canadian identity, depending on the particular situation.) In the place of this static ethnic identity, Victor perceives an identity that is an amalgamation of Italian and Canadian cultural elements and the result of chance experiences. He experiences a constant "panic of being thrown" into new and unknown situations, in which he feels "unsolid as air without contours" (213). The problem of assuming a stable identity is amplified by the expectation that Vittorio will fulfill his immigrant father's hope of continuity and achievement. Victor would be "the flourishing of [the family's] collective will, the one their hopes resided in" (252). Yet, to attain "some return to my truer self" (252), as Vittorio sees it, he must re-establish a sense of continuity with his immigrant heritage.

After graduating from university, Vittorio decides to go abroad, in this case to a country in Africa, a place that is very different from his frame of reference. His position as a school teacher puts him at higher social level in this new environment. In this place, Vittorio and his 'white' colleagues are considered to be European, regardless of their individual origins. Also, at the school, the white staff members, who hold positions of authority, are listed first, whereas the rest of the multicultural staff, such as staff members who are considered to be Indian and Pakistani are listed last (reflecting an actual African racial scale). The administration of the school seems to reflect historical positions of power, since there is a correspondence between ethnicity and the class structure. As a member of a higher social echelon, Vittorio indulges in his newfound sense of belonging. He is part of a homogenized "white" group of individuals, who "in our whiteness" discover that there is "less work to do to understand one another" (304). No longer feeling that he is an outsider and given the immediate social status that he has obtained in his position as an English teacher, the necessity to conform to established rules and to accept a set of cultural beliefs becomes unimportant to living there and interacting with members of his social group, for it is a "place without expectation that I should ever have to find the way to fit in" (308). In the process, he demonstrates an inability to interpret the behaviour and cultural patterns of other cultures that are not European and he shows a satisfying sense of superiority which is the result of his privileged position as a teacher.

It would seem that a kind of personal redemption comes in the form of a position of comparative social status. This form of empowerment provides a false sense of security because it is not based on a consistent set of values that he has incorporated into his life. Instead, his need to be part of a coherent social context continues to reinforce his sense of social disorientation. Vittorio's trajectory in the modern world is usually about giving in to extraneous forces and contingent situations, which puts him under the control of others — such as his father, the church people of Mersea whose world he tried to be part of, the social system at the university and the teaching staff in Africa. For him, there is a tendency to accept the existing social order while staying, at a particular level, disconnected from it. This disconnection maintains his resentment and anger towards others. Vittorio's general awareness of social reality is basically superficial, as a result of his disengagement. His insecurities and resistance constantly undermine the external perceptions, whether supportive or neutral, that others have of him. Therefore, his adult identity continues to be essentially unformed. His attempts at perceiving events and behaviour as well as himself from an external perspective are fed by the desire to see his own image reflected in the world. Thus, Vittorio engages in the contradictory process of wanting acceptance from individuals while recognizing that he does not want their validation. The following statement typifies his contradictory and confused emotional state: "I seemed under the full tyranny by now of the image I thought Marnie had formed of me, the complex dynamic of wanting her good opinion and not believing in it, and silently holding her in contempt for it and yet daring less and less to expose it to any risk" (222).

This predicament forms a recurrent pattern in the narrative. Vittorio feels the incongruities between the various cultural spaces that he is straddling. The book contrasts the reality of his marginal existence in small town Ontario to his position of social authority in a small village in Africa. Each experience deriving from a specific social situation stands in direct opposition to the previous one: in the former, the immigrant, working class outsider struggles to enter the middle class English Canadian mainstream and, in the latter, the English teacher is content to fulfill a privileged role in a class-based and racially stratified society. The dominant English culture in Ontario constantly reminded him of his ethnicity. In another country, even though he is technically an outsider there, it his "Englishness" that marks his social position. His English identity is the product of a strategic linguistic and cultural assimilation through his university education. Throughout the narrative, Victor is aware that he occupies subordinate and dominant positions in the power spectrum, first as an immigrant in Canada and then as a well-placed member among the foreign elite in a poor country. This awareness of his specific social status affects his emotional state and his attitude toward himself and other individuals. Despite this awareness, he does not consciously link his behaviour to the material factors that shape social relations in the given social context.

In Africa, he uncritically represents the power of a dominant minority. As Victor shifts into the role of a member of the white elite in Africa, certain particularities of his behaviour are emphasized, among which is his incapacity to interpret other cultures that are alien to his "Europeanness" and his satisfying sense of superiority, which he maintains through his status as a teacher. His attempts at perceiving other people and himself from an external perspective are motivated by the desire to see his own image reflected in his social environment. There is an impression that the protagonist upholds the social norms and cultural values of the dominant group which he aspires to be a part of.

Victor's identification with the dominant culture appears to be part of the subjective internalization of images transmitted through established cultural institutions, especially the mass media. As Alain Touraine points out in *Critique of Modernity*[6] the individual "is motivated by what is expected of him and not by self-interest." As such, the members of a community, especially newcomers, will fall into a specific definition of their status and their corresponding roles (352). Early in the novel, when Vittorio observes the Mexican workers who have been hired to work on the family farm, he comments that "[t]hey were our past, what we'd been when we first arrived here with their low wages and their subservience, insistence on working long hours" (254). Although Vittorio relates to their situation, he maintains a certain distance from the farm labourers, referring to them as "our workers" (254). He finds a kind of fulfillment in having a certain economic security and in being part of the dominant group.

For Victor, the city of Toronto epitomizes the presence of the dominant culture, giving the "impression of a hard immutability and rightness" (199) with its business ethic and commercialism. Vittorio's experience in this urban centre does not remove or mitigate his anxiety about participating in mainstream society. He cannot bring together the opposed parts of his identity: one part is tied to the traditional immigrant culture, another side of him wants to be integrated in modern, urban society, while there is that person in him that remains essentially ambivalent, standing outside of the ethnic and mainstream cultures.

He thinks that he has transcended his cultural alienation when he leaves Canada. Africa allows Vittorio to start again, "to be awakened like that to the world, attuned to every possibility" (308). It is only by distancing himself from Canada , from the source of his anxiety and confusion, that Vittorio can obtain some kind of emotional stability: "in this place without expectation that I should ever have to find the way to fit in" (308). In Africa, Vittorio recognizes in the other "white expatriates" a similar "subtle embitterment of the migrant at being out of place" (318). The shared sense of displacement allows him to feel a sense of normalcy.

The desire to overcome cultural dislocation leads to an idealistic view of society: "[It was] as if a new, more subtle colonization was taking place, self-contained and self-protective, not so much replacing the dynasties ... as slowly rendering them irrelevant" (306). This ideal state is contrasted to the fact that the retention of one's cultural heritage at this time in history is still steeped in the reproduction of stereotypes in Heritage Festivals that represent "the desire not so much to reclaim the past as to redeem it ... to recast it as the ennobled source of the present's happily-ever-after" (272). Vittorio's particular fears are circumscribed by a twofold threat since he must derive the knowledge of his own existence in either a suspended state of Italianness or in a process "toward an increasingly anonymous present ... [with] its mongrel heterogeneity" (270).

Vittorio's project of reinvention, of putting himself into the role of the European white male, is an attempt to find a stable identity. Yet he discovers that this imported role does not permit him to "break through to some truer level of exchange with people, become real, an individual" (306). Instead, to his unease, he notes that he is essentially estranged from the people that he is there to help. He realizes that the "the token reverence that came with [the role of English teacher] and its reverse, a kind of invisibility ... [t]hat seemed in the end what most defined my stay in the country" (306). Vittorio's awareness of his predicament urges him to break out of an oppressive situation, a somewhat alarming goal since "there seemed always a risk in the transition, a challenge to the accepted order" (306). Vittorio's reflections on the experiences of his own Italian immigrant community and on other cultural groups in the Canadian "mosaic" evoke a set of social realities, particularly in terms of "roots, hardships, foreignness," that are in contrast to the "founding mythologies" of the dominant culture. The condition of displacement creates a type of solidarity among displaced people, showing that cultural displacement is a process that is not strictly geographical, but rather, that it is the result of the socio-political disempowerment of minority groups by dominant powers.

Notes

1. Nino Ricci, *In A Glass House*, McLelland and Stewart, 1998.

2. Marino Tuzi explains this problem of disjuncture in his essay in this book, *Nino Ricci: Essays on His Works*: "Disjunction, Paradox, and the Deromanticization of the Old World in *Lives of the Saints*" pp. 1-8.

3. Note the author's comment :"There was definitely a strict code there of family values in the background, but mainly it was not one that was used in a positive, supportive way. It was a code in which success went unacknowledged, and failure was punished. This was the closest thing to encouragement that you would have." See Pino Esposito's interview/article "Nino Ricci: Life After Sainthood" in *The Eyetalian*, 1:1 Fall 1993, p. 21

4. Nino Ricci, and also Frank Paci (see *The Rooming House*, 1996) point to the fact that at this time in the novel, which would be the early 70s, there were few educated second generation Italians, and therefore a higher education was something of a privilege which would produce little "enclave[s] of privilege" (Ricci, 236).

5. Some of these fears are due to the support for Mussolini, who was apparently treated as a hero in the South because he had brought in schoolhouses and education to the people. This presents a worm's eye view of history, that is, from the viewpoint of a population that had never known anything but severe domination. We must also keep in mind that, during the Second World War, the Canadian Italian male population was interned in POW camps in Canada, as well as in England and the United States.

6. Trans. of *Une Critique de la Modernité* (Fayard: 1992) by David Macey, Oxford: Blackwell, 1995.

William Anselmi

The Theme of Cultural Displacement in the Novel, *Where She Has Gone*

WHERE SHE HAS Gone, the last novel in Nino Ricci's trilogy, suggests in its final moments, through a poetic dream, the continuation of the story of Victor Innocente. The enigmatic ending transmitted by the image-charged dream has a metaphoric quality that alters a linear reading, going against the expectation that the story is coming to a conclusion, and it hints at something mystical that lies beyond the small rustic village that has been described to the reader. Seemingly emblematic of Victor's life thus far, the dream of bonfires, "ten thousand of them burning away," spreads out like "messages ... [a]cross the valley like a code". (*Where She Has Gone*, 1997, 322). The trilogy developed through a series of recurrent themes: the departure for Canada in *Lives of the Saints*, settlement in Canada *In A Glass House*, and the return to the old peasant hometown in *Where She Has Gone*. At the end of the novel, *Where She Has Gone*, Vittorio's view of himself and his place in the world is presented ambiguously through the depiction of the startling dream of bonfires. Everything that has happened up to now is transcended by this expansive dream, in which the character appears to dissolve into a universal, sorrowful humanity.

The dominance of the bonfire dream leaves open the possibility that the whole narrative is part of an unending dream, something like a fable akin to *The Neverending Story*. The muted ending opens up a myriad of other possible meanings and narrative themes. Is the text suggesting that the words of any narrative, after its first reading, burn out, like the bonfires, and that the code (its meaning) is irretrievable? Is the text implying that the messages in a story are subject to the personal interpretation of the reader? The open-endedness of the narrative, amplified by the numinous quality of the bonfire imagery, suggests possible scenarios in the continuation of Vittorio's story. Will he ever find the courage to confront the older German man about his relationship with his mother? Will he resolve his incestuous affair with his sister? Will he ever make it back to Canada, given his almost aimless travels in Western Europe? The break from realism at the end of the novel also infers aesthetic questions: Is the trilogy dealing with a conventional rendition of the immigrant story interwoven with tragic elements or is the novel really an allegory about life as a personal voyage and as a process of self-discovery?

Vittorio's yearning for something beyond the ordinariness of life seems to inspire him to conjure an atavistic vision of burning fires bringing light to the primeval darkness. Presented in retrospect, coming just after Vittorio's attempted suicide in England, shortly after he had left Italy permanently, the dream of bonfires appears to anchor him psychologically — if only temporarily — to the land of his birth — to that sparsely populated village of his childhood. Vittorio's return to his hometown follows a series of complicated and dramatic events (which encompass *Lives of The Saints* and *In A Glass House*): his mother's affair, his sister's birth, his complicated love-hate relationship with his father, and his ambivalent relationship with his sister, in which love and cruelty are intermixed, and his essential isolation in English Canadian society, even including his years as an undergraduate student, during which his academic success cannot create the basis for social integration. Throughout the narratives, the reader is reminded of Victor's unreliable memory, since many of his recollections are faulty or at least imprecise, tilted towards his own emotional interest. Often his recollections of past events do not match the details of what actually happened in the past. This situation is continually made evident to the reader in *Where She Has Gone*, when the main characters end up giving different readings of the physical spaces and situations that are recalled, as if the mental and physical worlds are separate from each other. The gap between memory and reality pushes back any memories of cultural displacement. Despite the inconsistency and unreliability of memory, *Where She has Gone* seems to be concerned with the necessity, on Victor's part, to recall details from his Italian childhood so that he can reintegrate this history of that childhood into his life. This is one of the important motivations for his return to the village of birth.

In *Lives of the Saints,* an incongruity arises that is not addressed until the third novel. This incongruity is not resolved in *Lives of the Saints*, as if time had no linear aspect, or, as if time were compressed in a continuous present, the present of a mythical time and not of an historical time. When Vittorio's mother, Cristina, becomes pregnant four years after her husband's departure for America (eventually Canada), the German soldier is implicated as the impregnator. The narrative is told through the voice of seven-year-old Vittorio Innocente and the events take place in the early nineteen sixties, decades after the end of WWII. It is not clear if, like a Japanese soldier wandering around, dazed, in the jungles of the Philippines, the German soldier was unaware of the end of war. The interpretation that the Italian villagers give of the event involving Cristina and the German soldier in the barn in Valle del Sole is attached to both the religious and the mythical realms. According to the local peasants, Cristina was bitten by a snake in the stable. So given this explanation, the metaphor does not cover up the sexual act but actually reveals it to the community. This response, which is a superstitious reading, does not have to compete with the real explanation that Cristina has found a lover. Through the minds of the villagers, the mythical moment absorbs the real event. After being bitten, Cristina is ostracized by the villagers not only for being someone who has transgressed the close-knit sexual rules of the family and the community, in this traditional, peasant village, but also for having been the object of the snake's attentions. In folk superstition, the bite of the snake is related to the bite of the tarantula spider in Southern folklore. In this southern Italian tradition, it is the women who are bitten by the tarantula, and the physical reaction to this bite is a transgressive dance, the enactment of a repressed sexuality, which finds the public forum to reveal itself as sexual desire. The community accepts the transgression, which is the manifestation of an irrepressible sexual desire in the form of a possession. According to superstition, it is an outside source, from the animal world, in this case the tarantula, that infects the healthy body of the woman and changes it into something other than what it is acceptable socially, in terms of its individual characteristics, as indicated in the physical frenzy of the dance. In a Christian sense, the bite of the snake is a re-enactment of the first transgression in Eden, of a person succumbing to the sexual allure of the other—the seduction of knowledge by sexuality.

In the *Lives of the Saints* trilogy, below the everyday world, there is a current of influences, comprised of the religious dimension and its opposite, sexuality, that affect the characters and makes them act accordingly. In this situation, a diluted Catholicism, never simply ethical but always morally embedded, and a suppressed (but not for long) sexual energy, become the negative and positive charges that animate the behaviour of the main protagonists. The mythological and historical domains are not totally integrated, although the narrative suggests that the characters are unique individuals and that they are representations of a greater humanity.

In A Glass House, which follows *Lives of the Saints* and is the second novel of the trilogy, describes to a great extent the experience of Vittorio's cultural and social displacement. The book focuses on the relationship between his real father (who had immigrated to Canada before him) and his half-sister, whose father was Cristina's unknown lover. Cristina had died while giving birth to her daughter, Rita (Vittorio's half sister), aboard the ship to America in the last part of the first novel. Compared to the first novel, the social context of *In A Glass House* is wholly English Canadian. The life of the immigrants in this new social context is well represented, particularly with respect to their various linguistic, material, and emotional hardships and their experience of the loss of their sense of community. *In A Glass House*, the development of Vittorio's life, whose Canadian name becomes Victor, includes his movement from the small world of a farming community to the large urban, intellectual space of a university in Toronto. Throughout this novel, the character portrayal of Vittorio continues to emphasize his almost obsessive self-reflection.

While doing his studies at the university, Victor immerses himself in mainstream, urban, English Canadian society while he maintains a problematic attachment to his ethnic background, represented by his father and half sister. This complex social and psychological condition sets up the narrative links to the third novel, *Where She Has Gone*. This novel is partly centred on his adult relationship with his half-sister, Rita. Rita's own life has been marked by familial estrangement and social and emotional dislocation. As a young girl, Victor's father could hardly bear the presence of Rita, his wife's illegitimate daughter, in his house. Rita was to him the living emblem of his wife's unforgivable betrayal. Her step-father is not reluctant to accept her adoption by a middle-class English-Canadian couple. This occurrence emphasizes Rita's marginalization from her own family and ethnic community. The experiences of Rita generate a series of representations that support a portrayal of social and cultural displacement. The novel contrasts the two different families: the English atomic unit with its emphasis on individual development and refinement and the fragmented, working class, group-based Italian family. Through this dramatic contrast, the novel emphasizes the different and conflicted perspectives of Victor and his half-sister. Victor's way to escape from his debilitating sense of cultural displacement is to find another place to live, in this case a country in Africa, where he will be able to find temporary peace as an English schoolteacher. For Victor, the irony of the new situation becomes slowly evident to him during his stay in this seemingly exotic, foreign land. He is teaching the English language to local school children, a language which he mastered while doing his university studies. He discovers that the local village people are themselves socially and politically marginalized in their own country. He comes to realize that in any country there is always someone who is at the low level on the socio-economic scale. Through his participation as an English teacher at a local school in a country, which is a former British colony, in Africa, Victor finds a momentary balance in life. Before settling down at the local school, he could not overcome the tension between the difficulty to fully integrate, no matter how Anglicized one was, in Toronto and the impossibility of permanently divesting himself of his ethnic identity. Thus the experience of linguistic and cultural reinvention in this new mysterious space, in a village in Africa, temporarily fulfils his desire to belong to a particular place.

Where She Has Gone continues the exploration of the recurrent themes of movement and displacement that are developed in *Lives of the Saints* and *In A Glass House*. Given the trilogy's thematic patterns, it is possible to identify a Lazarus Syndrome with respect to the Italian-Canadian experience. The Lazarus Syndrome offers a Catholic reading of the multiple elements present in the process of displacement. Basically, when talking about the immigrant, two types of immigrants are present: a) the political immigrant, who refuses the political system at home and searches for a better life, and b) the economic immigrant, who is refused by the economic system at home and also searches for a better life. Of course, both situations can apply to a single person. In both cases, the negativity of the experience in the country of origin is evident. In the first situation, the political immigrant rejects his homeland and in the second, the economic immigrant is rejected by the homeland. Yet, the immigrant is rejected not only by the homeland that does not want him or cannot feed him but also he is at some level rejected by the newly acquired "home" perhaps because of such problems as inadequate language skills, differences in social mores and in even physical appearance. We can imagine the years it could take in a new country to come to terms with the social and cultural dislocation, which might not be acknowledged by the motherland. The immigrant wanders about in the new land, forever reminiscing about what he has left behind. The initial departure from the homeland serves as a funeral, with relatives and friends wailing, lamenting, and creating the walls of the tunnels towards another state. Any return to the place of origin is in the form of the living dead, like a Lazarus figure. Friends, relatives, and acquaintances, all will have to deal with the loss of time from the day of the person's departure. There is only one possibility to deal with this loss and that is to tell stories, but these stories deal with the past, and not with the present, and never with the future. It is the weight of the past that binds the returned immigrant to his pseudo-death — to his spiritual and cultural absence. It is a past told a thousand times over by others and the memories shift precariously, so that, upon his return, the immigrant is twice in limbo: he has been symbolically killed by his community upon his departure, and he suffers a kind of death — a cultural vacuum — upon his return. There is only one possibility of escaping this tragic cycle: some kind of rebirth is necessary, but it has to be a divine rebirth, not of this earth so that the immigrant can avoid the irretrievable stories, which flicker away in the night like fires.

In this sense, *Where She Has Gone* suggests displaced

protagonists, who are sentimentally attached to an Italian world that can never be regained. It is a world that is altered by a memory whose recall is forever outdated, out of time. It is also an idealized memory of the past that will be destroyed by the individual's confrontation with the reality of the return to his home. This parable of displacement resembles the narrative of the lost paradise. Thrown down in the world of work and sweat, the sullen mass can prostitute its humanity in any sacrificial way, only to discover that the return (the heaven to be regained) is always another reality, complete in its essence, as if each departure had made that idealized world less accessible, thus more impermeable to any discourse. The last novel's depiction of cultural displacement provides a metaphysical reading, which does not negate the return home. However, this depiction of the possibility of the return is about some personal, essential experience and not about the multiplicity that erupts out of a displaced subjectivity, akin to "the potential of the multitude" (Hardt and Negri, 2001). This depiction of the process of displacement verges on a kind of mixed response to one's ethnic past — wherein negative nostalgia is attached to an emotional hopefulness, resulting in a dream retold, composed of fantastic images penetrating the night.

Also it is important to understand the role of religion /Catholicism in helping to put together this ambiguous but not nihilistic depiction of the return. I have already referred to this influence in Catholic terms as the ghost that haunts the narrative. The reconstruction of the place of origin (earthly paradise — the harmonic, happy world of the beginning, of Eden) is connected to the myth of the original sin. Original sin resides in the collective memory of what caused the separation between the human being and the divine. The blame for the original sin is self-assumed and its constant expiation drives our religious worship through the world. Only through long acts of confession can the guilty try to be redeemed for committing the original sin. All sinners must endure, in their way, innumerable trials and tribulations without any promise of ever obtaining salvation. Victor's final descent into what psychologically speaking can be called "hell," both in his private and public life, begins with his own recollection about half-way through the novel. In his contemplation of the return home, he reiterates the recurrent symbolic and religious elements:

> I hadn't told my family yet about my going. When I was a child, a return was always a matter of certain ritualized formality like a funeral: those returning would sit in wait in their kitchens or recreational rooms the night before their departure and all even-ing long people would come to them like petitioners with their envelopes or little packages to be carried back to their relations. It had always stuck me how little joy there had seemed to be in these events, as if a return were a matter of grave risk or threat or as it were a sort of judgment against those who remained behind, a source of quiet humiliation (162).

In *Where She Has Gone*, a negative view of cultural dis-location becomes apparent in the form of the funeral metaphor. Returns, then, are as terrible as departures, not only because the same funereal atmosphere domin-ates, but also because the symbolic loss of life in the leav-ing is doubled on return.

The point of view offered by Italian graphic artist and writer Alberto Montanucci provides another way of looking at cultural dislocation or displacement. In his book, *Sudden Reversal (Colpo di coda*; literally: *A Flick of the Tail)*, Montanucci makes this interesting observation:

> [H]aving as destination social perdition, continuous dislocation as a complete alternative to the hermit's life. With the good luck that, while traveling you cannot really feel the ugly you find around, because you are looking at it externally, a thing that selfishly diminishes anger and increases serenity" (folio 14, p. 31).

There is the full realization that the person is intentionally engaging in dislocation. This intentionality is fruitful because the lived structure of (cultural) space becomes apparent to the participant. This cultural formation that inhibits the emergence of critical multiple dimensions (the positive side of displacement) is bypassed in favour of the gaze, of the participant, that encompasses the inner and outer socio-cultural formations. This is the binary system (between departure and return) that is acquired (with respect to cultural polarization) though the gaze of the participant. In the end, the relationship involved in dislocation is always tertiary. The subject encompasses the experience of departure and return and that something else that is the result of the person willing to accept displacement as a new form of behaviour ("continuous dislocation as a complete alternative": Montanucci). However, it is wilful dislocation that facilitates critical detachment from everyday life, even from a cultural past with which we have an ambivalent relationship. As Alberto Montanucci notes:

> Even the tone of this text I believe is influenced by distance and the time spent in being away and in different

places, so that one is detached by things, which does
not mean to say one is above them, but rather that
one considers them amongst other things ... allowing
us to freely say to those who try to dominate us that
we feel them as fastidious, meddlesome lice itching at
the groin (folio 21, p. 17).

At the airport, while the security officer checks his passport, before allowing Victor into the country, Victor feels
a kind of anonymity, as if the technical details of his
place of and date of birth in Italy are inconsequential
and that he is just another visitor to the country:

At the passport control a young man in khaki thumbed
through my own with a languid circumspection, his
eyes resting for an instant on the details of name,
place of birth, but then moving on with what seemed
an almost wilful withholding of any welcomes as it to
say there was nothing special in me, he saw dozens,
hundreds like me every hour (166).

Instead of a sentimental depiction of the return (echoing
the mythical return of the Everyman or of Ulysses), the
reader is presented with a routine scene in which standard procedures are followed by uniformed, nameless
security guards. The suggested case of young male Italians returning home who are eligible for military duty
reinforces the bureaucratic nature of the re-entry into
the country of origin. For Victor, this experience sustains
his sense of intellectual distance and emotional disconnection from the country of origin. The feeling of displacement continues in Victor's discussion with the taxi
driver:

"I'm going near Piazza Navona," I said, in Italian.

"*Ah, è italiano.*" But it was clear from his forced smile that he'd in fact surmised the opposite, that I was a foreigner.

The taxi made its way into traffic already grown frenetic and thick, weaving through its laneless flow, the car wheels thump-thumping against the cobble-stone paving.

"*Americano?*" the cabby said. (167)

Victor finds himself taking an intuitively contradictory stance that he seems unable to repress. Victor was born of Italian parents in Italy and then he moved to Canada and in Canada he acquired his Canadian identity. He became a Canadian after his arrival to Canada. The narrative leaves uncertain, from Victor's point of view, what constitutes being a Canadian for him: is it becoming English, French, or Italian-Canadian, is it a question of language acquisition and practice, or are there certain cultural values and beliefs that support the idea of Canadian identity? It is as if by entering Italy, he is consciously standing back and observing both sides of his cultural identity: the Canadian and the Italian. It is a kind of wilful psychological dislocation that provides him temporarily and perhaps in an illusory way a "complete alternative" (Montanucci) to his habitual response to his immediate social environment.

In the last part of the book, memory is identified as playing tricks with Victor/Vittorio's mind: "but I no longer trusted myself, the tricks my mind played" (239). Confrontation with the reality of the Old World undermines any secure memory on which a cultural understanding is or was based on. The Old World is a sum of stories that turn out not to be totally verifiable. Thus any certainty about the world is thrown into question, since the implication is that the New World is as "story" oriented as the Old One. If an understanding of the world is a sum of stories, then truth becomes a possibility that must be agreed upon. This idea that truth is relative and that its existence relies on individuals or groups of individuals who are willing to accept it suggests a modern sensibility about the multiplicity and relativity of meaning. In the novel, from both the perspective of Victor and the other main characters, this modern view of what is truth pervades both urban, technological society and rural, agrarian areas in the world. The Innocente trilogy operates within this problematic framework, which is at once the recuperation of an encompassing, grand-scale narrative and a subjection of this narrative to ideological fragmentation. This fragmentation is reflected in Victor having been born elsewhere, of having lost his mother and father, of having had a half sister, who temporarily becomes his lover, and from whom he becomes estranged, and of Victor constantly being conflicted about his Italian and Canadian identity. It appears to Victor that the moral end-game is the will to end it all. Vittorio decides to move to London, England: "It was the following night before I reached London ... I stood outside the station thinking I might simply collapse there on the pavement: this was the end, there was nowhere further to go" (310–311). His attempted suicide has no finality, only a lingering non-lethal slitting of the wrists in an anonymous bathtub in a rented room. The confusion and desperation that at some point had pushed him to try to commit suicide is followed by his lack of commitment and insecurity after his failure to do so. Thus, the return in the novel does not provide an ideological explanation or an existential solution to the problem of living in the modern world, where the past cannot provide a guideline as to how one should live in the present.

Having returned to Italy together, Rita and Vittorio stumble upon a deserted archaeological exhibit near their hometown. The sign at the entrance reads: "Seven Hundred Thousand Years Ago, The Community Of The First Europeans" (262). Accompanying them is John, who has befriended Rita in Toronto and invited her to tour the world with him. He is an older man, who could also be Rita's natural father, the wandering German soldier of *Lives of the Saints*. At this point, the text refers to an analogy about the earliest dwellers of this region who were themselves nomads (the earliest possible migrants). This analogy hints at the nature of Victor's, Rita's, and John's visit to Italy. They like their prehistoric antecedents are travelers in the area; they form a small disparate group of visitors, who are themselves clandestine. Vittorio has avoided military service in Italy, Rita is a half-sister conceived in Italy during her mother's illicit affair, and John is possibly the solution to a number of questions (the German soldier in *Lives of the Saints* and Rita's father in *Where She Has Gone*) who is attempting to atone (once again the Catholic theme emerges with full force) by having guided her to her hometown to meet up with her brother.

The narrative forces us to consider the nature of the past. Who are the Europeans if not wandering souls? No one (not even a modern Ulysses) is at home anywhere. In response to Victor's question about why people search for the source of their origins, Rita states that finding out who you are is a kind of a game. The entire passage suggests that because most people are wanderers the only home they can claim is their current one. The text implies

that most people in the modern world share a common
sensibility since their origins are from somewhere else.
Thus, the trilogy concludes with an open-ended trajectory, with wondrous dreams about the origin of things.
But as Victor admits to himself, dreams are also invoca-
tions of hope and desire:

> Tell me your dreams, she might have said, and I would
> have told her, I dreamt I wrote you a letter and in it
> was everything. That is what I have wanted, to hold
> every nuance and hope, every smell, every bit of sky,
> though there hasn't been a single line I've written here
> that hasn't seemed untrue in some way the instant I
> set it down (317).

Works Cited

Ende, Michael. Trans. Ralph Manheim. *The Neverending
Story*. Garden City, NY: Doubleday, 1983.

Hardt, Michael and Tony Negri. *Empire*. Cambridge, Mass:
Harvard University Press, 2001.

Montanucci, Alberto. *Colpo di Coda*. Unpublished manus-
cript, 2002. Note: Perhaps, the following quote translated
from the original Italian best sets Alberto Montanucci's
work: "he even dared asking if the following pages
could maybe be inscribed in that 'modern novel-essay'
of which Dario Del Corno finds an antecedent in the
dialogue *On Love* where Plutarch 'moved by the interest
in the multiform reality of life' enlarges the argument
to 'autonomous, historical and biographical vicissitudes'". (Mascioni, Grytzko. *La notte di Apollo*. Milan,
Italy: Rusconi, 1990. *The Night of Apollo* by Grytzko Mascioni, Rusconi, 1990) This is the quote in Italian: "e ha

anche osato chiedersi se le pagine seguenti potrebbero
magari ascriversi a quel 'moderno romanzo-saggio' di
cui Dario Del Corno trova un antecedente nel dialogo
Sull'amore, ove Plutarco, 'indotto dall'interesse per la
realtà multiforme della vita', allarga l'argomento 'a vi-
cende autonome, storiche, e autobiografiche'". *La notte
di Apollo*, Grytzko Mascioni, Rusconi, 1990.

Note: these are the original Italian passages by Alberto Montanucci from *Colpo di Coda*:

1. "destinandomi alla perdizione sociale, al disloca-
mento continuo completamente alternativo all'ere-
mitismo. Con la fortuna che, viaggiando, il brutto
che si incontra non si sente proprio, perché si sente
di osservarlo dall'esterno, cosa che egoisticamente
abbassa le rabbie e aumenta la serenità..." (folio 14,
p. 31)

2. "Anche sul tono di questo testo credo che influisca
la distanza e il tempo dello stare lontani e in luoghi
differenti, per cui si prende un certo distacco dalle
cose, che non vuol dire snobbarle, ma considerarle
fra le tante che la paura di crepare non ci fa pren-
dere per quello che sono; così invece possono essere
prese con quella puzza sotto il naso che ci permette
di dire liberamente a quelli che tentato di dominare
che li sentiamo come invadenti fastidiose piattole
che prudono tra gl'inguini." (folio 21, p. 17)

Ricci, Nino. *Lives of the Saints*. Dunvegan, ON: Cormorant,
1990.

-----. *In A Glass House*, Toronto, ON: McClelland and Stewart,
1993

-----.*Where She Has Gone*. Toronto, ON: McClelland and
Stewart, 1997.

Jim Zucchero

Postcolonialism and Shifting Notions of Exile in Nino Ricci's Fictional Trilogy

We are old, Chevalley, very old. For over twenty five centuries we've been bearing the weight of superb and heterogeneous civilizations, all from outside, none made by ourselves, none that we could call our own. We're as white as you are, Chevalley, and as the Queen of England; and yet for two thousand five hundred years we've been a colony. I don't say that in complaint; it's our fault. But even so we're worn out and exhausted. (145)

— *The Leopard*, **Giuseppe di Lampedusa**

IN THIS PASSAGE from Lampedusa's classic Italian novel, the Prince tries to explain to the Chevalley (the representative of Garibaldi's new government of a unified Italy) something of the character of Sicilians and by extension southern Italians in general. The description is useful here for two reasons: first, because it provides a capsule history of colonialism in southern Italy and its impact on the collective consciousness of southern Italians; and secondly, because it points us toward important but uncertain issues of how writing by and about Italian immigrants to Canada can contribute to debates about postcolonialism in Canadian literature. Can Canadian literature be "postcolonial" and, if so, how does ethnic minority writing figure into this discussion? One

way to approach the question is to reframe it in the context of immigrant writing and ask: How is Canada postcolonial for immigrants whose experience of colonialism
may be quite distinct and varied? This essay discusses
the trilogy of novels by Nino Ricci as one example of contemporary Canadian fiction that examines shifting notions of exile and cultural identity[1] for one of Canada's
largest ethnic minorities. Ricci's characters, Italians and
Italian-Canadians, carry the baggage of their cultural
and colonial past into an uncertain and open-ended future in Canada; they are, like all immigrants, required
to refashion themselves, to create viable new identities
out of their cultural heritage in the context of their new
surroundings. Theories of hybridity and ambivalence
emerging out of postcolonial studies provide useful models and methods for examining the liminal features of
their immigrant experience, and for rethinking Canadian narratives of immigration by reorienting us to
ideas about diaspora, cultural identity and cultural belonging.[2] Furthermore, analysis of these texts contributes to the discussion of postcolonialism in Canada
because they help us move beyond the particularist/
universalist gap in fresh ways. I will argue that in Ricci's
novels sexual transgression, in the form of adultery and
incest, functions metaphorically as well as literally. These
transgressions reflect the shifting orientation of individuals to authority, the reversal of patterns of domination,
and the prospect of reconciling the influence of the past
with the possibilities of the future. Ricci's novels contribute to current discussions about identity politics, multiculturalism as a strategy of containment, and the problems of binaristic construction of margin/centre and
universal/particularist debates in postcolonial theory.

One function of postcolonial theory is to help us

examine the translatability of culture across borders. These borders are not only national but also linguistic, cultural, religious and ethnic. The specific conditions relating to immigration by Italians, most of them from the south of Italy, to Canada during various waves of migration over the twentieth century, form the backdrop against which Italian-Canadian writing has evolved and against which the question of Canadian postcoloniality must be measured. While conditions in Canada may have seemed agreeable to most Italian immigrants, still the discrepancy between the ideal fostered through official government policies of multiculturalism familiar today, and the realities of their social struggles (with language acquisition and prejudice, for example) must have resulted in some measure of dissonance and, for many, a feeling of living in exile. Eva Hoffman, in her essay "Wanderers by Choice," suggests: "In recent years, great shifts in the political and social landscape have affected the very notion of exile. Cross-cultural movement has become the norm, which means that leaving one's native country is not as dramatic or traumatic as it used to be" (46-47). While Hoffman's notion of our shifting concept of exile may be valid, it does not follow that because cross-cultural movement is more commonplace it is necessarily less dramatic or traumatic than it ever was. The drama (or trauma) depends a great deal upon the particular circumstances of the migration and the personal characteristics of those who migrate; moreover, the dramatic appeal of these stories of migration will depend upon the literary craft and sheer power of imagination of those who relate and record them.

To appreciate the particular critical concerns generated by much Italian-Canadian writing, and especially Ricci's trilogy, requires, first, an awareness of the social conditions in southern Italy at this time; and second, an understanding of the ways in which these social, political and economic conditions — the material conditions of production — contributed to the development of a particular sense of cultural identity. Ricci's novels describe how this sense of cultural identity is manifested by successive generations of Italian-Canadians when they are transplanted into a Canadian setting.

What is colonial about the condition of the characters and events described in Ricci's fiction? I would propose that these works lend themselves to postcolonial analysis in at least three ways — geographically, historically and psychologically — and that these three elements are connected organically, that they are inextricably tied. One way in which the Innocente family is colonial is in terms of the dislocation they experience following their migration from Italy to Canada. Dislocation is a central feature of postcolonial literature. "The term is used to describe the experience of those who have willingly moved from the imperial 'Home' to the colonial margin, but it affects all those who, as a result of colonialism, have been placed in a location that ... needs ... to be 'reinvented' in language, in narrative and in myth" (73), according to Ashcroft, Griffiths and Tiffin. They note that "the disruptive and 'disorienting' experience of dislocation becomes a primary influence on the regenerative energies in a post-colonial culture" (74). The volume and variety of immigrant writing produced in Canada support this claim.[3] Ricci's fiction is an example of writing from the Italian-Canadian community that contributes to re-inventing, in narrative and myth, the dislocated of his ethnic community.[4]

Ricci's novels describe the experience of a group of people whose history is steeped in colonialism, and whose experience of colonialism is deeply conflicted. A striking paradox characterizes the relationship of southern Italians to the very notion of colonialism: on one hand, they can identify, at least in a historical and mythical sense, with the ancient Roman empire; they can claim an affinity with an imperial power that conquered and dominated much of the known world in ancient times. On the other hand (as Lampedusa points out), they can point to the footprints and the landmarks left behind by countless conquering armies that marched across their land, occupied it, and ruled over them at various times over the past twenty-five centuries: Carthaginians, Greeks, Romans, Saracens, Normans and Bourbons. It is easy to imagine how such a complex past might give rise to feelings of ambivalence toward colonialism, and equally easy to appreciate the hybridity that might emerge from the convergence of so many cultural and historical influences. It is difficult to isolate and accurately describe the specific features that define the cultural identity of any ethnic group; nevertheless, in the case of the southern Italian community described in Ricci's novels, and particularly in *Lives of the Saints,* there are certain features, painted in broad strokes, that provide an unmistakable sense of the character of the place and the mindset of its inhabitants — their cultural identity. The psychological aspects of their colonialism are the most difficult to trace but they are also the most insidious and arguably the most important aspects for the purpose of this discussion.

The social and economic conditions in Valle del Sole, the fictional hometown of the Innocentes, are marked by poverty, a lack of opportunity or the prospect of social mobility. There is the sense that little can change here, that little can be hoped for and consequently despair and resentment seem to simmer just below the surface. Politically there is a sense of resignation and yet an abiding sense of suspicion of authority and authority figures; this curious disposition is manifest in what the Italians call "omertá" — silent non-cooperation. A deep sense of religious devotion to the Catholic faith is evident, but it is countered by a strong measure of cynicism toward the Church, and by an equally deeply rooted sense of superstition. There is a distinct tension in the clash of Christian and pagan ideologies and practices. Three factors — the colonial social conditions in southern Italy; the ambivalent historical orientation of southern Italians toward colonialism; and the immediate effects of their migration to Canada, with its ensuing sense of disorientation resulting from dislocation — these are the features that contribute most significantly to defining the colonial circumstances in which the characters in these novels function. These factors constitute a strong case for examining Ricci's novels in the context of postcolonialism in Canada; his writing lends itself to postcolonial analysis in terms of geographical, historical and psychological considerations.

I consider Ricci's trilogy here in the context of criticism by scholars like Kamboureli and Godard, who have examined Canadian literature from postcolonial perspectives, and with a particular interest in exploring questions of hybridity.[5] Applied to the diasporic subject, hybridity can provide insights into the historical materiality that is so important to the construction of identity; hybridity posits that the past is crucially important without being determinative of the future. Kamboureli suggests hybridity theory constitutes a new paradigm for the critical evaluation of Canadian literature and the machinations of multiculturalism in Canada. Hybridity, for Kamboureli and Godard, has replaced paradox, as a tool to conceptualize the condition of the diasporic subject. The immigrant exists in a liminal space symbolized on one side by his baggage — all of what has formed him and which he carries from the past; and on the other side by his expectations — all of his hopes and dreams, fears and apprehensions for the future. "Immigrant" describes both a condition of being and a set of circumstances. Hybridity can characterize not only the temporal condition, the in-between-ness of past/future, but also the gap between personal experience and the social and political milieu as the forces that determine the construction of identity. This dynamic is not binary but a web of interconnectedness. Godard notes that, for Kamboureli, hybridity "is the condition of diasporic subjects as distinguished from the binarity of ethnic subjects. Hybridity is also the haunt of the *angelus novus*, Walter Benjamin's angel of history, suspended between past and future in a violent storm of progress. The diasporic subject caught in this contradictory in-between ... like the angel, transforms the past into a future that will be" (Godard 240). Ricci's Italian-Canadian protagonists, Victor and Rita, manifest characteristics that Godard and Kamboureli associate with diasporic subjects; they are able to transform their past and project for themselves a future that absorbs the past but is not bound by it. They seem to emerge at the end damaged but, still, determined to 'move on'.[6]

Writing by Jonathan Rutherford on the subject of identity points to one way Ricci's novels contribute to discussions about postcolonialism in Canada. Rutherford suggests the relationship of the margin to the centre can be recast to avoid the binarism that "reduces the potential of difference into polar opposites" (21-2). He asserts: "[The margin] is more than a simple boundary marking the outer limits of the centred term because it functions as a supplement, marking what the centre lacks but also what it needs in order to define fully and confirm its identity" (22). His point, that the margin helps to define and confirm the identity of the centre, is provocative if we apply it to the case of diasporic writing in Canada, and it relates very directly to the writing of Kamboureli and Godard on this subject. It suggests that the totality of writing from ethnic communities and individuals, in all its diversity and asymmetry, constitutes an integral part of the Canadian national identity — as elusive a notion as it is. In Rutherford's view, "the Other, in its very alienness, simply mirrors and represents what is deeply familiar to the centre, but projected outside itself" (22). Canada is postcolonial to the extent it recognizes and embraces the otherness and difference that its ethnic writers and diasporic populations represent. Ricci's fiction speaks to the compelling human need to confront the past, not to escape it, but to absorb it and overturn it.

Over a period of seven years, Ricci wrote and published three novels that trace the movement and development of an Italian immigrant family in Canada: *Lives of the Saints,* published in 1990, won the Governor General's Award for fiction; it was followed by *In A Glass House* (1993), and *Where She Has Gone* in 1997. The trilogy traces the development of Vittorio (Victor) Innocente from his early childhood in a southern Italian village, through his immigration to rural southwestern Ontario, and finally to his migration to metropolitan Toronto. Collectively the three novels explore the construction of personal identity, particularly through reference to language acquisition, memory and cultural touchstones.

The story traces the geographic, cultural and psychic movement of the protagonist from the old world to the new world and from childhood to maturity. As an expanded depiction of one family's experience of immigration and settlement, Ricci's three novels resonate with many other migration narratives. The deep sense of alienation that accompanies the experience of cultural and linguistic dislocation, and the primacy of language as a tool for creating an identity are two of the most striking features of Ricci's writing. But above all, for Victor, the migrant experience is infused with a profound sense of ambivalence as he attempts to redefine himself in his new environment. This ambivalence and its effects — the hybridity that it engenders — will be the focus of my discussion of Ricci's work here. Victor's ambivalence is clearly evident in a variety of ways. For example, he is ambivalent in his sense and use of language; his knowledge of Italian dialect is of limited usefulness in southern Ontario and he struggles with self-expression as he learns to understand and speak English. His early experience at school and his agonized family relations, particularly with his father, provide clear indications of the ambivalence he feels as a young immigrant caught between two cultures and residing with a foot in each. But most of all, Victor's ambivalence is crystallized in his relationship with his half-sister, Rita.

Rita, the illegitimate child, is the product of his mother's adulterous affair with a mysterious stranger in the barn (in the old country), the episode that opens *Lives of the Saints* and sets off all the action that follows. Born during a violent storm at sea in the midst of their trans-Atlantic crossing, Rita becomes a metaphor for hybridity and for Victor's experience of immigration and assimilation. His feelings toward her are characterized by a profound ambivalence — his need to know her and embrace her, but also his need to recognize her independence and respect her autonomy. Their relationship is the focal point of the trilogy. I argue that their brief incestuous encounter functions symbolically to illustrate their disavowal of authority and a reorientation toward the past that is necessary for them to construct new identities for themselves in the new world. The reconciliation between Victor and Rita in the third novel suggests a degree of resolution, but it is, in the end, ambivalent and resists closure. I assert that the two sexual transgressions depicted — adultery and incest — operate as bookends in the first and third novels and provide the key to the interpretation of the trilogy as a whole.

My interpretation of Ricci's work engages with Homi Bhabha's writing about hybridity and ambivalence. Much of Bhabha's work emphasizes the psychology of the colonial experience; he adapts psychoanalytic theory to examine post-colonial subjectivity and the splitting of the subject in colonial settings. In his 1985 article "Signs taken for Wonders" Bhabha articulates his ideas about the nature of colonial authority and the dynamics of colonial power, including the concepts of hybridity and ambivalence. Aspects of Bhabha's theory can be applied usefully to Ricci's fiction; however, his description of colonial subjectivity at times collapses important differences that pertain to distinct kinds of colonial experience, including the marginality of immigrants in various circumstances. Read through each other, Ricci's work is illuminated by Bhabha's concepts; but equally important are the ways in which Ricci's writing resists certain aspects of Bhabha's descriptions or stretches his notions of colonial subjectivity, ambivalence and hybridity.

Bhabha investigates "the ambivalence of the presence of authority ... in its colonial articulation" (110). He suggests that the colonial setting opens up a space that becomes the site of "a strategy of disavowal" and "a process of splitting"; where "the trace of what is disavowed is not repressed but repeated as something different — a mutation, a *hybrid*" (111). Hybridity, according to Bhabha, is "the sign of the productivity of colonial power, its shifting forces and fixities; it is the name of the strategic reversal of the process of domination through disavowal" (112). I think that the strange twists and turns of plot that unfold in Ricci's novels exhibit a disavowal of authority and domination similar to that described by Bhabha. However, the disavowal evident in Ricci's novels takes on a particular shape and colour specifically because it emerges from the experience of immigration as one aspect of postcolonial subjectivity. The space that opens up to enable such disavowal is created by the process of immigration and movement from the old world to the new world. Specifically, Victor and his half-sister Rita revisit their mother's act of adultery — a transgression against the social and moral codes — and re-enact it as a brief incestuous encounter. This action, their incest, both mimics and mocks the adulterous affair; in Bhabha's terms, the disavowed action is not repressed but repeated as something different. But what is crucial to our understanding of their actions, what defines their act as reversing the process of domination, is the radically different effect of their encounter. Their transgression does not have the same crippling effect for them as their mother Cristina's deed had; rather, it is a social barrier that they pass through and supersede en route to forming viable identities for themselves in the new world. Their resilience and repositioning constitutes a form of hybridity. Bhabha suggests that "the display of hybridity — its peculiar 'replication' — terrorizes authority with the ruse of recognition, its mimicry, its mockery" (115). In this sense their transgression may be seen as a means of freeing themselves from the shadow of their own dark past. To illustrate my point I will examine the two scenes of transgression — the adultery and incest — and their repercussions in detail.

Lives of the Saints begins with: "If this story has a beginning ... then that beginning occurred ... when my mother was bitten by a snake" (*Lives* 1). The description that follows paints a scene of a rushed illicit sexual encounter in the family barn interrupted by the untimely appearance of a snake. Ricci uses the opportunity to expose the curious mix of Christian and pagan beliefs that inhabits the minds of the local peasants. So, for example, in the description of the stable scene and subsequent snake bite biblical and pagan images and associations are twisted and knotted together: the stable, traditional scene of the nativity, becomes the scene of adultery. The incident releases the peasants' penchant for superstition and the local lore of snakes is set out:

> Snakes, in Valle del Sole, had long been imbued with special meaning. Some of the villagers believed they were immortal, because they could shed their skin ... But there was a saying in Valle del Sole, '*Do l'orgoglio sta, la serpe se ne va,*' — where pride is the snake goes — and there were few who doubted that snakes, whatever their other properties, were agents of the evil eye. (*Lives* 11)

The scene is important because it establishes the association between Vittorio's mother, Cristina, and the unforgivable sin of pride. Predictably, the result of this illicit affair in the barn is Cristina's pregnancy. But to the townspeople it is not so much her transgression that offends them as it is her refusal to be shamed by her deed. Cristina is held in contempt by other women for her pride, her beauty, and her staunch refusal to conform to local standards. They demand a confession, or that she should take 'a cure', some act of atonement, some gesture, not only for her sake but to prevent the curse from settling on them all. But Cristina is steadfast. At a certain level they seem to wish they could be more like her, but they dare not; on this the social order rests — compliance with unspoken rules and standards. Bhabha notes that "the acknowledgement of authority depends on the immediate — unmediated — visibility of its rules of recognition as the unmistakable referent of historical necessity" (110). In Ricci's novels it is especially important to recognize the ways in which colonial authority is culturally grounded. First, we must acknowledge here the role of the Church as a model for imperial power and as part of the state apparatus that creates ideology. Also, it is important to note that in this instance, at the local level, colonial authority has devolved to a point where it is implied and imposed not by a ruling class but by the local peasants themselves. Their lack of any real power to change their circumstances has caused them to develop and submit to an arcane local authority characterized by its conservatism and reliance on superstition. Cristina attempts to resist the authority founded in her traditional culture and, in refusing to recognize such authority as necessity, she gestures toward the possibility of an alternate social order. That alternate order will be exposed and acted upon by Victor and Rita years later, in their need to contravene the authority's residual power in the new world. The effects of Cristina's defiance are far reaching and are most evident among the three generations of men in her own family.

The deep sense of shame felt by Cristina's father, the town mayor and a local favourite, provides clear evidence of the weight of cultural (and religious) authority in the old world. He resigns his public office and recedes into the shadows of town life, bitter and broken. Vittorio sees the profound change in him and comments: "Over my grandfather's face a film had formed, tangible as stone, which he retreated behind, like a snail into its shell, staring into space as if my mother and I were not there" (*Lives* 57). In a final act of defiance, before their departure for Canada, Cristina refuses to make amends with the townsfolk who come to see her off; she is vehement in her denunciation of them:

> 'Fools!' she shouted now. 'You tried to kill me but you see I'm still alive. And now you come to watch me hang, but I won't be hanged, not by your stupid rules and superstitions. You are the ones who are dead, not me, because not one of you knows what it means to be free and to make a choice. (*Lives* 184)

Cristina's position of dissent from her community is clear, but her pride, like her adultery, has consequences for others who are less capable of acting with impunity. In the aftermath of Cristina's scandal one of the local women asserts: "God will make his judgements ... It's not for nothing she was bitten by a snake" (*Lives* 51). And in due course Cristina's fate is decided: she delivers her baby during a storm at sea and dies shortly afterwards from excessive bleeding. To the local peasants Cristina's death during childbirth is a clear sign of the wrath of an angry God; conversely, it could be interpreted as easily as the more direct result of an incompetent, drunken ship's doctor. More importantly we are left to ponder the symbolic meaning of Cristina's death. Her rebellion and disavowal of local authority cannot be sustained at this point in time and in this locale; but it anticipates very different consequences of her children's disavowal, later on in the new world. As a consequence of her death, her cuckold husband in Canada finds himself charged with the care of not only his estranged son Victor, but also a newborn baby who is not his own.

In A Glass House is in many ways the record of the odyssey of immigration seen through a child's eyes. Vittorio, now known as Victor, struggles to establish a rapport with his father, Mario. His father, in turn, struggles to reconcile himself to the shame of Cristina's adultery, within his family and in the local Italian-Canadian community. Mario's complete inability to cope with the consequences of his wife's infidelity becomes clear. He is crushed by the disgrace and embarrassment heaped on him by her deed. Although he lives in the new world now, Mario has in many ways never left the old world in spirit. His grief is summed up in one line. Weeping in a field, he says: "It's better to be dead than to live like this"(*Glass* 28).

While relations between Mario and his son are strained, he fails to establish any rapport with young Rita. Mario is crippled emotionally and socially by the stigma of his wife's adultery, and the baby in the house becomes a perpetual reminder, a living sign of his grief. Irritable, gloomy and forlorn, he too is a broken man, stripped of his dignity and, he believes, haunted by a curse, as when his greenhouse is razed by a terrible fire. Eventually Rita is adopted out to a local Anglo family (the Amhersts) and with her departure Victor's family surrenders the illusion that they had a vital bond. The immigrant family has broken down; Rita is co-opted and absorbed into the Anglo fold perhaps symbolic of the tide of cultural assimilation. Rita's departure is described as an event in which no conscious choice was exercised. Victor notes: "It seemed no real decision was ever made about Rita, ... that we'd merely given ourselves over to what had happened as an act of fate, never daring, in our immigrant helplessness, to question what rules such matters were governed by here" (*Glass* 120). The manner in which Rita is surrendered, more by default than by wilful act of choice, conveys vividly the sense of "immigrant helplessness" that characterizes the Innocente family's status and the particular marginality of their colonial subjectivity. The consciousness of the presence of choice and the importance of exercising will becomes vitally important later on when Victor and Rita try to re-establish relations as young adults.

In the trilogy's final volume Victor and Rita slowly resume contact with each other in Toronto. The shift in the setting is important. Paradoxically, here in the crowded urban metropolis, they seem able to open up a space in which the old terms of authority, the inflexibility of their cultural heritage, can be cast off and they are free to seek out new patterns of behaviour that are devoid of the emotional scars of their past. The renewal of their contact signals their mutual need to articulate a mature relationship. The early chapters place a heavy emphasis on memory, ideas of home, and the dynamics of relationships. As Victor begins to spend time with Rita he struggles to find an appropriate range of emotional and physical responses to her. Once when she is upset he extends a tender, caring embrace to her only to find that he is later haunted by the memory of the impress of her body and the heat of her skin. There is the lingering sense that intimacy between them is both desirable (even necessary) and dangerous; called for, but forbidden. Their relationship becomes a social and emotional conundrum.

In an effort to find quiet time together Victor and Rita take a road trip and their destination, Niagara Falls, seems a fitting one. The famous Canadian landmark, with its torrents of rushing water, is the physical setting for a watershed in their personal relations. Here, before the great chasm and cascade, the emotional barriers between them begin to fall away and they are, for the first time as adults, able to achieve a sense of comfort in each other's presence: "We had come to the Falls ... I stood behind her and instinctively opened my coat to enfold her within it, ... it was clear, in the way I held her, in the way she leaned against me, that some line had been stepped over, that some emotion that had been hovering between us barely acknowledged had grown suddenly real" (*Where* 48). The description of the physical contact that takes place between Victor and Rita at the Falls hints at their movement toward personal and emotional reconciliation. When they return home and part with a kiss there is a mounting sense of both intimacy and danger. Their relationship is charged with a profound sense of ambivalence. Here we might recall Bhabha's description of ambivalence, a term borrowed from psychoanalytic theory and used to describe a continual fluctuation between wanting one thing and its opposite; or, the simultaneous attraction toward and repulsion from an object, person or action. In the complex ambivalence evident in Victor and Rita's relationship Ricci moves beyond the notions of ambivalence that characterize the two earlier volumes — ambivalence toward local superstition or toward assimilation into a new country and culture. Victor and Rita's ambivalence enables Ricci to explore questions directed not toward the past or the present but toward the future: not merely who we are but who we can become and how to relate to each other in a new environment. The ambivalence of their relationship, in many ways a metaphor for their experience of migration and assimilation, will be worked through by the choices that they make, following their own dark descent.

The description of Victor and Rita's incest is full of contradictions and paradoxes. Rita comes to Victor's apartment and they examine their past relationship and current feelings toward each other, their sense of possessiveness, abandonment and belonging. In a moment of genuine reconciliation Rita asks to be held and their embrace unleashes in both of them a deep sense of the need for the warmth of human contact that each has lacked for so long: "I held her. There was a moment then that was like falling into a kind of human darkness, like the two of us opening a door in a dream and stepping out; and then we were kissing. There seemed no decision in this, just a giving-in to the darkness, to the falling" (*Where* 70). Their embrace and kiss, both awkward and tender, is emblematic of their yearning for a sense of acceptance and their hopefulness for fulfillment in their new surroundings. There is a clear sense in this scene that their passions, once released by their embrace, have a force of their own that will not be denied.

Victor describes their incestuous encounter in language that suggests a mental state of confusion and disorientation:

We were still falling. There seemed no distance between us now, just this awful relinquishing as if everything

> were unfolding at once unreal and yet inevitable, hav-
> ing nothing to do with us and yet what our lives had
> always been moving toward ... and then I was ... doing
> things and being inside of the doing of them and yet
> seeing them as if their reality were merely a mirroring
> of something already lived through, that had already
> long ago been done and atoned for. (*Where* 70-1)

The "awful relinquishing" that describes Victor's emotional response to his experience with his half-sister also
serves as an apt description of his sensibility toward his
own experience of immigration. Because the episode is
related by Victor, the first person narrator, we lack the
benefit of insight into Rita's impressions of their encounter. But what is striking from this description is the sense
that their communion was inevitable, pre-destined and
that, in a sense, they are repeating history. The suggestion that these events are "a mirroring of something already lived through" clearly invokes the memory of their
mother Cristina's catastrophic transgression — her act of
adultery. Victor and Rita's transgression is described in
terms that render it simultaneously knowingly wrong
and perfectly right:

> There was something almost ruthless in us then,
> hopeless, the instantaneous mutual admission of
> wrong and its flouting. There would be this one time,
> we seemed to say, when the world would split open
> and every unspeakable hope, every desire, every fear
> would be permitted. (*Where* 71)

The language of this passage recalls Bhabha's description of the split subject in a colonial setting. Furthermore, the conflation and inseparability of hopes and

fears here is the sort of paradox that is illumined by Bhabha's description of colonial hybridity. He notes that:

> Hybridity is not a third term that resolves the tension
> between two cultures ... in a dialectical play of 'recog-
> nition' ... Hybridity is a problematic of colonial rep-
> resentation and individuation that reverses the effects
> of colonialist disavowal, so that other 'denied' know-
> ledges enter upon the dominant discourse and estrange
> the basis of its authority—its rules of recognition. (113)

Viewed in this light, Victor and Rita's incest seems not
right or wrong but both, not an act of fate or will but
both; it seems as necessary as it is inevitable, the acknowledgement of their hopes and fears for each other
and for themselves.

As much as the incest between Victor and Rita reflects Bhabha's concept of hybridity, it also gestures toward ways in which immigrant colonial subjectivity
resists containment. Smaro Kamboureli has suggested
that "[d]iaspora, and the cultural difference that it entails, cannot be studied in terms of Us and Them, in
terms of sovereign and minority subjects; it must be
examined within the web of complexities that inform
ethnic subjectivity and its representations" (43-44). In
the case of Ricci's trilogy, the "complexities that inform
ethnic subjectivity" arise not only across national, cultural and linguistic borders (Italian and Canadian) but
within the scope of Italian-Canadian-ness as the hybrid
cultural ground in which these characters develop. What
becomes clear is that for Victor and Rita (and for others
of their generation) the struggle to create an identity is
as much a struggle against the "Us" of their ancestral
cultural heritage as it is a struggle against the "Them" of

the Canadian culture into which they have been transplanted. Their disavowal is as much a symbol of resistance to their own cultural heritage as it is an expression of their desire to create a new home for themselves in their Canadian surroundings.

In the aftermath of the incident Victor's reactions are scrutinized more extensively than Rita's. The day after the encounter he wanders out in the streets of Little Italy and stumbles upon a street procession — the passion play. It is Good Friday, the day of atonement for Christians, and Victor is swept away by memories of Easters passed as a child in Italy. Suddenly the full impact of his actions is felt and he is filled with remorse:

> I was a child again in a small village church in Italy ... what had I wanted then, what would the boy that I was have seen in the man I'd become? My head was filled with a rush of images, my whole past seeming to tumble through me like something to be taken away, that there was no going back to; and then I was crying.
>
> My god, I thought, my god what have I done? (*Where* 84-5)

But Rita seems better equipped to deal with the fallout from their affair. When they finally broach the subject and Victor confesses that he doesn't know what to do, she counters simply: "There's nothing to do ... I don't want you to think it's your fault ... I'm not a kid. We both did what we wanted. We could look at it that way ... Except that it was a mistake" (*Where* 113-114). Rita's comment that they chose this is crucial. Just as, in her view, they have chosen this course of action, so too they can choose not to disclose its occurrence to anyone — an option that did not exist for their mother Cristina. But their decision to keep their illicit encounter secret is a sort of double-edged sword: on one hand it enables them to retain control and "authority" over their transgression. It is not surrendered to public scrutiny for judgement against any social or moral standard. So they have, in a sense, mastered the authority; they answer only to themselves and to each other. However, in doing so they must internalize their actions and their struggle and assume responsibility for management of it in the future, a commitment whose unpredictability could be terrifying. Their situation is emblematic of their status as first generation immigrants: they have asserted their independence, their freedom of choice in an attempt to overthrow their past. But it is unclear to what extent their past will resurface to influence and affect their new lives.

In a recent article that discusses the strength of exile fiction in the Canadian literary scene, Pico Iyer suggests that the reconciliation of a troubled past with an open-ended future is a distinguishing feature of contemporary Canadian writing that deals with exile. He notes: "If the one great question that America asks of every newcomer is 'What will you do with your future?' Canada adds to it the more difficult ones, 'What will you do with your past? How much will you abandon everything that made you what you are and join in a sea of other pasts from Somalia, Barbados and South Africa?'" (46). He points out that Canadian writers are producing some of the "strongest (and most quietly radical) novels" of our time, a trend that he ascribes directly to the nature of our multiculturalism (46). When he accepted the Governor General's Award for English-language fiction in 2000, Michael Ondaatje—another acclaimed Canadian writer with ties to immigration and exile, said: "Nothing is more thrilling than recognizing one's own world in a book, one's own self-portrait in an invented story." The struggle of the immigrant, at the heart of the contemporary Canadian literary scene, (and at the centre of the Canadian literary canon), is an effective metaphor for the struggle that Canadians undertake in creating, and recreating themselves as a society, a process still very much in flux. The challenge now is to recognize the invented stories of Canada's immigrants and ethnic minorities as integral to the self-portrait of Canadian national identity and central to the study of postcolonialism in Canada.

Notes

1. I use the term "cultural identity" here to refer to what I conceive of as a sort of psychic space, a mental framework that combines the intellectual and emotional orientation to events and encompasses both conscious and unconscious influences and motivations.

2. It is a cliché to say that Canada is a nation that was built largely by immigrants. With the exception of aboriginal writing, all Canadian writing is immigrant writing and "ethnic" writing, whether it emerges out of the dominant majority culture or from a minority ethnic group. The history of immigrant writing in Canada is well documented; writing by immigrants and about the experience of immigration covers every period of writing in Canada and springs from a vast array of cultures. Critical response to immigrant writing has been a hallmark of the Canadian critical tradition as evidenced by the work of Northrop Frye, Margaret Atwood, John Moss and more recently writers like Enoch Padolsky, Sneja Gunew and Smaro Kamboureli.

3.   Many of the most popular Canadian novels of the twen-
      tieth century, by writers like Mordecai Richler, F.P.
      Grove, Laura Salverson and John Marlyn, examine,
      from various ethnic perspectives, the experience of im-
      migration and settlement in Canada and the assimila-
      tion that follows. Writing that deals with the experience
      of migration continues to be a prominent feature of the
      contemporary Canadian literary scene, as evidenced
      most recently by works from Rabindranath Maharaj,
      Yann Martel, Wayson Choy, Fred Wah, and others.

4.   Ricci has, at times, expressed his frustration with the
      problems that arise from writing about the experience of
      immigration. See "Laying to rest 'this whole immigrant
      thing'," *Globe and Mail* 13 Sept. 1997, C10. The article ad-
      dresses some of the difficulties that accompany being
      labeled as an ethnic writer and highlights the problem
      of minority ethnic identity as a strategy for containment.
      Notwithstanding these factors, Amanda Mullen notes
      that Ricci's fiction has been instrumental in marking the
      contribution of Italian immigrants to Canadian nation
      building; she writes: "In using his fiction to recreate the
      suffering of Italian immigrants, Ricci adds their stories
      to Canada's national narrative and thereby recovers a
      lost history and claims a place in the nation for Can-
      adians of Italian origin" (40). (See her essay "Neither Here
      nor There" in *Canadian Ethnic Studies*, Summer 2004.)

5.   Two important critical works that focus on issues of
      diasporic writing in Canada in relation to matters of
      multiculturalism, the politics of representations of eth-
      nic identity, and postcolonial concerns such as hybridity,
      are Smaro Kamboureli's *Scandalous Bodies: Diasporic
      Literature in English Canada* (2000) and Barbara Godard's
      essay "Notes from the Cultural Field: Canadian Litera-
      ture from Identity to Hybridity" (2000).

6. The reading of Ricci's trilogy I offer here is an optimistic interpretation of what is, admittedly, at times a rather dark tale. Ricci's novels are complex; they invite and support many interpretations. I approach his texts here with a particular focus on issues of memory, authority and the past, and find narrative turns and details of characterization that support my reading; however, I recognize that Ricci's novels also problematize a range of other issues such as family relations, patriarchy and male power. The strained relations between Victor and Rita reflect other problematic relationships between Victor and his father, between Rita and Mario, between Victor and John. Each of these relations can support readings that highlight distinct social and moral issues, such as shame and betrayal.

Works Cited

Ashcroft, Bill, Gareth Griffiths and Helen Tiffin. *Key Concepts in Post-colonial Studies.* London: Routledge, 1998.

Bhabha, Homi K. "Signs Taken For Wonders." *Race, Writing and Difference: Special Issue of the Journal Critical Inquiry.* Ed. Henry Louis Gates Jnr. Chicago: Chicago UP, 1985. Rpt. in *The Location of Culture.* London: Routledge, 1994. 102-22.

Godard, Barbara. "Notes from the Cultural Field: Canadian Literature from Identity to Hybridity." *Essays on Canadian Writing* 72 (Winter 2000): 209-247.

Hoffman, Eva. "Wanderers by Choice." *UTNE Reader* July-August 2000: 6-7.

Iyer, Pico. "Exile Fiction." *Saturday Night* Dec. 1999/Jan. 2000: 46.

Kamboureli, Smaro. *Scandalous Bodies: Diasporic Literature in English Canada.* London: Oxford UP, 2000.

Lampedusa, Giuseppe di. *The Leopard*. (1958) Trans. Archibald Calquhoun. New York: Collins, 1961.

Loriggio, Francesco. ed. *Social Pluralism and Literary History: The Literature of the Italian Emigration*. Toronto: Guernica, 1996.

Mullen, Amanda. "Neither Here nor There." *Canadian Ethnic Studies*. Summer 2004 Vol 36, Issue 2, 29-51.

Ondaatje, Michael. "My thank-you note to Canada." *Globe and Mail* 15 Nov. 2000, natl. ed.: R2

Ricci, Nino. *Lives of the Saints*. Dunvegan: Cormorant, 1990.

-----. *In A Glass House*. Toronto: McClelland & Stewart, 1993.

-----. *Where She Has Gone*. Toronto: McClelland & Stewart, 1997.

Rutherford, Jonathan. "A Place Called Home: Identity and the Cultural Politics of Difference." *Identity—Community, Culture, Difference*. Ed. Jonathan Rutherford. London: Lawrence & Wishart, 1990. 9-27.

Howard A. Doughty

The Novelist As Anthropologist: An Essay on the Fictional Work of Nino Ricci

Thou shalt not sit
With statisticians nor commit
A social science
    —W.H. Auden

REVIEWS AND DISCUSSIONS of Nino Ricci's trilogy commonly focus on two themes.[1] One theme is the inner conflict and psychological anxiety of the protagonist, Vittorio Innocente. The other is the accuracy of Ricci's "thick description" of the supporting characters and settings.[2] Beginning with *Lives of the Saints*, the "customs and narrow ways" of the Italian village of Valle del Sole are meticulously disclosed. Its "rural, superstitious, clannish, pagan"[3] inhabitants are genuinely depicted and sensitively rendered "with a tenderness that avoids sentimentality."[4] Ricci, we are told, "has created a real place, has populated it with real people."[5] Ricci himself described *Lives of the Saints* as "written in a high realist style" and added that it "relies on a detailed representation of the world of the story for its effect."[6] The world that is represented in the first novel is defined by one commentator as "an inbred little community" wherein "peasant Catholicism" melds "with paganism."[7] It is this second theme, the delineation of the collective social context rather than the complex individual psychological states, that most concerns us here.

Cultural anthropology can initially be painted as an inquisitive eye looking at human attitudes and actions both from without and from within the social community. Objective observers examine societies from the outside in an attempt to create a science of culture corresponding to the theories and methods of natural science. In the alternative, subjective interpreters argue that genuine understanding (*verstehen*) must give strong recognition to the meaning of thought and behaviour as experienced and understood by the people under study. The first is commonly called an "etic" approach; the second, "emic."[8]

Nino Ricci's method is congenial to the emic and particularistic strain in anthropology that seeks to reconstruct cultural history accurately without yielding to the temptation to employ a more ambitious comparative or evolutionary framework that would facilitate the development of general laws of cultural development. In *Lives of the Saints*, the mores and folkways of Valle del Sole are recollected from the childhood memories of Vittorio, then living through his seventh year. The sequel, *In a Glass House*, shifts the setting: first, to an immigrant Italian farming community in south-western Ontario; next, to a suburban university in Toronto; and then to an African boarding school. The stops along the way are mediated through Vittorio's increasingly mature gaze. Despite radical shifts of place and circumstance, and notwithstanding the personal growth and development of his main character, Vittorio Innocente, Ricci's admirers say that the writer's powers of observation are abidingly keen and that his precise representations of community life remain accurate and evocative. Even in the third novel, *Where She Has Gone*, the increasingly intense psychological dimensions of the story, emanating from the violation of the antediluvian taboo of incest, do not detract from the persistent attention to cultural detail as Vittorio, now a young man, returns to his birthplace, a reluctantly modernizing Valle del Sole. There, he encounters half-remembered characters from his childhood, including his former playmate Fabrizio with whom he shared the original venial sin of smoking cigarettes. Fabrizio has worked in Roman restaurants, but has chosen to pass his life under the clear Apennine sky. Self-consciously choosing the security of a government job and the vocation of tending his "Garden of Eden," Fabrizio is happy to deliver mail and content to be a missionary gardener caring for his small, uncorrupted parcel of local land. Seeking reassurance from Fabrizio, Vittorio finds dissonance instead: "Every contradiction of how I remembered things was like having a part of me torn away."[9]

The reality of "high realism" is a negotiated reality. A traditional community is not necessarily a static community. In Valle del Sole at the time of Vittorio's birth, automobiles may be unreliable, but they do exist. So, the emic (subjective) understanding of the community depends upon an awareness of differences in subjective perceptions between women and men, old and young, to say nothing of particular personalities. The emic anthropologist and the novelist thus share an interest in the unique, richly textured, more-or-less distorted, psychologically repressed, or simply false apprehensions and memories of individuals. The more scientific interrogators of meaning, on the other hand, shun the singular and unreliable and search always for verifiable patterns. Setting aside the personal, mental and spiritual aspects of the novels, even Ricci's critics acknowledge his skill in describing generalities. "Superstitions, politics, hard work and dreams of America that pervade the village," says one, "are rendered with an almost anthropological rigor."[10] A major element in all three books is the author's capacity to give imaginary life to cultural environments that are both true to his characters and accessible to readers lacking personal knowledge of rural Italy, Leamington, York University, and Nigeria.[11]

The Task at Hand

In this essay, first, I wanted to consider whether Ricci's novels conformed to the findings of social scientists who study life in traditional Italian villages, the cultural dislocations of immigrants in new societies, and the adjustment problems encountered by those who attempt to go home again. Second, I wanted to discover if the writer's work contributed any insights that might be useful to social scientists researching these and related questions. In short, was Ricci's self-professed "high realism" realistic? Undergraduate textbooks now commonly connect forms of literary criticism to social science. Literary critics including Roland Barthes, Jacques Derrida and Umberto Eco are frequently cited by anthropologists, and anthropologists such as Clifford Geertz and Claude Levi-Strauss are often shoehorned into discussions of literature.[12] The lines are blurred, for example, in Italo Calvino's "claim that he finds Northrop Frye's anthropological criticism more convincing than structuralism ... and his belief in the epistemological importance of literature."[13]

What Is Anthropology?

Classically, anthropology "sets for itself the general problem of the evolution of mankind."[14] Currently, its "goal" is identified as "the comparative study of human societies ... to describe, analyse, and explain ... how groups have adapted to their environments and given meaning to their lives."[15] The discipline is divided into two main areas, physical (or biological) and cultural (or social) anthropology. Physical anthropologists investigate biological evolution and topics ranging from palaeontology and population genetics to evolutionary psychology and forensic anthropology. At their most ambitious, writes English teacher David Hawkes, physical anthropologists suggest "that competition for Stone Age sexual favours continues to dictate our behaviour, despite the enormous historical and cultural distance which separates the post-modern from the Pleistocene, leaving 'middlebrow' readers awash with claims about the discovery of the 'rape module' or the 'aggression gene.'"[16] Physical anthropologists suffer a lack of consensus as to the parameters of their subject matter. What, unambiguously, is a human being? Do we mark our origins in terms of physiological characteristics such as brain size (intellect), vocal chords (speech), or the use of technology (an opposable thumb)? Ought the locus of inquiry to be at the level of genetics, individual organisms or the species itself? What is the precise structure of our "family tree"? Is there an uncontested line that separates *Homo sapiens sapiens* from our primate kin? Cultural anthropologists study cultural evolution, whatever the much-debated and much-debased term "culture" may be said to mean. The muddle over the meaning of human culture is perpetually troublesome.[17] Cultural anthropology is where the emic/etic division is most relevant, and where interpretative rather than analytical techniques are emphasized.

There are several core questions that arise whenever anthropologists squabble about which among them are getting it right. Perhaps the mightiest of these relates to the relationship between anthropology and imperialism. Are academic inquiries into the lives of "other" people anything more than intelligence-gathering missions for empire builders? Another has to do with social values. Does the discovery of enormous diversity of human attitudes and behaviour compel ethical relativism? Or, do anthropologists have a moral obligation to protect or to help transform societies in which accepted customs upset modern sensibilities? Finally, anthropologists worry more than most about the "nature-nurture" controversy. Are not human beings genetically engineered for specific kinds of behaviour (female passivity, male hostility, for instance), or are we socially malleable and capable of improvement (whatever we may believe that to be)?

It is important to be aware of these issues and the controversies that they entail, for they often constitute the *real* criteria according to which an anthropologist's professional judgement will be evaluated. It is not so much that ideology trumps empiricism; it is that ideology defines what will be accepted as evidence. So, too, the novelist, for both are rooted in the same humanistic soil, both are branches of the same intellectual tree.

What Is Literature?

"Ontological" issues are often at stake in debates about whether or not literature is necessarily restricted to imaginative or fictional writing. Some scholars, for example, still worry about whether *The Holy Bible* or Machiavelli's *The Prince* count as literature. As Terry Eagleton points out, "nineteenth-century English literature usually includes Lamb (but not Bentham), Macauley (but not Marx), Mill (but not Darwin or Herbert Spencer)."[18] According to Eagleton, literature is defined according to socially determined and historically variable structures of belief. Those unhappy with such blatant socio-economic determinism may invoke aesthetic standards. Others, focusing on the writer as artist, take literature to be the product of a distinctive kind of activity which, whether its product be reckoned superior or inferior, at least has a *prima facie* claim to be called "art." It exists in "its concreteness." It is "faithful only to itself." Peter McHugh, for one, contends above all that literature must be treated "independently of its history, context, or social circumstance."[19] One of the primary, legitimate tasks of art and, hence, of literature is the act of representation.

As has been mentioned above, the fictional trilogy by Nino Ricci examined in this essay, utilizes the various techniques of "realism," a traditional form of literary representation. The writer reproduces in a detailed fashion diverse settings in the old country and the new world and provides descriptions of the physical appearance and mannerisms of the many characters in the trilogy. This adherence to literary realism has been confirmed by the writer himself and by literary critics who have highlighted the importance of the use of extensive detail in the trilogy to build plot, characterization, and theme.

Tradition and Modernization

What we call literature is as old as what we call civilization. Indeed, among the earliest bits of evidence for civilization are the myths and legends of antiquity. The social sciences are rather recent additions to the humanist's tool-kit. They were fashioned as a part of that modernizing process itself, and took some time to gain respectability as a legitimate form of knowledge. Their invention was part of the same process as the main social theme in the Innocente novels, the transition from traditional to modern society. The broad social landscapes painted by many early social scientists, for example, had much more in common with romantic poetry than with contemporary displays of statistical virtuosity as in, for example, the aptly named technique of multiple regression analysis. There was a preoccupation with the life of the city and the country, with tradition and progress, and with the loss of community and the triumph of market society.

Much nineteenth-century social science fell squarely in the radical tradition that began with William Blake's condemnation of the "dark, satanic mills" of industrialism. It viewed the factory system of industrial capitalism as an historically unprecedented, wicked and tyrannical exploitation of mind and body (and even Adam Smith considered the modern corporation a fundamental perversion of economic organization). By casting an eye back to simpler societies, untainted and untarnished, anthropologists furnished social reformers with the kind of contrast they needed to facilitate a moral censure of the proletarian misery and bourgeois decadence of life around them.

If such progressives entertained naïve ideas of noble savages, sturdy peasants and idyllic pre-industrial life, the "high realism" in Ricci's trilogy appears to be the flip side of the anthropological coin. Unsentimental and non-judgmental, the writer's simple recording of Vittorio's failure to find happiness in the big city of Toronto and the return of a young man such as Fabrizio to tend his garden in the old village combine to provide ample "data" to support the suggestion that the promise of an upscale urban lifestyle may be hollow.

The trilogy does not embrace the visceral myth of barbarian virtue. Although many students of literature recoiled from the late nineteenth-century triumph of science, and some took up the spiritual exaltation of the "stupefied peasant." The writer of the trilogy seems to reflect the orientation of social scientists. These social scientists brought the tools of the academic trade to the study of their contemporaries as they struggled through the transition from tradition to modernity. Most sociologists and anthropologists who are concerned with problems of transition do their "field work" in remote and romantic locations, such as the rain forests of South America, the deserts of southern Africa, the idyllic islands of Melanesia, and so on. Some, however, work on the close fringes of modernity. One of these is Edward Banfield, a controversial scholar whose book, *The Moral Basis of a Backward Society*, contains a very ugly account of bucolic Italian peasants in the late 1950s, at precisely the time when the fictional Vittorio was growing up in Valle del Sole.

Edward Banfield turned his study back upon tales of ignorance in the recesses of European development, in the nooks and crannies missed by the Marshall Plan.[20] By using a combination of neo-Freudian psychology and structural-functional analysis, duly confirmed by the application of Thematic Apperception Tests, Banfield sought to explain the social values and the economic, political and social problems of Montegrano, a town in Southern Italy, not much different from Valle del Sole. Like the later work of Oscar Lewis, including his famous monograph, "The Culture of Poverty," Banfield's efforts helped establish the contemporary neo-conservative fashion of "blaming the victim."[21] He attributed the "backwardness" of his backward Italian town to amoral familism, by which he meant a tendency to look out for one's immediate relatives and not contribute to the general good. More than appearing merely economically underdeveloped, Banfield's subjects were pseudo-scientifically shown to be morally inferior to the bulk of post-World War II western Europeans, who had seized upon modern technology, individualism, the work ethic, and the spirit of capitalism.

For his part, Nino Ricci, while telling a tale about similar people and at the same time as Banfield's account, presents a non-judgemental view of the peasantry. His purpose, after all, is neither to condemn nor to reform extant social arrangements, but to set the stage for the psychological study of individual behaviour while examining ideas about morality. The effect in this case, however, is paradoxical, for it is Banfield, the "scientist," who is transparently burdened with ideology, while Ricci, the writer, appears more disinterestedly "scientific."

In contrast to Banfield's fierce adherence to the norms of modernity in his account of a peasant village, the fictional trilogy by Ricci appears to present neither an affinity for inherent human traits that are resistant to social evolution and behavioural change, nor for the urban ideals of a gentle and genteel future that would be available through correct child-rearing practices. If the trilogy clings to any universal theme, it is the universal experience of shame and, perhaps, the theological despair that accompanies it; but his concentration on this theme is upon emotional (almost existential) responses, not upon the extant cultural causes. The trilogy does not condemn traditional societies, nor does it celebrate them. The writer does not appear to adhere to the notion of an ineluctable human nature, nor does he indulge in either romantic retrospection or the optimism of progress.

In this context, Ricci neither joins with Banfield in denouncing the depravity of allegedly primitive societies, nor does he turn a blind eye to their unpleasant characteristics. He simply writes an effective imaginary ethnography. Once again, he can be depicted as a better social scientist than many who practice the crafts of sociology, anthropology and the several varieties of human studies. Instead, he has much in common with those anthropologists and other social scientists who recognize that "the relationship between modernity and tradition is not dichotomous but dialectical," and that the path to modernity is not linear but involves "a dynamic process, a give and take between new conditions and old social forms."[22] Not every change is an improvement; not every loss need be mourned.

The struggle within anthropology has been between the soft-hearted, nurturist, relativist, liberal, epistemologically flexible cultural anthropology and the hard-hearted, naturist, authoritarian, conservative, ontologically rigid sociobiology. The trilogy seems not to present either view. Instead, Ricci's trilogy can be viewed as an imaginative exercise in participant-observation, the anthropological technique of becoming seemingly at one with the native inhabitants in order to produce a more absorbing account of the meaning of their lives. Balancing the etic (social or objective) and the emic (personal or subjective) approach to social documentation, the writer calls forth the life of Vittorio Innocente without insisting on a particular viewpoint. This approach, however, might be seen in any work of fiction that tries to be factual, that attempts to describe the vicissitudes of social life with some degree of accuracy. In reference to the original question of whether or not Ricci's self-professed "high realism" is realistic, it is fitting to note that the work is realistic. His descriptions would certainly resonate with those who hold his characters up for dispassionate scrutiny. He calls attention to both sides of the modernizing dialectic. Yet, it is necessary to probe still a little deeper into the politics that underlie contemporary scholarly practices in order to better locate the anthropological dimension of the fictional work of Nino Ricci.

Representation and Culture

It is important to understand how scientific and artistic conventions of story-telling work, and to realize, with anthropological icon Claude Levi-Strauss, that, "although the really vital unity of science and art lies in the ways of understanding reality, we should not overlook the important similarity of the means of representing reality in the arts and sciences."[23] A scientific study can be a work of art, and a work of art has much in common with a scientific study. This fundamental epistemological assertion flies in the face of those, like McHugh, who hold that "the rule of art is that [it] is nothing but itself, i.e., not to be confused with whatever else than itself it brings to mind. There is no 'operationalism' in art in the technical sense ... art need not 'represent' anything whatsoever: the reality of art is in no way contingent upon its connection with something else that is real."[24] Like much of literature that is representational, the trilogy is consistently realist in its depiction of social reality. In the opinion of one reviewer, *Lives of the Saints* "finds its fullness in a particular and peculiar time and place," where Ricci displays his "brilliant descriptive powers."[25]

The representative dimension of Ricci's work builds on, among other subjective experiences, his own small experience as an apprentice social scientist. "At university," he tells us, "I interviewed approximately 150 Italian immigrants as part of a project."[26] In the trilogy, Vittorio, at university, does likewise. Vittorio becomes engaged in a small research project in which he must interview Italian immigrants about their lives. Vittorio's work seems to be self-absorbed, perfunctory and academically inept. He asks sterile questions. His subjects pretend to answer them. He pretends to believe their answers. All the while, "sensitive questions" are "thrown out from the start."[27] The interviews are mediated by technology: "Whatever eccentricity there might have been seemed levelled by our [tape] recorders — the mood changed at once when they clicked on ... The recorder itself became a presence, a silent official in the room ..."[28] Vittorio himself is less intrusive in this process. He feels an "unease" that grows "more insistent."[29] Both understanding and representation are allowed to collapse as he retreats from engagement with his putative subjects. As far as practical research techniques are concerned, Vittorio is an ineffective social scientist since he appears unable to get a clear sense of the true values and emotions of the subjects being interviewed. This situation seems to hint at Ricci's understanding of the complexity of the immigrant experience.

Like science, literature need not strive to reproduce authentically only what passes for reality, as did, for instance, socialist realism. Just as science is not limited to description but becomes genuinely exciting only in experimentation, so literature must also be an imaginative exercise equally at home in factories, in houses of ill repute, on streetcars winding their way through crowded cities. But, even when dealing with utopias, drug-induced hallucinations, or self-conscious language games like those in Christian Bök's *Eunoia*, something (an act, a perception, or a desire) is being represented by the writer.[30] All stories have the potential to test reality, to probe conventional boundaries, and to see literally what they can get away with.

Stephen Amidon writes: "*Lives of the Saints* is an honest and well-detailed story, evoking the everyday life of an Italian peasant community with commendable accuracy."[31] Ricci's own attribution of important influences on his work, however, shows that he is not only interested in literary realism. "Realism," says Terry Eagleton, "aspires to a unity of subject and object, of the psychological and the social."[32] On balance, though, Ricci's ethnography is less concerned with the community than it is with the individual. It is less obliged to anthropology than to psychology. He pays homage to Robertson Davies' *Fifth Business* and acknowledges his debt to Northrop Frye, who taught him to weave the story of an individual into larger mythological patterns. As well, when acknowledging his intellectual debt for assistance in creating the community of Valle del Sole, he confesses: "I drew from my reading of Freud and Jung in imagining how that kind of community would operate."[33] For all his scrupulous detail, his descriptions are influenced by psychological theory, not presented simply as gritty fact. He acknowledges his primary debt to Freud insofar as the crucial event of *Where She Has Gone* is concerned. "You could argue," he says, "that civilization began when this [incest] taboo was created, that the guilt that created led to civilization. And there's something formative about the incest taboo. Anthropologists have found that it was one of the first taboos."[34] If not quite "the original sin," the representation of incest in the novel comes close to it. The entire trilogy, says Roland Merullo, "is a brilliant study of the way shame is passed down through generations. Like any inherited illness, shame grows silently in the innocence of childhood, then stifles the victim's own blossoming, never allowing him to see this beauty in himself or to allow others to see it."[35] According to Merullo, "Nino Ricci understands this dynamic, and gives it its rightful place in the pantheon of human misery." Also Ricci's depiction of the Innocente family is "without a tinge of preaching, without the mercy of even a momentary joy," yet Merullo concludes that at the end, Vittorio is allowed to "reach a sort of peace."[36] "Northrop Frye," adds Jeffrey Canton, "provided a key for Ricci's exploration of myth, ritual and superstition."[37] So, Ricci's *Lives of the Saints* is declared a "lyrical and evocative portrayal of rural life in the Apennine mountains of Italy."[38]

Unlike most anthropologists, Ricci persists in displaying symbolic and material culture and to illustrate personality configurations in different settings. In so doing, he effectively demonstrates the plasticity of human behaviour. Still connected by memory to the traditional world of Valle del Sole yet implicated in the amorality of postmodernity, Vittorio is not silenced by the predicament of seeking to define his moral code but by his ambivalence in choosing among the structures of moral codes themselves. Vittorio is conflicted between a morality based on ahistorical verities, such as they are embedded in the religious language of sin, and what has lately been called "situation ethics." Ricci shows how, in a remarkably short period of time, not only Vittorio Innocente but most of the main characters in his novels are compelled to adapt to changing circumstances. Even though he alludes to and most often describes material circumstances, the writer does not clearly provide explanations of the relationship between those ecological, economic, reproductive and technological circumstances that anthropology seeks to generate in its study of social reality. The writer gives us data, within an imagined world, to which anthropological theory could be usefully applied. In the fictional trilogy, the language game of the fiction writer is not yet identical to the language game of the social scientist.[39] In contemporary society, it is impossible for an artist or a social scientist to claim to express an unassailable truth about any aspect of the human condition. As Vittorio notes, "Language seems sometimes such a crude tool to have devised, obscuring as much as it reveals, as if we are not much further along than those half-humans of a million years ago with their fires and their bits of chipped stone; though maybe like them all we strive for in the end is simply to find our own way to hold back for a time the encroaching dark."[40]

Notes

1. Nino Ricci, *Lives of the Saints* (Dunvegan: Cormorant, 1990), *In a Glass House* (Toronto: McClelland and Stewart, 1993), *Where She Has Gone* (Toronto: McClelland and Stewart, 1997).

2. The phrase "thick description" is borrowed from anthropologist Clifford Geertz, whose studies involve detailed treatments of semiotics as the basis for the analysis of cultures. See "Deep Play: Notes on the Balinese Cockfight," *Daedalus*, Vol. 101, No. 1 (Winter, 1972), pp. 1-37.

3. Jim Bencinvega, "A Little Boy's Sense of Justice," *The Christian Science Monitor* (July 5, 1991), p. 13.

4. Ann Copeland, Irene McGuire and Paul Stuewe, "A Circle of Clarity," *Books in Canada*, Vol. 20, No. 3 (April, 1991), p. 19.

5. Jonathan Yardley, "Breaking Old World Ties," *The Washington Post* (May 8, 1991), p. D-2.

6. Nino Ricci, in an interview with Jeffrey Canton, *Quill and Quire*, Vol. 56, No. 7 (July, 1990), p. 55.

7. Roy MacSkimming, "Two First Novels," *The Canadian Forum*, Vol. LXVIV, No. 791 (July-August, 1990), p. 30.

8. The emic strain in cultural anthropology includes a legion of cultural idealists, symbolic interactionists, phenomenologists, ethnomethodologists, and sundry eclectics and obscurantists. A singular example was Franz Boas (1858-1942) of whom Marvin Harris said: "it is obvious from the research strategy [that Boas] followed throughout his career that he was perfectly content to continue his particularistic studies in complete independence of their nomothetic payoff." *The Rise of Anthropological Theory: A History of Theories of Culture* (New York: Crowell, 1968), p. 262. From the mind of Boas grew the more ambitious Margaret Mead.

9. Ricci, *Where She Has Gone*, p. 199. Fabrizio did not go to America nor take university classes, but he is, however briefly, among the more sympathetic characters in the trilogy. The "path not taken" by Vittorio may lead to genuine grace.

10. Stephen Amidon, "Romanzo Paradiso," *The Listener*, Vol. 124, No. 3184 (September 27, 1990), p. 33.

11. Regarding disciplinary boundaries, I empathize with Kurt Vonnegut, former anthropologist and novelist: "I visited the Anthropology Department of the University of Chicago a few months ago. Dr. Sol Tax was the only faculty member from my time who was still teaching there. I asked him if he knew what had become of my own classmates ... Many of them, ... he said, were practising what he called 'urban anthropology,' which sounded an awful lot like sociology to me. (We used to look down on the sociologists. I couldn't imagine why and can't imagine why.) If I had stayed with anthropology as a career, I would now be doing, probably, what I *am* doing, which is writing about acculturated primitive people (like myself) in Skyscraper National Park." *Fates Worse Than Death: An Autobiographical Collage for the 1980s* (New York: G.P. Putnam's Sons, 1991), p. 126.

12. See Martin McLaughlin, "The laconic partisan," a commentary on Italo Calvino's *Lettere* (Milan: Mondadori, 2002), in the *Times Literary Supplement*, (14 December, 2001), p. 23.

13. A representative example is Robert DiYanni, *Fiction: An Introduction* (New York: McGraw-Hill, 2000), pp. 373-410.

14. Franz Boas, "The History of Anthropology," *Science* 20 (1904), p. 523.

15. Serena Nanda and Richard L. Warms, *Cultural Anthropology*, 7th edition (Belmont: Wadsworth/Thomson Learning,

2002), p. 1. Similar definitions can be found in most introductory texts.

16. Fed up with postmodernists and various species of subjectivists, Craig B. Stanford joins other "biological anthropologists" who say that "in an era in which the concept of culture has been so widely appropriated by groups all over the intellectual and political spectrum" and in which "attempts by anthropologists to define culture have devolved from a lively, genuinely intellectual debate into a petty squabble over whose thinking is in fashion and whose is outmoded ... it may be a good idea [to] ditch the word altogether." See "The Cultured Ape?" *The Sciences* (May/June, 2000), p. 43.

17. David Hawkes, "Free will, at a price," *The Times Literary Supplement* (11 January, 2002), p. 5.

18. Terry Eagleton, *Literary Theory: An Introduction* (Minneapolis: University of Minnesota Press, 1983), p. 1.

19. Peter McHugh et al., *On the Beginning of Social Inquiry* (London: Routledge and Kegan Paul, 1974), pp. 157, 159.

20. Edward C. Banfield, *The Moral Basis of a Backward Society* (New York: Free Press, 1958).

21. *Scientific American* (October, 1966).

22. Virginia Yans-McLaughlin, "A Flexible Tradition: South Italian Immigrants Confront a New York Experience," *Journal of Social History*, Vol. 7, No. 4 (Summer, 1974), p. 430.

23. Claude Levi-Strauss, "Anthropology: Its Achievements and Its Future," *Current Anthropology*, Vol. 7, No. 2 (1966), p. 126.

24. Peter McHugh et al., *op. cit.*, p. 155.

25. Barbara Grizzuti Harrison, "The Evil Eye at Work," *The New York Times Book Review* (June 2, 1991), p. 7.

26. Ricci, *loc. cit.*

27. Nino Ricci, *In a Glass House*, p. 276.

28. *Ibid.*, p. 275.

29. *Ibid.*, p. 276.

30. Christian Bök, *Eunoia* (Toronto: Coach House Press, 2001)

31. Stephen Amidon, "Romanzo Paradiso," *The Listener*, Vol. 124, No. 3184 (September 27, 1990), p. 33.

32. Terry Eagleton, *Heathcliff and the Great Hunger: Studies in Irish Culture* (London: Verso, 1995), p. 149.

33. Nino Ricci, "Recreating Paradise," an interview with Jeffrey Canton, in *Paragraph*, Vol. 13, No. 3 (1991), pp. 2-5.

34. Quoted in Brian Gorman, "Getting Weird and Ugly with Nino Ricci," *Today* (6 December, 1997), downloaded from www.canoe.ca/JamBooksFeatures/ricci_nino.html, 5 December, 2001.

35. Roland Merullo, "End of Innocente: Nino Ricci's 'Where Has She Gone,' concludes a trilogy of immigration," *Boston Globe* (5 July, 1998), p. F-1.

36. *Ibid.*

37. Jeffrey Canton, in a review of *Lives of the Saints* in *Quill and Quire* Vol. 56, No. 7, p. 55.

38. Ann Copeland, Irene McGuire and Paul Stuewe, *op. cit.*, p. 16.

39. One of the most praiseworthy and clearest explications of the scientific method as applied to human culture can be found in Marvin Harris, *Cultural Materialism: The Struggle for a Science of Culture* (New York: Random House, 1979).

40. Nino Ricci, *Where She Has Gone*, p. 320.

Marino Tuzi

Subjectivity, Ideology, and Culture in the Fictional Trilogy of Nino Ricci

FICTIONAL TEXTS, AS theoreticians of literary representation have asserted, are infused with sets of beliefs and ways of organizing reality that do not simply stem from the particular subjectivity of the writer. Assumptions about what constitutes social reality and what is considered to be normative behaviour may be rethought and even refuted by a given writer either deliberately in the process of presenting or as a consequence of articulating a particular view. However, readings of social reality are at some level shaped by the social context in which the writer is located. Although the writer is not a mechanical reproducer of an existing social order, whose development is usually historical and its contents tend to be contradictory and multifaceted, he or she still cannot avoid, even if he or she wishes to do so, the external influences that form perception and affect the imagination. The writer hopes to deploy elements of literary form as a means to probe the layers of contemporary reality and through that literary form construct a sense of reality not obviously evident to everyone, if it is evident at all. Literary texts are not material reality per se but representations of reality. Yet, by investigating the nature and meanings of given social realities, fictional texts and their writers participate in helping to shape not only how internal and external phenomena are perceived. Equally important, the writers and their work at some level help to build if not legitimize the social framework that holds psychological and social phenomena in place. Parameters and boundaries are redrawn or discarded, resulting in the affirmation or the contesting of established social structures.

Ideology then is not simply a factor in the construction of a literary work. (Ideology can be generally defined as a system of beliefs that not only guides human action but also organizes what is perceived to be real, acceptable, common sense or even natural.) Rather it is more accurate to state that, without ideology, without some linkage to past and present beliefs, a literary work could not be referential. Thus, for a work that is attempting to be referential, to be representational, it somehow needs to connect itself to an identifiable social reality. In general, literary and social theorists would assert that all literary work, whether it is non-referential, self-referential, or referential, issues from some identifiable social context, evolved through time and space. The literary imagination can creatively reorganize elements of human experience and even invent elements never before experienced. Such an imagination cannot transcend in absolute terms, even if it wished to do so, the time and space of which it was a part and from which it obtained selectively the materials to do its work. It is very difficult to prove that human actions exist apart from the physical and social conditions that circumscribe them and that limit human potentiality. It is an insurmountable task to argue convincingly that human actions stand outside the external conditions that they are meant to respond to and even change. Since the human imagination is strongly grounded in a social terrain, its reference points are not just aesthetic but also ideological.

This is not to reduce literary activity to a mechanistic reproduction of specifically designated social realities, realities ranging from the mainstream to the marginal. Literary form can transform established perceptions of reality, presenting the reader with sometimes radically different ways of envisioning the world. The literary imagination, by probing the deepest realms of a given situation, can expose layers of complexity often hidden from view, suggesting the illusory nature of any given experience. Literary form and the literary imagination have their own vitality and a sort of independence from external forces. Sometimes the emotional, psychological, and aesthetic power of a particular narrative style can in itself be much more critical to a literary work than its actual message or even social content. But this observation does not exclude the notion that within a given literary form itself are imbedded ideologically based assumptions of what constitutes human experience and human reality.

Social and literary theorists have rejected an essentialist view of human existence, asserting that social reality and social and cultural identities are socially constructed. But, in asserting this constructionist point of view, they have not denied the political usage that essentialism can be put to, evoking difference and marginality in a dominant culture or among competing cultural and social groups. Such social theorists also have not repudiated the legitimacy of authentic, lived-in experience, occurring at different levels of consciousness, whether it is non-rational, non-cognitive, or intuitive; neither have they denied the emotional and psychological power of beliefs and symbols. The rejection of essentialism, the rejection of the idea that various dimensions of human experience exist outside of an identifiable time and space and that they are inchoate, somehow beyond human intervention, is not itself a rejection of the authentic emotions and beliefs that are attached to the various elements of human existence. The claim that insists on the asociality, purity, and absolute autonomy of literary form and the literary imagination is one that accepts an essentialist view of human action. It is in rejecting such an essentialist view of art and the imagination in general that one can state that ideology, composed of a set of socially defined beliefs with their attendant emotional and psychological effects, is an intrinsic part of literary production.

What is notable about the fictional trilogy of Nino Ricci — *Lives of the Saints, In A Glass House,* and *Where She Has Gone* — is the consistency in its development of a discourse about ethnicity and identity. In the trilogy, the shifting of cultural terrains, pierced with contradictions and uncertainty, is simultaneous with the changes in literary styles and ideological frameworks. The intense dramatization of social displacement and existential angst, in cultural surroundings without fixed and reliable signposts for human meaning and action, is underlined by the notion that the dubiety associated with ethnicity (as cultural experience) and identity (as to what content constitutes the self) are themselves symptomatic of an overarching ontological problem adumbrating postmodernity. The novels do not intend to make of their central character, Vittorio/Victor Innocente, a representative of the conventional second-generation Italian Canadian. (Technically, it needs to be mentioned that Vittorio has been born in Italy and arrives in Canada

when he is a boy. So the use of the term second generation here is a way to denote the linguistic and social assimilation of Italian immigrant children in English-
speaking Canada.) Nino Ricci constantly inveighs against
some socially conditioned expectations of the reader in
the development of the personality traits of Victor Innocente. These expectations deal with a set of factors,
such as a commonality of socioeconomic experience, cultural values, social attitudes, and recurrent behaviour,
which are supposedly typical of second-generation Italian-Canadian males. The inability and unwillingness of
an assimilated Victor/Vittorio to adhere to the norms of
his immigrant community and his ambivalence about
the relevance of mainstream middle-class beliefs produce an irresolvable tension inside of him. This internal
conflict is the cause of the gap between what he thinks
and feels he should do and what he actually does in response to evolving social circumstances.

The psychological conflict is emblematic of the ideological contradiction rife in the trilogy in which the connection to ethnicity and group experience, with its
incipient teleological trajectory, cannot mesh with that
space where desire and personal freedom, uninhibited
by social boundaries, can cultivate a sense of self. In the
postmodern era, there is almost pervasive reflexive scepticism towards any claim about the complete efficacy of
any kind of social or technological system to solve the
ongoing problems of human existence. Equally important, postmodernism is marked frequently by its adamant
refutation of authenticity, of organicism, or of essentialism. Much of postmodern discourse does not accept any
sort of conceptualization of human experience that exists
outside of an identifiable social framework. For many
postmodernists, prehistory may have predetermined the

biological limits on human abilities, but it is the social
and technological achievements of the human species,
within preset material, biological boundaries, that matter
the most in the study of human behaviour. Consciousness (awareness) and cognition (intellect and thinking)
have been instrumental in helping to shape the world in
which we live. In the process, the dialectical relationship
between the mind and materiality (including nature) has
formed our view about what encompasses our distinctive place on the planet. Through language, culture, and
technology, cognition has made the past knowable to us
and has allowed us to continue to build the foundations
for sociality. The conceptualization of a time in prehistory before the constitution of a cultural consciousness,
even if such a time produced informal, small social
groupings of people, cannot be relied upon to provide a
full explanation of the basis of human experience. It is
the fact that the vast majority of peoples live in societies
(in human designed environments) that is central to the
analysis of human behaviour. In this context, notions
about culture and individuality are relentlessly changeable depending on the given circumstances. Ideas about
individualism are endlessly malleable ideological and
cultural constructions, whose emergence and validity
depends as much on the positioning (subjectivity) of participants as it does on the structures that have been put
into place to sustain historically and geographically
specific beliefs.

There is a thematic pattern, which begins with *Lives
of the Saints* and is sustained throughout *In A Glass
House* and *Where She Has Gone,* that involves several
interconnected issues related to culture and identity.
The trilogy explores the irresolvable contradictions inside immigrant culture and urban society. The three

books also dramatize the central character's inability to reconcile himself to his ethnic past and to fit into contemporary society. References to an ancient past, bordering on pre-historical, nomadic non-sociality, and allusions to pre-cognitive, inner states of desire and to mythic dream-worlds are opposed to a cognitive, socially hierarchical present that reduces such atavism to deluded romantic yearning, to a kind of nostalgia for a way of life that is no longer feasible in the postmodern era. The first book, *Lives of the Saints*, details an apparently distinct view of social reality (which in this case involves a late1950s rural Italian culture) and then the rest of the trilogy counter-poses this ethnic perspective to a restless, undefined individualism that is associated with urbanism in the host society. In the second and third books, *In A Glass House* and *Where She Has Gone*, the transformed identity of Victor Innocente is forged out of his disillusionment with his parents, who engage in self-destructive behaviour, and through his assimilation of selected elements of an urbanized English Canadian environment. Victor developed a new non-ethnic self in reaction to what he perceived to be the restraints and excesses of a traditional agrarian, working class Italian culture, whose members, as epitomized by his immigrant father, have insulated themselves from modern life to cope with the challenges of immigration.

The trilogy does not seem to imply that Victor's rejection of his original culture is just the result of the mental confusion that he experienced when he tried to negotiate a space between two opposed cultural traditions. His rejection of his Italian peasant heritage is at a certain point in time, especially when he is a university student (in the second book, *In A Glass House*), so extreme that it leads him to a nervous breakdown. It is arguable

that Victor manages to recover fully from this emotional collapse, through which he discovers his inability to
cope with the pressures of living an ordinary life. The
portrayal of the social dislocation of the secondary characters (some of these characters are English Canadian)
in the *Glass House* narrative is linked to an absence of
moral rectitude and to the social relativism of a culturally heterogeneous urban society. The generalized sense
of displacement indicates that social disorientation and
the constant rethinking of identity are common features
of what is loosely referred to by cultural theorists as "the
postmodern condition." (This postmodernism is typified
by constant social and technological transformation, the
multiplicity of viewpoints, cultural relativism, subject-
ively based truths, and anarchic individualism that is
self-referential.) The trilogy is disinclined to present a
resolution to Victor's contradictory attitude to his rural
Italian heritage. He wants to form some kind of attachment to his Italian culture through his family, first
through his father and after his father's death through
his half-sister, but he cannot get rid of his fundamental
unease towards the family-based values of his immigrant culture. At university and during the succeeding
years, Victor finds provisional safety through a chosen
solitariness that is facilitated by him living in an urban
milieu in which people are essentially detached from
each other. In this urban setting, individuals belong to
specific social networks that have no direct connections
to a larger, cohesive community. Despite the relative
calm that this individualistic and asocial existence provides him, Victor remains uncommitted to the beliefs
and ways of life of mainstream, technological society.
Through linguistic assimilation, the English Canadian
social context allows Victor the personal freedom to

decide how he will sustain his ethnic ties to the Italian immigrant community. Unlike the narrow collectivism of the Italian village and its embodiment through the family unit, the multiculturalism and openness of Torontonian society permit Victor to re-imagine his cultural identity according to his emotional and intellectual inclinations. The primary factor that offers Victor the opportunity to revise his relationship to his ethnic past is the individualism that is at the core of modern, urban, liberal society.

In Nino Ricci's trilogy, the privileging of the authority of the self, through which meaning in the world allegedly derives, appears to be associated with the fundamental irresolution of the crisis of essentialist ethnicity in postmodernist society. It is this state of cultural crisis, initiated by immigration, that propels the plot structure and the development of the main characters in the entire trilogy. The obsession on the part of the protagonist, Victor Innocente, with recovering his lost self frequently escalates to a level of self-indulgence that verges on solipsism, as especially is the case in the second book, *In A Glass House*. This leitmotif about cultural identity is combined with the notion of the obstinate influence of the diasporic experience, which is dramatically revisited in the last book of the trilogy, *Where She Has Gone*. In this third novel, Victor and Rita, who are following their separate itineraries, restlessly move around in Europe, eventually return to their ancestral home, but their stay in the small town does not rekindle for them emotionally and imaginatively a definite sense of place that they are searching for to remedy their social dislocation. The life-long consequences of the dispersal of extended family and community members, through immigration, invest homelessness with a sort of permanence that becomes an ontological state for the minority subject. Geographical relocation and cultural adaptation prevent the transplantation of a genuinely indigenous culture. In the trilogy, the recurrent thematic patterns concerning identity crisis and cultural deracination sustain and continually intensify the unremitting, sombre mood and grim, unrelenting message related to personal loss and existential despair. The final vision in the trilogy verges on a kind of romantic nihilism near the end of the third novel, *Where She Has Gone*. The invocation of human existence on the brink of some inexplicable nullity is achieved through the unsettling image of tiny, flickering campfires, stoked by weary shepherds who are dispersed precariously in the impenetrable pitch darkness of rough mountainsides. The persistence of unfulfilled desire and the seriousness invested by the trilogy in the presentation of cultural irresolution serve to elevate the narrator-character's story of displacement to the status of a metaphysical drama. Yet, the trilogy avoids acceding to a classical tragic vision because it refuses to accept the basic premise of such a vision. Within the moral scheme of the trilogy, which is supported by the critique of feudalism in *Lives of the Saints*, an individual is not forced to perform a prearranged role in order to fit into society. In the modern world, within certain limitations, individuals choose from among different ways of living. Therefore, people are not obligated to fulfill a specific, preordained destiny, whose primary function is to reinforce their roles and placement in a stratified social system. There is no specific kind of punishment meted out to those people who are non-conformist, especially since social roles and norms of behaviour are very complex and continually changing. Instead, existence, despite one's particular point of origin, is random and unpredictable. Everything is ultimately temporary, predisposed to a slow, usually undetectable, insidious process of antiquation, even disintegration. In such a situation, tragedy assumes a different form, given that stability is never assured and that any kind of established truth is finally unreliable. Freed from strict, narrow social constraints, the individual can imagine ways to achieve a sense of identity that will permit him to fulfill an array of personal desires.

Given this kind of viewpoint, the trilogy, through the form of a first-person narration, is not only a studied, extremely self-conscious investigation of the dilemmas of a particular ethnicity, but it is also a story whose intention is to probe with gravity some of the pivotal questions about existence that have infused Western discourse since the inception of philosophy in ancient Greek civilization. The inference from this interpretation of the trilogy is that this literary work employs historicity and cultural data as material to construct a narrative whose ultimate purpose is not cultural but philosophical in orientation. Because it wants to confront subject matter that is informed by established western values and beliefs, the trilogy then is in some sense quite ideological in its representation of social reality. This ideological stance is especially evident in situations when the books try to reconstruct time and place from within an arguably revisionist perspective. External reality (such as village life in Italy, reproduced in *Lives of the Saints*, or small town behaviour in rural Ontario, depicted in *In a Glass House*, or even the quality of current urban existence in Toronto, described in *Where She Has Gone*) is refracted through the consciousness of Victor Innocente and through the consciousness of the other main characters, namely Victor's mother and father and his half-sister. At the same time, the perspectives of these characters and that of secondary characters are mediated through the consciousness of the narrator-central character, Victor Innocente, whose presence is the foundation of the entire trilogy. The reader knows about the thoughts, feelings, and actions of the characters only through the filter of the central character. In the trilogy, without the objective distance provided by an omniscient narrator, the use of first-person narration has the effect of not only supporting the ongoing solipsism and existentialism of the saga of Victor Innocente. This narratological device also serves to emphasize the notion that subjectivity and individualism are central to the postmodern conceptualization of aesthetics and social reality. The reader cannot dissociate the representation of the thoughts and feelings of the various characters from the underlying bias in Victor Innocente's perspective. In order to separate the perspectives of the various characters from the consciousness of Victor, the reader must attempt to detect contradictions in the ways that Victor conveys the individual perspectives of the various characters. There is also another component to the representation of external reality in the trilogy. Often, the depictions of particular settings, events, and actions take on allegorical aspects, in which the narrative moves beyond realistic renderings of these elements and details in Italy and Canada. The use of imagery, symbols, and metaphors that establish non-linearity and non-rationality, as if the reader is entering a particular psychological state, ruptures the realism of the trilogy, resulting in a different way of looking at the construction of ethnicity. The allegorical qualities suggest a plane of existence that transcends the ordinariness of daily life, exposing the metaphysical dimension inherent in any local reality. The

Lives of the Saints trilogy as a form of literary discourse advances an outlook in which ethnicity positions itself within a postmodern sensibility in its preoccupation with the process of meaning and the nature of subjectivity.

The dramatization of the unresolved, ideological, contradictory stance of the trilogy is conducted mainly through the depiction of Victor Innocente's thoughts and actions. The trilogy is an extended narrative of a personal journey in which the voice of the central character is indistinguishable from his role as the narrator of the story. One of the effects of having the narrator as the central character is that it not only blurs the boundary between the act of storytelling and the mediated subjectivity of the characters. It also undermines the presence of an external reference (in the form of a detached omniscient narrator), which normally allows the reader to test the claims of the narrator-character. Instead, the narrative situates the reader solely in the subjectivity (with its attendant epistemological limitations) of one individual, whose story is a kind of self-confessional in which the confessor admits to the impossibility of any culturally sanctioned redemption. To do penitence for his real and perceived sins, Victor would have to accept the ethical foundation for his sense of guilt that is found in his Roman Catholic, superstitious, peasant, working class upbringing. He would have to embrace an ethnicity from which he is estranged or he would have to turn his back on this retrograde, soul-destroying heritage and then acknowledge the merits of living in a diffused but liberal, mainstream Canadian culture. In the trilogy, the autobiographical approach to cultural experience evokes the postmodern emphasis on the personal as a vehicle for expression in an environment where an essentialist notion about truth has been replaced by a fixation with relativity and multiplicity. Moreover, the construction of a narrative based on personal history foregrounds the view that any kind of truth is only a projection of the self, which is fleeting and incomplete. This view suggests that subjectivity, as a compendium of contradictions and varied elements, is by its very nature unable to arrive at any final meaning. Imprisoned by his mind, where the conscious and unconscious constantly intertwine, as is evident in *In A Glass House* and *Where She Has Gone*, the adult Victor is as much at war with himself as he is with the cultural milieus that have produced him. His various cultural beliefs and his complex emotional states are constantly in conflict with or stand in opposition to each other. The cause of some of this psychological conflict is the divergence in values between two historically different cultures. The values of the adopted English Canadian culture, which is almost post-industrial and thoroughly urbanized, are not compatible with the norms of the traditional agrarian Italian culture, which was never really touched by industrial capitalism. But as the trilogy seems to imply, the basis for this internalized cultural conflict is not simply immigration, but it is to be found in the way consciousness becomes aware of itself in the world. In being conscious of alternative modes of existence, both ethically and behaviourally, Victor cannot commit himself wholly to one cultural lifestyle. This is the fundamental dilemma experienced by the ethnic subject in the aftermath of the collapse, in the host society, of centrality of the old value system, whose authority had been protected by the insularity of its rural community.

As *In A Glass House* attests to, the cultural cleavage between the old and the new cultural values reinforces the intergenerational gap between father and son in

Ontario. It is a division of views and values that is as much the product of parenting as it is a result of immigration and subsequent assimilation. Ironically, while Victor has not accepted his father's beliefs, he has unconsciously inherited many of his behavioural traits, along with his father's gloominess. It is a negative outlook, which borders on manic depression and which, in his father's case, makes him susceptible to suicide. *Where She Has Gone* suggests that the self-destructiveness that Victor internalized from his father, while not being fatal physically to him, leads to equally devastating results. This self-destructive behaviour, operating at a reflexive, unconscious level, is epitomized by his tortured, dysfunctional relationship to his half sister. Rita is the only person with whom he has any real emotional bond since the death of his mother, when he was a boy. Ironically, it is the premature birth of Rita, causing Cristina's death, on the passenger ship headed for Canada, which established the basis for Victor's problematic relationship to his half-sister. It is a relationship that is typified by an unrelieved ambivalence in which the arrival of a sibling resulted in the end of his symbiotic connection to his beloved mother. The contradictory nature of the feelings associated with this ambivalence, spanning from affection, protectiveness, and loyalty to anger, bitterness, and aversion towards his sister, is never resolved in the narrative. This convoluted emotional state underpins the crisis that takes place in the last part of the trilogy, *Where She Has Gone*, and drives the narrative to its apocalyptic-tinged conclusion. Victor's unintended but callous exploitation of Rita, emotionally and sexually, permanently destroys the trust that is the basis of their renewed relationship.

The event, which occurs close to the beginning of *Where She Has Gone*, is very important to the development of the remainder of the story. The sexual encounter has unshakable psychological effects on the two main characters. Equally significant, the event helps to shape the plot and thematic movement of the third novel, while having a critical influence on the thematic and ideological meanings of the conclusion of the trilogy. In its depiction of incest between a half-brother and a half-sister, the text generates a series of contradictory significations, which remain entirely unresolved. Victor and Rita are almost strangers to each other when, as adults in their early twenties, they meet in Toronto, after having led separate lives for many years. From late childhood to early adulthood, Rita was brought up by a middle-aged, English Canadian couple in a small town in rural Ontario, where her stepfather, Victor's father, had eventually settled after his immigration to Canada. Her stepfather eventually allowed her to be adopted by an older, childless couple, affirming his lack of emotional and familial commitment to her because he knew she was the daughter whom Cristina had with her German lover. As young adults, the unexpected attraction between Rita and Victor is simultaneously physical and emotional. She is a kind of narcissistic projection of his physical features and sense of self-image. They are similar in certain aspects of their physical appearance because they had the same biological mother. Victor's attraction towards Rita is in some fashion an unconscious actualization of his underlying desire for his mother, expressed in the cave scene in the first novel, *Lives of the Saints*, in which Cristina is presented as a kind of goddess figure, bathing sensually in a pool of water. Young Vittorio stares at her, mesmerized by the power of her physical presence. The sexual activity between Rita and Victor is a form of emotional sharing that is based on a chronic emotional neediness on their part. Through physical contact, they provide support for each other, having been wounded psychologically as children by the breakdown of their respective parents' relationships and the emotional absence of their parents in their lives as children.

The narrative accentuates the tenderness and sensuality that surround the scene of their lovemaking by stylizing the sexual act to the point that it is a kind of physical gesture, relying on suggestive language for its meaning. The narrative reduces the event to a basic movement, omitting a graphic depiction of the sexual encounter that would have led to a kind of voyeuristic sensationalism and to a sexist objectification of Rita's body. Despite this narrative reserve, the scene cannot escape the ethical implications that underlie one of the most profound forms of moral transgressions in modern, liberal society. The minimalism in the presentation of the scene does not mitigate the sense of shock that accompanies it and the heightening of its disquietingly disorienting effect on the reader. The psychological impact of the event is associated with the idea that a great amount of the sexual tension and murky eroticism of the scene derive from a sense of sexual repression. Such suppression of sexuality seems to flow from inexpressible, pent-up emotions festering in the two individuals. In addition, the social prohibition of incest appears to intensify the repulsive psychological effect of the scene. The impression is that much of the disturbing eroticism of the event is the result of a combination of several contradictory factors. The implied understanding that the impending act is socially reprehensible is in sharp contrast to the depiction of the benign, casual way that Victor and Rita interact with each other, as if they were two ordinary people who had spontaneously come together.

Divested temporarily of its serious sociological context by the immediacy of the strong feelings that are shared for each other, their subsequent lovemaking is described in a conventional manner, involving passion, consent, and reciprocity between the two participants.

The pathology issuing from the sexual encounter is tied to the larger logic of the narrative, in which cultural displacement caused familial breakdown and consequent social and emotional dysfunction. The incest is at once symbolic of the destructive inwardness, rigidity, and oppression of patriarchal Italian immigrant culture and it is symptomatic of the fundamental, irreversible damage done to the emotional makeup of individuals, whose identities have been fractured to such an extent that they plummet into states of confusion and desperation. Yet, there seems to be an unequal power relationship between Victor and Rita. He is older than his half-sister and therefore he is in a position of authority over her. Also, despite his father's deleterious detachment towards him, Victor has benefited financially from his membership in a patriarchal, ethnic family by obtaining his father's estate after his father's unexpected suicide. In contrast, Rita was orphaned as a result of her mother's death and her biological father's unexplained disappearance. Subsequently, in Canada, she was unfairly ostracized by her stepfather because of her illegitimate parentage and excluded by him from his household. Whatever benefits she accrued socially and educationally, as the adopted child of reasonably prosperous, English-descended foster parents, these benefits were undermined by the strictness and rigidity of her foster parents. Because of her troubled origins and emotional neediness, her adopted parents constantly reminded her that she was somehow inadequate as a person, both morally and psychologically. Alienated and emotionally vulnerable, as a young woman, Rita turned to her brother for guidance and support, thinking that through him she could reconstitute a sense of family. On his part, Victor was first very appreciative of Rita's re-emergence since he had once thought that he would never see her again after her adoption, having lost his connection to his biological family.

The incest is an enactment of the internalization of Victor's experience of helplessness, originating in the unintended abandonment by his mother through her death and the disinclination of his father to create a paternal bond with him in Canada. Robbed of his right to have the emotional support of his parents, Victor tries to reclaim in his relationship with Rita the power they had over him as a child. In part, he absorbs his parents' harmful attitudes towards him in order to preserve his fragile identifications with them. By repeating in his own way their selfishness and irresponsibility, he becomes like them, assuming their terrible authority, in his treatment of his half-sister. Meanwhile, by seeking the protection and sympathy from Victor that she did not receive from her biological mother and father and her stepfather, Rita temporarily gives in to Victor's seductively comforting presence. Victor expresses his misogyny, which is part of his link with his father, unconsciously yet selfishly imposing himself on his half-sister at a time when she is exceedingly vulnerable emotionally. His sexual engagement with Rita is also a kind of deviant, desperate attempt to rejoin his mother, whom Rita resembles physically, reinforcing his Oedipal longing for Cristina, which was evoked in the cave scene when he was a child. The deep desire to overcome the loss of his mother, whose nurturing presence ambiguously had intermixed tenderness and eroticism, attains its monstrous actualization through his twisted yet temporarily soothing sexual involvement with his estranged, half-sister. A critical part of the dramatic effect of the incest scene is the ethical issues that it raises in terms of the novel's attitude toward this kind of anti-social behaviour, as it is represented by Victor, and in terms of the depiction of such a form of prohibited sexuality in a literary text written by a male. The incest scene recapitulates in a strongly negative fashion a fundamental problem with patriarchal, Italian peasant culture, whose phallocentrism devalues femininity and objectifies the female body. Within the trilogy's thematic scheme, the incest scene, as a kind of culturally based, intensely psychological moment, functions symbolically as an extremely dramatic instance of the sense of attraction and revulsion, of the feelings of affection and self-hatred experienced by the protagonist, Victor Innocente, when he makes direct contact with his ethnicity through the presence of his forlorn half-sister.

Soon after the incident, his sister abruptly departs from Toronto without telling him where she is going. Through her mysterious departure, the book raises symbolically a critical question about the future of ethnicity as a mode of living in a world where time and space have been compressed by incessant immigration of people. Victor is seized immediately with a sense of guilt that further erodes his already low self-esteem. He undergoes a severe depression over what he has done to his half-sister. Disregarding his own mental and physical health to make amends, he travels to England and then to Italy, like a detective furtively following signs of Rita's movements, so that he can attain some form of forgiveness from her. He believes that even if she forgives him for his transgression such absolution will never transpire because of his unwavering self-hatred. Victor will not allow himself to be freed from the underlying guilt and shame that have festered inside of him since childhood. He perceives himself to be an outcast, in self-imposed exile, disconnected from his inner self and the world around him, unable to cure the pathology that has made him act the way he did towards his half-sister.

The text's minimalistic presentation of the sexual incident forestalls any implication of an exoticized, culturally specific decadence or a sensationalistic rendering of erotic love. The event is not invested with any kind of positive meaning in terms of its long-lasting effects on Victor and Rita. Instead, within the logic of the trilogy, incest functions as the ultimate signifier of familial breakdown, caused by marital discord and social upheaval. The permanent separation of brother and half-sister, which occurs after the incest, marks the final disintegration of the Innocente family unit in Canada. The fallout from the separation reduces Victor to an almost moribund state. He is socially marginalized, without any kind of family support, and profoundly alienated from himself, filled with an incurable self-hatred that casts an enormous, heavy, shadow over his journey toward some kind of self-revelation. The grim erasure of family ties is evidence of the fundamental incapacity of immigrant culture, because of its implied narrow codes of behaviour and rigid gender roles, to cope with the pressures of social displacement. In traditional, Italian proletariat culture, the family was the basis of social values and it was supposed to control the actions of individual family members. In contrast, in Canada, the immigrant family is mostly self-regulating, surrounded by an urbanized, diverse social environment that does not reinforce the norms and values that have maintained the ethnic family in the country of origin.

In relation to plot and character development, the incident of incest is deployed as part of the excruciating delineation of the steady, incremental, mental decline of the narrator-character. Victor's morbid, psychic deterioration becomes worse after this incident. Following the clues of Rita's movements in Western Europe soon after their horrid separation, in a somewhat somnolent state, Victor travels across Europe, from England to the European continent, in search of a European past that still affects his life. As he gets closer to Italy, he falls deeply into an emotional depression that threatens to immobilize him mentally, while slowly taking away his will to live. Eventually, without planning it out clearly, as if he is compelled by some irrepressible inner force, even though he discovers that Rita has gone there, Victor re-enters his place of birth, Valle del Sole, which has been transformed into a ghost town, since many of its inhabitants have emigrated and those that remain are elderly and decrepit or eerily lifeless. The progressive ruination of the isolated, mountain village makes Victor aware of the impossibility of ever reconciling himself philosophically and emotionally to his dysfunctional family and, through his family, to the traditional culture that had created it. The fatalism that permeated the lives of the peasants in the old country and that was transmitted to him through his father's harsh stoicism seems to have finally overtaken the small town. As he examines the ruined sites and abandoned fields of this ancient village, Victor is unable to discern any residual positive, humanistic quality that can help him to reduce his psychological torment and to question his belief that life is essentially meaningless. Considering the hopelessness that overwhelms Victor in that shrunken, devastated medieval village, the reader senses that the incest incident was part of an inevitable movement toward ruination. All the assorted, imperfect elements that comprise immigrant peasant culture systematically are intended for some type of annihilation.

The incest scene in *Where She Has Gone* also serves another very important purpose in terms of the ideological discourse in the *Lives of the Saints* trilogy. The taboo sexual activity between brother and half-sister, in which both participants are partially complicit, alludes to the presence of an anarchic individualism that has a problematic relationship to social reality. There is no doubt that Victor's decision to become sexually intimate with his half-sister is reflective of his sterile inwardness. In giving in to his impulse to fulfill his immediate emotional and sexual needs, he discards his ethical obligation not only to his half-sister but also to the civic society that protects and supports him. At another level, in terms of ideological signification, Victor's anti-social behaviour is part of the trilogy's exploration of the dialectical interchange between human subjectivity and external reality. A central aspect of the trilogy's representation of this dialectic is related to questions about what is the nature of human desire and how this desire is actualized in the world. One idea about desire is that desire comes into being at the moment when a child (in this case a boy) develops an emotional bond with the mother figure. The bond is both nurturing and erotic, an ambiguous condition that captures the complexities inherent in desire as central to the life force. Eventually the boy separates from his mother through the predictable process of individuation. This individuation is socially motivated, resulting in a definable identity. Through its various institutions of socialization, such as the family and the education system, society requires that individuals develop unique attitudes and skills that will allow them to conform to prevailing social norms, attaining eventually social and economic independence. The individuation process is simultaneously phenomenological because it entails the development of a separate consciousness. Consciousness becomes cognizant of its existence through an awareness of the world outside itself. By comprehending what it is not, by understanding the presence of the other, embodied by the external world, consciousness knows of its existence in the world. In this situation, the boy becomes aware that he is not his mother; that she is the other infiltrating his consciousness. Human consciousness asserts its presence in the world, giving meaning to whatever it apprehends. Yet, the desire for oneness with the mother figure, the craving for comfort and pleasure critical to the life force, is lost because individuation necessitates breakage from the mother, who is the source of that initial desire. In part, this separation leads to a contradictory situation: the boy continues to be attracted to his mother, but he is now also disgusted by her, seeing her nurturing behaviour as cloying, stifling behaviour that threatens his independence. When he becomes a young man, the boy will continue to experience desire, but the desire will be displaced, it will be projected onto something else, since that state of oneness before individuation, before the emergence of a separate consciousness, is not retrievable. Desire turns into a fractured, repressed urge, which can be experienced only in an exaggerated, monstrous form, because desire is projected onto an object or person that is external to the consciousness of the subject. In this process of projection, desire loses its original purity and becomes something that is prurient, that is corrupted by its desperate need to experience desire as end in itself. In this context, desire becomes a complicated and contradictory experience. Pleasure, which is retained from the child's former attachment to the mother, is intermixed with pain and revulsion, which ensued when the boy/young man detached from his mother, losing the state of oneness with the mother, because he developed a separate consciousness.

The need to fulfill one's desire and the knowledge that such fulfillment will not ever be complete distort the nature of desire, encouraging the objectification and organization of the experience of desire. Desire is made possible when a person uses the kinds of objects (such as elements that are connected to people and specific physical items) that a person's consciousness chooses arbitrarily from a host of eroticized or sexualized objects available in a given social context. These selected objects (such as a type of clothing or a particular part of the human body) become the stylized forms through which desire is activated. Often, the need to experience desire as fully as possible becomes excessive, resulting in self-destructive, extreme behaviour. In this obsessive striving for fulfillment, both the desire and the object of the desire, which are inseparable from each other, are corrupted, or degraded, or reach a state of what is called "abjection." The quality of the desire is debased steadily and the performance to achieve gratification can turn into a form of perversity, in which the technical components of the performance are transformed into the primary elements to facilitate desire. The enactment of desire becomes a desperate act and it takes on over-wrought, extreme forms so that the individual can compensate for the disappearance of the idealized desire of childhood. Throughout this entire process of experiencing desire and attaining some type of self-actualization, some sense of identity, through desire, the subject grasps that it is consciousness and the way that consciousness operates that make everything possible or even impossible. Desire comes to life in a state of suspended disbelief. Consciousness creates an artificial, deformed dream-state to reproduce the idealized desire that is forever lost. It is only through a fetish, an object substituting for what is desired, such as a type of dress or a particular setting, that desire manifests itself in the world. Thus, desire is about the wish for oneness in the self. It is a kind of oneness that is achieved through certain ways and forms. Idealization, approaching a dream-state, is what consciousness is attempting to produce. Since this idealization is a production of consciousness and since consciousness is constantly remaking itself, the subject knows that any kind of idealization, any dream-state, is basically provisional. The knowledge of this provisionality incites the subject to objectify desire, rendering it static, through fetishism, which distorts the nature of one's yearning. But since a particular fetish reifies and confines the way desire is experienced, the subject discards one fetish and invents a new fetish to temporarily satisfy his desire. Often, the new fixation is a preposterous, much more graphic version of the former fetishized object.

In *Where She Has Gone*, Victor's sexual encounter with his half-sister is suffused with complex significations because it holds in its fashion many inconsistencies that have shaped identity formation so far in the Victor narrative, including the first and second books. The incident sharpens his awareness of the fact that he is perplexed about the composition of his cultural identity. Victor realizes that the confusion is not just the product of contradictory positions, but that the experience of intangibility, of desiring fullness but knowing that such fullness cannot ever be attained, is fundamental to the nature of subjectivity. It is not simply the external world that dictates what an individual feels and wants. Just as important is what the individual gives meaning to, what he projects into the world through the self, that shapes the needs and wants of that individual. There is a deeply agonizing, existential feature to Victor's sordid sexual encounter with his half-sister, who appears as the medium of his yet unfulfilled desire for oneness, as the means to ultimate cultural and psychic transcendence. He knows that what he is doing is wrong, in turning her into an object of his desperate need to experience desire in its pure form. However, he persists with his sexual objectification of her, treating her as the exotic other, in order to enter a state in which he can feel the urging inside of him. He knows that finally satisfaction is not possible, that adulthood, despite the difficulties of maturation, requires individuation and responsibility and the destruction of unity with the mother figure. Victor engages in his grotesque act of desire because through such an act he wants to reunify the fractured parts of his cultural identity. Yet this abject, debased, enactment of desire cannot eradicate the semiotic void in consciousness that is the paradoxical effect of consciousness being capable simultaneously of meaning and meaninglessness. According to postmodernist sensibility, because there are no ethical and ideological absolutes, there cannot be any essential, sustainable truths. Since there are no reliable spiritual and cultural guidelines to living in the modern world, the ethnic identity of the subject remains unfixed, without any real clarity or focus, and it is incessantly changeable.

Continuously, at a subliminal and symbolic level, as the *Lives of the Saints* trilogy implies, much of the cultural disjunction is linked to a basic human condition, which is typified by the inability of the individual to find meaning and emotional stability in the world. This primary existential situation goes beyond the specificity of a particular social order. Yet, it is only by observing how the problem with meaning is made obvious locally that the narrative can describe the powerful qualities of this epic drama. For instance, in *Lives of the Saints*, the non-rationality of the central Italian peasants (a non-rationality that is marked by its lack of empiricism and scientific knowledge) relies on ritual, myth-making, superstition, rudimentary Roman Catholicism, and established quasi-feudal arrangements to make sense of external conditions that are inherently antagonistic towards them and brutalize many of them to the bitter end of their lives. This non-rationality verges on irrationality, on a kind of inchoate fear of unfamiliar patterns of diurnal activity and on an endemic distrust of the motivations underlying the actions of individuals living in the local village and in the surrounding hamlets. This inbuilt paranoid-schizophrenic-like mental state is simultaneously a defensive mechanism against adversity and an internalization of the peasants' subjugation by an obstinately rugged, subsistence, agrarian landscape and by a ruthless, hereditarily based ruling class, whose origins go back to the Germanic tribal invasions after the collapse of Roman administrative hegemony. The beleaguered psychological condition, which governs the behavioural patterns of the adults and the acculturation of the children, is the psychic fabric from which materializes the acute pessimism of the peasants, resulting in borderline manic depression. Idiosyncratically manifested through the various attitudes and actions of the local villagers, the collective psychosis stands as the historical, root cause of the emotional volatility of the parents, the dispossessed Cristina and her estranged husband who is living as a migrant worker in rural Ontario. The working class parents instil unconsciously the emotional features of this psychological instability, laced with manic depression, in their impressionable, sensitive children, Victor and Rita. In the trilogy, each character's precarious mental state generates situations of neurosis that veer unexpectedly towards prolonged moments of debilitating psychosis. In Canada, although the material factors that created the fear and anxiety in the immigrant characters are no longer present, the main characters, Victor and Rita, continue to unravel emotionally, plunging into a kind of emotional and intellectual stasis, when they are faced with the challenge of taking responsibility for the way they live, because they cannot consciously modify psychologically their relationship to a cultural past that has shaped their identities.

By foregrounding the idea that the influences of the country of origin are transposed by immigrants into the host society, the trilogy suggests that migration has been a fundamental part of human existence since prehistory, when groupings of people left their birth places to seek opportunities in distant lands that were seemingly accessible to them. The notion of constant movement as a characteristic of the human condition, which is based on conventional anthropological and archaeological studies, is reiterated in the second and third book of the trilogy. Near the end of *In A Glass House*, after he completes his university studies in Toronto, Victor voluntarily immigrates to Nigeria, a country located on the West African coast, to teach English in a small impoverished, war-torn community. This journey to Africa is a fore-shadowing of Victor's trip to Europe in the last novel of the trilogy, *Where She Has Gone*. Victor travels across Western Europe, finally returning to his hometown, in a desperate search for personal enlightenment after his disastrous fallout with Rita. The Nigerian trip and the return journey to Italy, through the western European continent, echoes the references to ancient migration, conquest, settlement, and post-war working class immigration to Canada that are described in the opening narrative of the trilogy, *Lives of the Saints*. In its invocation of social and cultural flux, the first book emphasizes a sense of timelessness in terms of the ongoing process of migration and settlement. *Lives of the Saints* conjures up descriptions of an ancient past when the Abruzzi region was the centre of a highly advanced indigenous civilization. The trilogy refers to the way of life in Abruzzi before Roman legions finally defeated militarily, after many centuries of warfare, the warrior, mountain-based civilization of the Samnites, who were the ancient, legendary ancestors of the downtrodden peasants in Valle del Sole. The military victory of the Romans over the Samnites began a chronicle of invasions by foreign peoples, from the Romans in ancient history to the Germanic tribes and their descendants in the middle ages. The unending struggle of people looking for a place to live is reiterated in the conclusion of *Where She Has Gone* through the allusion made to the primordial, inhospitable mountain terrain of the Abruzzi region, which is still populated by small villages, whose inhabitants are barely able to make a living for themselves.

From a postmodern perspective, through its movement through time and space, the trilogy universalizes the basic notion that society, as a hierarchical, bureaucratic social organization, is essentially coercive and repressive. Society is systematically antithetical to human desire and destructive when it comes to personal freedom, flattening out and distorting individuality to the point that the behaviour of individuals is symptomatic of the pathology that is inherent to a given society. The involuntary absorption of norms and values not only represses personal freedom, but the maintenance of this repression results in a chronic psychological dysfunction in the individual, a psychological dysfunction whose persistence makes behavioural abnormality the common condition of socialized individuals. It is only by having an emotional disorder, a neurosis or even a psychosis, some kind of serious psychological breakdown, that an individual obtains an understanding of the existence of a repressed inner self, telling him/her that something is definitely wrong in his/her relationship to the external world. The repressed side of the self exists as a negative reference point to the status quo or it is perceived as a type of emotional absence. Individuals are forced to live in society to survive physically and economically. Therefore, social relations are predetermined by some type of social structure, regardless of its level of complexity. Since an individual can never break away fully from the control that society has over him or her, there cannot be any authentic form of individualism. Given this situation, any kind of administratively designated individualism is primarily ideological, serving certain political and social designs. Individualism is not permitted to exist simply as a means for liberating human impulses and potential to the benefit of the entire society. There is definite value to this postmodernist critique of an officially sanctioned individualism that acts as an ideological construct to legitimize consumerist, corporate capitalism.

But this postmodernist approach has its limitations as a form of social and cultural analysis. Some postmodernist thinking tends to distance itself from Marxist, class-based analysis while maintaining its support for concepts that are related to traditional phenomenology. This type of phenomenologically oriented postmodernist investigation, in its own highly qualified manner, believes in the existence of a freestanding individualism. Emancipated individualism is envisioned as a cognitive-based subjectivity that is supposed to have a reciprocal relationship to ideology. Although the subject is the object of ideology (in other words, the individual is subjected to ideological indoctrination), the subject is also the creator of ideology, participating actively in the development and implementation of particular societal beliefs. In this case, ideology is considered to be more than a specific, mechanistic social, political doctrine. Ideology, as a general term, signifies an open-ended process through which there is the generation, acceptance, and revision of ideas and beliefs that help to shape external reality and to give meanings to actions and events in the world.

According to such a phenomenologically-based postmodernist analysis, in the examined trilogy by Nino Ricci, the presence of a repressed but authentic (socially unconstrained) individuality is metaphorically conveyed as a kind of indescribable darkness in the soul, as a profound spiritual absence in the self. This dire existential state is typified by extreme despair, which becomes especially acute for Victor in *Where She Has Gone.* It is only by experiencing a terrible hopelessness about finding meaning in the world that the individual can free himself from the oppressive constraints of society, finally recognizing that his extant identity is an inauthentic, socially constructed entity. However, this kind of postmodernist interpretation of the three texts assumes that the trilogy has committed itself to an ideological position that is highly problematic in its effort to pinpoint the nature of ethnic identity. Any kind of individuality undergoes in some way continual social negotiation; therefore an individual is incapable of avoiding completely a process of socialization. Also, the emphasis on a freestanding individualism presupposes that external reality is fundamentally subjective. External reality has been brought into existence by the sheer will of the individual and it is not representative of historically specific, evolving material forces. From a purely phenomenological vantage point, historical moments are not reducible to the constant interaction of material factors, which are contained in hierarchical, institutional structures, involving the economy, politics, and the military. Instead, history is mostly about the movements and revolutions in consciousness, manifesting themselves in the ceaseless conceptualizations of reality undertaken by diverse groups of individuals. Radical postmodernism deconstructs and repudiates what it considers to be totalitarian social norms and it privileges an anarchic, individualistic subjectivity. According to this type of neo-romantic elevation of the individual, the world is only accessible to and obtains its meanings for individuals through their consciousness. However, this neo-romanticism slides back inadvertently towards a kind of essentialist view of human experience, in which consciousness precedes any type of reality. As such, from a postmodernist phenomenological standpoint, the trilogy has exchanged one form of oppressive essentialism, a collectivist, immigrant culture that nullifies individuality, for another equally problematic form of essentialism, in which an individual's identity is a sort of empty vessel that is to be filled

in not by the elements of a culture issuing from a particular human experience. In this context, individuality becomes totally self-referential, implying a self-created identity, without a locatable past and in effect without any
reference points to contextualize itself in the present.

Yet, in attempting to answer the questions that it
has raised about ethnicity and its relationship to free
will, the *Lives of the Saints* trilogy refuses to embrace
fully a subjective view of reality in its representation of
the cultural history of working class Italians. The trilogy
seems to be uneasy about supporting a specific, comprehensive philosophical perspective. The ontological ambivalence of the trilogy mirrors Victor's aversion towards
any established doctrine, whether it is religious or cultural, ironically suggesting a (postmodern) refutation of
any kind of essentialist viewpoint. In the development of
characterization, especially in reference to Victor Innocente, it is obvious at times that the narrative sets up a
dialectical relationship between consciousness and external reality. The story complements instants of sheer
inner experience, disconnected from the outside world,
with narrative passages, such as in *Lives of the Saints* and
In A Glass House, in which the landscape or external environment has its own separate existence from human
consciousness. Also, as is the case in the two books, *In
A Glass House* and *Where She Has Gone*, there are sections of narrative in which the main characters exist
in relation to each other and to the surrounding social
context. In order to build its social settings, the trilogy
makes imaginative use of extra-textual references, or
verifiable documentation, such as sociohistorical studies
of the peasantry in central Italy and of Italian immigration and socioeconomic adjustment in Canada in the
post-war decades.

In the second and third books, *In A Glass House* and *Where She Has Gone*, the practices of the imported culture of the immigrant characters periodically prove to be inadequate in responding effectively to the demands of contemporary, urban life in Canada. The new metropolitan, industrial surroundings require the rearrangement of social roles and sometimes even the jettisoning of some of the underlining beliefs attached to these social roles. The adaptive insufficiency of a number of the transplanted practices and beliefs originates in the old country. As *Lives of the Saints*, the first text in the trilogy, implies, there is little evidence that the traditional, quasifeudal, non-secular, and residually pagan rural culture was ever completely socially stable and consistent in its customs and beliefs. Unpredictable economic and political conditions, in various degrees, intermittently disrupted and modified familiar agrarian based patterns. In *Lives of the Saints*, part of the story about the peasants concedes that their overall socioeconomic circumstances had remained relatively unaltered since ancient time, consequent to the many centuries after the devious Romans had conquered militarily their advanced, prosperous agrarian and artisan ancestors. Constant struggle, bodily deprivation, culminating in hunger, disease, and death, were the realities of the countless, successive generations of subsistence farmers and goat shepherds residing in small enclaves strewn among mountain ranges. This unforgiving regime fostered a sort of defeatism in which the peasants regarded severe physical, economic hardship as a normal condition. Confined by an inert, rigid, nearly feudalistic system, these people internalized their impotence and misery by succumbing to a frame of mind of unmitigated pessimism. Their uninspiring fatalism melded with the puritanical bent of the Roman Catholic Church, with its stress on sin and guilt, which was reinforced by the worship of a host of gruesomely martyred Christian saints. This negative outlook on life was extended by the pre-Christian belief in the presence of supernatural beings that cast misfortune on and haunted the sleep of the weary peasants. In *Lives of the Saints*, the resignation of the peasants to their lowly stations functions as a component of a medievalist, caste-based worldview, which promoted the passive recognition by a person of his/her predetermined position. Conditioned to accept their place at the bottom of the socioeconomic order, the peasants believed that their social status had been pre-ordained by a supreme force that made its will known to them through the doctrines of the Roman Catholic Church and the irrevocable authority of the land-owning aristocracy. Through its ideological authority, the privileged class, which was comprised of the Church hierarchy, the administrators of the state, and the hereditary aristocracy, endorsed its permanence by maintaining that the status of the peasantry was a natural human state. In the novel, the acquiescence of the peasants to the ruling class carries with it a kind exaggerated piteousness that suggests muted resistance to an oppressive system. The work of fiction inserts a kind of inconspicuous pathos in its vivid delineation of the predicament of the villagers, underlining subtly their basic humanity. The sympathetic but guarded rendering of the plight of the peasantry is part of the way that the novel illustrates the villagers' conceptualization of their existence. These superstitious people envision a malevolent cosmos that persistently spreads incalculable chaos while being brutally indifferent to their distress. For them, despite their practice of Roman Catholicism, this unrelenting malevolence in the end divests human exist- .

ence of any enduring value. The distinctly pessimistic worldview of the peasants strengthens the multifaceted portrait of an isolated, stagnant, rural cultural community that has been bypassed by any type of social progress. The text infers that the weariness of the villagers and their negative historical consciousness are products of the constant social, political, and economic upheavals that have affected life in rural central Italy, and by implication most of Western Europe in general, from the ancient past up until the end of the Second World War. The post-war era heralds the beginning of the influences of modernism on impoverished towns and hamlets located outside established, regional urban centres. *Lives of the Saints* continually alludes to an underlying sense of social turmoil, in which people are pitted against external forces that are determined to eradicate the basis of their existence. The text uses an array of intertwining elements to portray an unromantic bucolic setting that because of its internal instability seems to be on the brink of collapse. Also, the narrative explores the acceptance of a state of flux through a non-rationality that reveals the villagers' steadfast devotion to the spiritual mysteries of an unknowable universe. Their superstitious attitude borders on a kind of mysticism, in which the causes of disastrous events and the motives for human action are often considered to be beyond rational comprehension. As well, the peasants tend to filter their conceptualization of Christianity through a lingering pantheistic sensibility that challenges the legitimacy of Roman Catholicism as the only form of acceptable spiritual worship. Guided by an almost prehistoric ethos, the villagers constantly build and rebuild their meagre infrastructure, utilizing the skills of a rudimentary artisanship and re-honing their techniques for subsistence agriculture. Against entrenched privation, they behave like a biologically preprogrammed colony of indomitable ants in their reassembly of pieces of an ancient agrarian system, yet they are never entirely successful in their work to defend themselves against the next cataclysm.

The combustive forces of history inscribe themselves in *Lives of the Saints* through the perspectives of the characters and the descriptions of particular historical events, unusual social situations, aspects of the landscape, and arresting physical sites. The heightened scenes from daily life in the village, which produce a kind of hyper-realism, the depictions of violent suffering, in terms of the stories of mutilated saints, and the meshing of dream-states with wakefulness break through the realism of the novel, injecting it with elements of allegory that indicate that the story is more than an imaginative interpretation of the process of immigration. The accumulation of juxtaposed images and esoteric symbols is not intended just for a conventional realist depiction of a specific time and place. Instead, this aesthetic strategy, which transmits allusions to ideas about the interface between a traditional way of life and modernism, points to a larger philosophical view of human experience. In raising fundamental questions about the role of subjectivity in the construction of social reality, *Lives of the Saints* indicates that ideology functions as an important part of its literary discourse. The novel depicts a world that is undergoing radical cultural change: the forces of modernism are slowly reshaping the foundations of a quasi-medieval, rural society. Through the perspectives of the major characters and the dramatization of specific events, the work of fiction investigates opposed belief systems that attempt to provide explanations of what constitutes social reality and an individual's relationship to this reality. The different ideological positions are presented through the references that the text makes to various forms of social organization, including collectivism and the emphasis on group identities, patriarchal structures and predetermined gender roles, the jurisdiction of the Roman Catholic Church, hereditary land ownership, and subsistence agrarianism. Along with references to these social institutions and social processes, there are allusions to ancient, pre-Christian society, such as the clan-based nature of village life, to elements from ancient mythology, and to the practice of ancient superstitions. The references to divergent social and cultural models, which have their own explanations of the role of the individual in society, are set against the pressures of modernity, in which the emphasis on individual self-determination, as exemplified by Cristina's struggle for female independence, is a major feature of the cultural transformation that is taking place.

The portrayal of the incongruity of values and beliefs, in *Lives of the Saints*, establishes the ideological parameters of a literary discourse about the minority subject. In the two subsequent novels, *In A Glass House* and *Where She Has Gone*, the representation of ethnicity situates itself in an urban, industrial society, where the position of the individual has immediate points of reference. The inaugural novel, *Lives of the Saints*, anticipates much of the familial instability that will transpire in Canada in its story about Cristina's (Victor's mother's) striving for true love and social independence. Despite the sanctions against her self-actualization, Cristina is encouraged by her knowledge of the public tolerance of unconventional behaviour and the opening up of social opportunities in the nearby city, which is not very far from the tiny village of Valle del Sole. The crisis in her role as a woman in a patriarchal structure is precipitated by her incautious romance with an ex-soldier of German origin, who is hiding in the barn on her farm, and by the subsequent birth of their daughter, Rita, on a passenger liner that is crossing the Atlantic Ocean on its way to the eastern coastline of Canada. As demonstrated by the storyline in the subsequent novel, *In A Glass House*, the destabilization of the traditional roles of the parents in the Innocente household, through Cristina's self-destructive iconoclasm, sets the tone for the further deterioration of family relations in Ontario. It is made evident in this second novel that ethnicity, as a kind of specific cultural phenomenon, with its historically evolved traits, undergoes constant modification, forced to adapt to different circumstances by deploying novel strategies to sustain itself in the new social context. In each part of the trilogy, the specific crisis undergone by the given character (Cristina in *Lives of the Saints*, Victor's father in *In A Glass House*, and Victor in *Where She Has Gone*) concludes in some complicated form of personal failure. Informed by a modernist sense of tragedy, the trilogy insinuates that failure is rooted in a sort of incapacity of the individual to revise his/her expectations in ways that are compatible with a changing world, whether it is the onset of modernism in the old village or the emphasis on individualism in industrial, capitalist society in Canada. Although the cause of this personal failure is partially the result of structural barriers, there is also the inference that the way that each person handles his/her fears and anxieties is equally critical to what happens to him/her in the end. A case in point was Victor's father's treatment of Rita when she was a girl living with him in a small town in rural Ontario. Unable to admit to his failure as a husband and a father, he ostracized Rita, eventually giving her up for adoption, when such an act was not economically necessary, since he had the resources to take care of both her and his biological son, Victor. Another plot development that supports the idea that failure is largely self-produced concerns Victor's contradictory attitude towards his half-sister. Victor seemed to share Rita's feeling of familial abandonment, in particular the cold distance that his father maintained with them as children, but Victor still could not create a strong familial bond with Rita, as if he had internalized his father's aversion towards her. By blurring the boundary between Victor as a victim of his father's manic depression and Victor as the victimizer in his sexual encounter with Rita, the two books, *In A Glass House* and *Where She Has Gone,* avoid a singularly deterministic approach to the depiction of human behaviour. Even though difficult situations may provoke strong feelings that can greatly affect the type of judgments that the main characters make, these individuals retain some degree of choice when they arrive at their decisions in response to circumstances that challenge their self-interest.

The *Lives of the Saints* trilogy takes an essentially ambiguous stance in its exploration of the dialectical relationship between external conditions and personal freedom. Although it draws attention to the significance of material factors in shaping emotions and attitudes, the trilogy does not pursue a strictly deterministic portrayal of the interaction of the individual with society. Instead, the trilogy appears to stress through its use of plot and characterization that the actions of individuals and the meanings that derive from such actions combine to make up the dramatic content of the narrative. Stylistically, the trilogy consistently sustains its focus on the subjective perspective of the central protagonist, Victor Innocente, from which the narration unfolds. Through its storytelling mode, in which there is no clear differentiation between omniscient narration, with its convention of objectivity, and first person narration, the trilogy implies that the external world is not the dominant force is the construction of consciousness. The philosophical implication of the exclusive use of first person narration attaches the trilogy to a postmodernist sensibility that underscores the notion that through acts of consciousness the subject produces not only meanings in the world but also he constitutes in the process a sense of identity. This idea about the crucial ability of consciousness to organize social reality by generating meaning is part of a definition of what is meant by individualism in a liberal democracy, such as the kind of liberal democracy found in Canada. But many social and cultural theorists have argued that this type of individualism is also associated with an ideology that encompasses capitalism and consumerism, in which social relations are primarily relations of the marketplace, oriented towards entrepreneurship, towards economic innovation and individual effort. The origin of this form of capitalist-based individualism is to be found in the tradition of liberal humanism, in which the liberation of human potential is supposedly the basis for not only social progress but also economic prosperity. As an ideological system, liberal humanism contains many of the ideas about the relativity of cultural and social values that support much of postmodern theory about subjectivity and the construction of social reality.

In *Lives of the Saints*, the allusions to facets of liberal humanism originate in an Italian cultural context that harkens back to the philosophical teachings in Greek and Roman antiquity and in a postwar Italian society that is prepared to accept modernism as an alternative to its failed sociopolitical models of centralized authority. When the narrative shifts from Italy to contemporary Canada, beginning with the second book, *In A Glass House*, the Italian-based humanist sensibility is linked to the cultural liberalism in English Canadian society. By permitting opportunities for the expressions of personal freedom, this Canadian version of liberalism increased the cultural gap between Victor's father and Victor and Rita as the two children became linguistically and culturally assimilated into urban Canadian society. This cultural assimilation is made obvious in Rita's attraction to the middle-class refinement of the childless English Canadian couple, who adopt her and integrate her in the new society and in Victor's reluctance as a young man to accept any kind of dogma, such as Catholicism or Christian evangelism, as a means to give meaning to his life. *In A Glass House* makes connections to a liberal humanist tradition, which is in general terms the foundation of western philosophy and western definitions of individualism. *In A Glass House* also acknowledges in its rendering of ethnicity that this liberalism cannot be easily integrated with a traditional culture, through its extended family structure, that requires its members to conform to social norms that exclude the type of individualism that is common in liberal societies. In the last novel of the trilogy, *Where She Has Gone*, the central character, Victor Innocente, is portrayed as a person who for the most part has absorbed the prevailing values of a liberal, individualist English Canadian culture, through his formal education and socialization in mainstream society. At the same time, after almost a lifetime in Canada, he has not been able to completely detach himself emotionally and intellectually from some aspects of his former, immigrant, Italian culture, which stood against unconstrained individualism. To some extent, as a result of circumstance and partially out of personal choice, the central character seems unable to fully comprehend the basis of his relationship to the modern world because of the constant transmission of contradictory, culturally based meanings. Such cognitive and semiotic confusion arises out of an indefinable existential condition, in which the minority subject remains uncommitted to any specific set of cultural values and beliefs. In its representation of subjectivity and culture, the examined trilogy by Nino Ricci communicates to the reader a kind of ideological irresolution that is emblematic of the complex situation of the minority subject in the host country. Equally significant, in terms of the overall discourse in the trilogy, this ideological irresolution serves to advance the view that there does not exist an authentic, preferred cultural perspective in postmodern society, whose essential liberalism has become supportive of the relativity of different cultural models.

Bibliography

Lives of the Saints. Dunvegan, ON: Cormorant Books, 1990 .
In A Glass House. Toronto, ON: McClelland & Stewart, 1993.
Where She Has Gone. Toronto : McClelland & Stewart, 1997.

Brian L. Flack

The Gospel According to Nino Ricci:
An Examination of the Novel *Testament*

IT TOOK A while, some 2,000 years, but there are now five Gospels in the New Testament: Matthew, Mark, Luke, John and *Testament*, which is Nino Ricci's fourth novel. In this new Gospel, there are four further Gospels. One is according to Yihuda of Qiryat, Judas Iscariot. The second is according to Miryam of Migdal, Mary Magdalene. The third is according to Miryam, Jesus's mother, she of the mythical "immaculate conception" and "virgin birth." And the fourth is according to Simon of Gergesa. This last narrator is, in many ways, the most interesting of the lot in that he appears to be an invention, a character with no counterpart in the traditional mythology. Together with his picaresque travelling pal, Jerubal, he seems to represent a trinity of individuals. He is a pathetic shepherd without belief in the one true God. He is also, quite possibly, Simon of Cyrene—for the reason that when Jerubal is crucified beside Jesus it is his cross that must be carried by a bystander, not Jesus' cross and surely there is some symbolic connection in this. Lastly, he is representative of the thief who is saved at the crucifixion. It is a fascinating compilation of roles if not an entirely convincing one.

What Ricci has done, in his rather idiosyncratic and Catholic, but highly entertaining way, is reinvent the New Testament Bible story. It is a risky, but not un-elevated task that few have attempted — talk about setting oneself up for dissection at the hands of religious zealots — and one at which few of the dubiously courageous have been successful. Perhaps the best-managed retelling of Biblical "history" in recent years is Joseph Heller's riotous portrayal of King David in *God Knows*, also his fourth book. In it, he presents a King David posterity hardly knew: warrior, philanderer, psalmist, chip-on-his-shoulder Jewish boy, cocksman, liar, and much plagiarized creator of Great Literature:

> At Nob I told some lies and eighty-five priests were slain. Not only that, but all of the men, women, and children in their households, and all of the livestock in that sacred city, were put to death as well. Who is to blame? ...
>
> Me? Where do I come in for any of the guilt? How can anyone reasonably assert that the responsibility should be mine? I was running for my life and had never, not once, done anything wrong.[1]

He is portrayed as a character in many ways not unlike Ricci's Jesus who is also a man posterity hardly knew.

Heller's novel is told in the first person, a perspective fraught with potential sinkholes as the author attempts to present, from the protagonist's point of view, exactly what happened, when it happened, and to whom it happened. Ricci, bravely, and to his credit, copies the form. He allows each of his four narrators to tell what s/he knows, what s/he saw, what s/he felt, and what s/he thought about the life of the subject: Yehoshua, or Yeshua, or Jesus as he is alternately referred to by his assessors.

But before getting into a more detailed examination of Ricci's accomplishment, it is necessary to say something about the appearance and immediate life of the novel itself. As this essay is being written, it has been some five months since the book's publication. Not a lot of time, but enough time for more reviews of the book than has been written and said about it. In fact, the paucity of attention paid to this novel is startling, especially given the subject and against the backdrop of the times in which its readers live.

The book has been reviewed in all the right places, although those reviews have been surprisingly short and to the point. More importantly, these assessments have managed only qualified praise for the book. There have been a couple of newspaper commentaries discussing the effort, but that is it. This is the case in a time when religious zealotry seems to be at a fever pitch, with fundamentalists of every colour and stripe bursting the seams of almost every culture. Yet, here is a writer who takes on the Biblical tales and conceptions of the Christian Messiah and hardly anyone has anything to say. Moreover, what he has to say about Jesus, the way he presents this man and against what historical realities, fairly cries out for attention. Still there is none to speak of. At this point in time, the book seems to have dropped off the literary radar.

For all its multi-narrational convolutions and overlapping perspectives, the story is fairly straightforward. Four compatriots of Yehoshua/Yeshua/Jesus take it upon themselves to relate, from their own points of view, inasmuch as each is privy to what the others saw and heard, essentially the same tale. It appears to cover the last one to three years of Jesus' ministry, mainly in Galilee. From his home in Kefar Nahum (Capernaum), Jesus troops through the countryside spreading the wisdom he has acquired over a life spent first wandering with his parents through Israel and Egypt, effectively banished by their families, and then at the knee of the prophet Yohanan (John the Baptist).

There are, however, a few rather salient facts presented about the man's life that define in rather unorthodox ways who he is and what he is doing. First, his family's banishment has come about because he is illegitimate. He is not the product of a virgin birth; no angels appeared to anyone to announce the coming of this holy man. He is simply the product of the rape (although there is much in scripture to suggest that what Ricci is offering is not so much a fabrication), by a visiting Roman legate, of Miryam, the daughter of a minor political official at the court of Herod the Great.

> One of these, a legate awaiting orders, my father befriended and presented me to, leaving us several times alone. In the end, because I was young and did not know better and because he threatened me with harm, I was forced to yield to him. I was never able to forget the smell of him—he did not smell like a Jew but had a perfumed odour underlain with a stench like rancid fat. ...
>
> The legate did not take me as his wife as my father had planned, but abandoned me the moment he had received his commission. When he had gone it grew clear that I was with child, and so was disgraced.[2]

She is then fobbed off on an older man, Yehoceph (Joseph), a mason, who has no sons and wishes to have them. He agrees to take her, pregnancy notwithstanding, along with a considerable dowry, which bankrupts her father, and promises to keep her if, after she has delivered the baby she is carrying, she is able to produce sons for him.

What's mildly radical about this situation, though, is that from a very early age, Jesus knows the circumstance of his birth. He does not try to hide it, and at the end of his life, he openly admits it to his followers, in a chilling scene that comes about after he is asked by a temple official, "Who was he, your father ... I might have known him" (409). This occurs shortly before Jesus is arrested in Jerusalem at the Passover, tried, and crucified. It seems fitting, somehow, that at this late date in his ministry he comes clean with his adherents who, understandably, do not take the news well.

> He [the temple official] stood there in front of Jesus, giving him time to answer, but still Jesus didn't say a word. The silence grew eerie then. ...
>
> Jesus had remained standing where he was with the dead stillness he had.
>
> "It was my mistake to come here," he said now, "and to bring any shame to you. But it's not because of what I've taught or what I've done but because of something I can't change, which is that I don't have any father but my god, and am a bastard.
>
> Joseph went white as marble. We all stood in silence and it seemed the walls of the place might fall in. ...
>
> "I'm sorry to have brought any trouble to you," Jesus said ... (409)

Still, it is curious that he is illegitimate, a bastard, for bastards were barred from the assembly houses (synagogues) and temples during these times. In other words, he had no standing in the Jewish community. Yet, he is presented as a Jew, thinks of himself as such, and preaches accordingly. One has to remember that Christianity had not been invented to coincide with his lifetime. He is just an individual spreading a philosophy of peace,

understanding, and love for one's fellow man, all attitudes perfectly consistent with Jewish belief.

He is often brooding and given to bursts of temper
but just as often lively and open to all who seek his time
and energy. This is not the common portrait of Jesus. He
is seen in Biblical literature as a man filled with the milk
of compassion and understanding, a man who existed
without a contrary bone in his body. Yet, in Ricci's universe, he is this and also the antithesis. He has favourites,
he can be terse, he yells at people, and he punishes them,
not physically, but with a withering eye and demeanour
that renders them nearly helpless when he turns on
them, as he does more than frequently.

In this regard, he is also something of a tyrant. His
sect has rules and regulations that he enforces strictly.
When he wants something done or someone to be somewhere or someone to accompany him, he is not above
saying so and then demanding it be done, often without
explanation. The subtext is that he is the master and
he must be obeyed. This is not the Jesus of conventional
scriptural mythology. This is a man who has much
trouble living and has as many human foibles as the rest
of the human race. The trinity of questions that arise in
the midst of this portrayal are clear: Is he simply a man,
or is he a godlike man, or is he God's son?

There is another aspect that this lines up closely behind: the fact of his illegitimacy. This version of Jesus
flaunts the separation of the sexes in the society of his
day. Not only does he allow women to be inner circle
members of his group of followers, he trusts them implicitly and worships with them. This is not a way of life
that is corroborated by the New Testament nor is it very
reflective of the place women held in the world of 30 CE.
Does this make Jesus a man ahead of his time? Does it

make him material for holiness? This is not necessarily the case. But it does make him very different. He is almost always, in Ricci's text, presented as a man who had ideas that did not mesh with his times, but also as a man who was certainly a sympathetic character. He was a man who had something revolutionary to say and who had a revolutionary way of saying it. As Yihuda of Qiryat (Judas) says of him:

> I had visited a dozen nations, and heard tell of a hundred philosophies; but what had most struck me in this was how little of value there was in the world, how men were deceitful and base and would espouse to you the loftiest ideals in one breath and contradict them in the next. When the chaff was sifted from things there seemed only further chaff, the same tired notions, the same predictable vice. Thus when I considered what it was in Yeshua that had held me to him, it seemed exactly the hope of something new: a new sort of man, a new way of seeing things. I thought, if there was a single person who had found the way to speak the truth, perhaps the rest was worthwhile; if there was someone whose vision was truly more than hope for his own gain or greater glory, then perhaps God had not made us simply animals, a pestilence the world would be well rid of. (121-122)

This is high praise indeed for a man so flawed in his origins and behaviour.

Given his wholly quirky presentation of the man called Jesus, as described above, it seems that in this book Ricci has not focused on the obsessions that marked his first three novels: *Lives of the Saints* (1990), *In a Glass House* (1993), and *Where She Has Gone* (1997). These three novels comprise the chronology of the life and times of one Vittorio Innocente. In fact, he both has and has not. On the surface, Jesus and Vittorio seem, in many ways, to be one and the same person. There appear to be overlapping (one cannot get far from this literary technique) circumstances in the lives of both central characters.

Where, as a child, Vittorio is an immigrant from Italy to Canada, Jesus, because of his conception and birth, becomes an emigrant from Israel to Egypt. Where poor Vittorio must live in the shadow of his mother's sexual indiscretions — it is this that precipitates her self-imposed exile from her family home, so too does Jesus suffer from his mother's similar, but not identical, sexual sins. Where Vittorio is treated as little more than an outcast in his new home by his relatives and his father, Jesus is similarly marked as a boy and must, because of this, remain outside the normal course of human interaction. Where Vittorio spends much of his childhood, adolescence, and early adulthood searching for some meaning to his life, some reason for what has befallen him, so too does Jesus wander from place to place and person to person seeking a sense of who he is, conscious, for the most part, only of his difference, his status as pariah, whether because of his birth or because of what and how he thinks.

In essence, Vittorio seems a being who is at once two people: he is the lost boy, the victim who has suffered mercilessly for the missteps of others, and the penitent who is seeking expiation for them. On the other hand, he is the sad-faced messiah, a man who careers through life seeking to understand his beginnings, touching those — his sister in particular — in whom he wishes to inspire a sense that there is hope that will mitigate the disrepair of their lives. Nowhere is this more evident than at the close of *Where She Has Gone*. He sees himself among shepherds (surely a messianic image) and as he leads himself out of the darkness, so too will his experience be a beacon to lead others:

> But that night I had a dream: I was walking along a mountain path, and behind me the shepherds had gathered in their flocks and pitched their tents and started their music because the night was coming on, but still I continued to walk, with that peculiar feeling of lightness the mountains give, the sense that just ahead some new vista will be revealed, or some new freedom hitherto unimaginable offered out. The path I was on was neither gentle nor steep, the darkness that was gathering was not the black of blackest night nor yet quite without threat; and the music drifting out from the shepherd's camp had an ancient, primitive sound as if some great sadness was contained in it, and lifted away. Then as I walked, small flickers began to appear in the valley beneath me ... [3]

Jesus, like him, is more than just a man who has been victimized by forces beyond his control, although he is that. He is, in addition, a being who vacillates between the role of a man and that of a god, even if his god-like qualities are most often seen through the eyes of his adherents who choose to see him as he, himself, cannot. At one moment, he is a crazed beggar who is near death from starvation and who must be rescued by Yihuda of Qiryat. At another, he is a man infected with a wisdom that exceeds all bounds, relating cryptic parables to those more confused about life than even he, a man who appears to have access to the divine. At another, rather than taking sustenance from a man like Yihuda, he is seen dispensing it: curing lepers of their affliction, causing a man who was crippled to walk, raising a man who has died back into life. Like Vittorio, Ricci's Jesus manages what he does without being touched by the convoluted political/social relationships that whirl all about him. It's like he is encased in glass, daring to emerge only when he deems it necessary or propitious to make an appearance, for a purpose he judges worthy of his attention. Jesus neatly parallels the arrogance and self-assuredness coupled with panic that Vittorio evidences in his life.

There is, though, one difference between the two. Vittorio is, at the end of the day, maddening. He tries the reader's patience in scene after scene, situation after situation. He is not a character one feels particularly close to, with whom one empathizes. He makes one angry and frustrated, at his egocentrism and at his failure to see what is plainly visible for him to see and which he repeatedly misses. Ricci's Jesus is not like that. This is where the maturity in character building makes itself apparent. Jesus is the opposite in every way. He emerges from the same kind of familial morass but he makes more of his opportunities, makes the reader understand more about what it is to be the outsider. He is not just the pathetic victim; he is the individual who is given a wall to scale and who finds a way to do it, with honour and certitude. Others benefit from his journey, whereas no one benefits from Vittorio's.

In all its intricacy and high-minded obsessions and curious parallels to the Catholicism of Ricci's previous novels, *Testament* is a success in what it does. This is not to suggest that the book is perfection attained. It's hard to imagine how it could be. But it works and it works well. It is a book that in this difficult time should be talked about more widely than it is. Ricci's Jesus is a character who has embodied in him the opportunity to see important things that are relevant today.

In part, this is because it is so evident that Ricci's research has been meticulous. He points out in a "Note" at the book's close that this is a work of "fiction," that "it does not purport to be an accurate historical representation of that [Jesus] figure." He also says that he has "made every effort to work within the bounds of historical plausibility, based on what is known to us of the time and place in which Jesus lived" (457). One could argue with the use of the term "historical," but that is not really the issue. What is the image of the man that is painted here? He is an icon begging to be considered in a way he has perhaps not been considered before. He is a representation of the cliché "in the eyes of the beholder." It's not so much that this interpretation is accurate or that it is not as much as it is a measure of what is intelligent, humane, and wise. Ricci has studied the scriptures well. He has immersed himself in the work of the Jesus Seminar. He appears to be as up to date as anyone on the current thinking about his subject, but that's only part of the story. It is, rather, like Simon of Gergesa says at the close of his oration:

> It won't be long, of course, before everyone has forgotten the man, or remembers only the trouble he had with his women or how he died a criminal or that he was a bastard, which sooner or later is sure to get out. But however things get remembered, you can be certain it won't be how they actually were, since one man will change a bit of this to suit his fancy, and one a bit of that, and another will spice it to make a better story of it. And by and by the truth of the thing will get clouded, and he'll be simply a yarn you tell to your

> children. And something will be lost then because he
> was a man of wisdom, the more so when even some-
> one like me, who when I met him didn't know more
> than when the crops came up and how many sheep it
> took to buy a bride, had come to understand some-
> thing of him in the end. (454)

He only knows Jesus for a week of his life, and his story, or at least his version of what he saw and what he heard, is as different from Yihuda's version as Miryam of Migdal's story is from Miryam's view, Jesus' mother. So, even among the followers, in the immediate wake of Jesus' crucifixion the story has already begun to metamorphose. But, as Simon also says at another point, what Jesus inspired in him was similar to what Elazar (Lazarus), who was raised from the dead must have experienced: the opportunity to "wonder what further realm there might be that we see nothing of" (456). This is the accomplishment of Nino Ricci. It is a worthy one at that.

But there is more to the success of this novel than even the inspiration it urges the reader to embrace. Principally, it has an entrancing, four-part, overlapping narrative structure, memorable, if deeply flawed, characters, and a rich use of language to recommend it.

The use of four narrators in the first person gives rise to the natural speculation that Ricci is simply modeling his narrative form after the original and that is undoubtedly true, at least in part. Although the scriptures are not first person, Matthew, Mark, Luke, and John attempt to get the tale right. Each story evinces a different perspective; each embodies different assumptions; each has its own agenda. Nothing is very much different in *Testament*. But, whereas the original assayers of the truth were trying and failing to be historical (only a non-believer could write this), the narrators in Ricci's book have a greater purpose, even if they don't know it. Only Ricci does and that's just fine. To grasp this purpose, though the fact every one of the principals is first and foremost human and as such a victim of all those things that are human, one must understand that the Gospels of the New Testament are not literal truth. Hardly anything said in them can be accepted at face value. This is true of Ricci's narrative as well. This fact cannot be forgotten when considering either the structure of Ricci's novel or the characters who propel it.

Ricci does not write in a vacuum. He knows that what this book says — the truths, the half-truths, and the idiotic statements that appear in his characters' mouths — is going to be measured against those first scribblings. A reader has to suspend his or her disbelief before reading the original Gospels and then must try and read them for their symbolic content at best. But a reader of Ricci's book has an option. S/he can take that former route, and likely get little if anything out of the experience of reading, or s/he can step back and follow the thoughts of four average and believable 1st century CE people who are simply relating what they know about a man of their acquaintance, not a god and certainly not the Son of God. There is more room to manoeuvre here because it is a novel and not some pretentious document that purports to be the truth. It is a "telling," an attempt to give some perspective to a story that originated over 2,000 years ago and that has been adopted as something divine. Ricci makes no such claim to divine truth.

Consider, for example, the raising of Lazarus from the dead. In the "Gospel of St. John," the story is told this way. First, Jesus lets Lazarus' sister Martha know that he is "the resurrection and the life: he that believeth in me, though he were dead, yet shall he live: / and whosoever liveth and believeth in me shall never die." After he gets her to admit that he is "Christ, the Son of God," Jesus heads out to where Lazarus has been interred and gives his instructions:

> 41 Then they took away the stone from the place where the dead was laid. And Jesus lifted up his eyes, and said, Father, I thank thee that thou hast heard me.
>
> 42 And I knew that thou hearest me always: but because of the people which stand by I said it, that they may believe that thou hast sent me.
>
> 43 And when he had thus had spoken, he cried with a loud voice, Lazarus come forth.
>
> 44 And he that was dead came forth, bound hand and foot with graveclothes: and his face was bound about with a napkin. Jesus saith unto them, Loose him and let him go. [4]

One needs to compare that version with Ricci's comparable evocation of the "miracle":

> ... he took the fellow's head in his hands and started to feel all around it, as if it was a baby's. This went on for quite a while ... it looked as if Jesus had put his fingers right down inside the man's skull, right through the bone like that, and after he'd felt around in there for a bit, something gushed out from the fellow's head into Jesus's hands , dark and alive ... when Jesus tossed the thing into the fire it sizzled and squealed like there was something dying.
>
> For a moment then Jesus knelt there with the fellow's head still in his hands looking down on him grimly as if he was thinking, Too late. And that was

> when it happened, and we all of us saw it, that the man
> simply opened his eyes, and was alive. (400-401)

Apart from the nature of the telling, there is much different in the circumstances of the telling. In "St. John," the "miracle" occurs about ten days before the Passover. Lazarus is the brother of two sisters who are acquainted with Jesus, and it is these sisters who send for Jesus that he might help their brother in his sickness, before he dies. But Jesus arrives four days too late. The man is dead. So he is forced to bring him back to life. In Ricci, this Elazar (Lazarus) character is clubbed during a riot in the marketplace in Jerusalem. His sisters become concerned later when he starts talking nonsense and finally passes out. Someone, an unidentified courier, is sent to fetch Jesus — he is in Jerusalem for Passover — but by the time he gets to the man's house the fellow is dead, or at least appears to be. He is stiff and is not breathing. So Jesus does what he does.

Is it a blood clot he taps into and relieves or is it a divine moment inspired by Jesus' singular relationship with God? Which version is more acceptable to the inquirer seeking after something that makes sense? Which is told with more empathy for the victim? Which leaves open the debate as to what, or who, exactly, this man Jesus is? It is not hard to make a choice. This is but one example among many that could be cited to make the case. The novel presents four human perspectives that provide four opportunities for the reader to make up one's mind about the man who is being examined. The four narratives are attempts to arrive at the truth.

Perhaps, the most compelling aspect of the structure of the novel, though, is the overlapping perceptions of common events. The book begins with the story of

Yihuda of Qiryat, Judas Iscariot, the Biblical traitor, the luster after pieces of silver. He is no such man here. Rather, he is a political rebel, a man dedicated to the overthrow of the Romans and all they stand for, a man who happens upon a beggar, Jesus, starving in the street:

> I first saw him in the winter of that year at En Melakh. A town of a few hundred just north of the Salt Sea. He had come in out of the desert, people said — from the look of him, his blistered face and the way his skin hung from his bones, he'd passed a good while there ... His hair and beard were scraggly and short as if recently shaved for a vow — they gave him a boyish appearance but couldn't however quite take the dignity from him, which seemed to sit on him like some mantle someone had laid over him. (3-4)

He befriends him, helps him bury a man killed by the soldiers of Herod Antipas, and they become uncomfortable allies. He begins the storytelling about the storyteller, involving the series of parables about the maker of parables. This is followed by the story of Miryam of Migdal, including an examination of her unreciprocated physical desire, in addition to her returned spiritual love for Jesus. After that Miryam, his mother, examines his early life and her ultimate reconciliation with her son just before he is crucified in Jerusalem. Finally, Simon of Gergesa presents his uncertain revelations of Yihuda's questionable interpretation of all that happened, in the process giving all the details about Jesus' last days, including the crucifixion.

Taken together, the novel's components, these four expositions, are the essence of a biography, a biography of one man's life, the details of which none of the tellers can agree on. It is in this that the charm and the true sense of who and what Ricci believes Jesus might have been emerges. He was to each individual what each wanted him to be, not what he wanted them to believe he was, not what some skewed mythological portrait that has come down through the ages in scripture insists he was. Simon, in the passage quoted above that sums up his feelings about both the man and his legacy, makes that perfectly clear. These storytellers are alive, as alive as Jesus is. They fill the reader with wonder. They are both mystifying and complex in their apparent simplicity.

Arguably, what all of them seem to be after is truth. It is truth about identity, no matter how varied the results of their inquiries may be, no matter how varied their interpretations of observed phenomena. They seem to be seeking, as Jesus himself was, in his words and his wanderings, the man's qualifications for messianic status.

Interestingly, this is not fundamentally different from what is observed during a reading of Ricci's previous trilogy of novels. Vittorio, himself, seems to possess a messianic vision that plays itself out in ways that see him, too, displaced from human society much like a cow is cut from a herd. What this does to him, as it does to Jesus and the narrators of each section of this book, is lead everyone to the precipice of truth.

Although there is no replication of it in *Testament* at the moment Jesus is being judged, conventional lore has it that Pilate asked, once, during a trial, the central question of this novel: "What is truth?" The fact is, as this novel beautifully reveals, there is probably no such thing as absolute truth.

Vittorio, in the trilogy, discovers this certainty because he is unable, after a harrowing search for it, to use what he thinks the truth is to bridge the gap between him and his mother, between him and his father, or between him and his sister, the gulf that haunts him the most. In like manner, the several narrators, each seeking the truth of Jesus, are left, at the end of their opportunities, flailing about in a wilderness that offers them no hope of anything resembling a unified opinion of the man who so obsesses them. Was he a blasphemer against God and an inciter against Rome as the "historical" Sanhedrin (religious Supreme Court) found him to be? Or was he not a blasphemer and inciter? Was he innocent of treason as Pilate found him to be — his trial before Pilate almost certainly a political rather than a religious hearing? Or was he not innocent?

In the end, as it was with Vittorio, the truth, whatever it is, does not matter: not in the Bible and not in *Testament*. In the end, Jesus suffers on the cross because he wanted to suffer on the cross. It was his choice. His silence when the possibility of relief from the charges is before him cements this belief. It is the final expression of his truth, of his helter-skelter, highly convoluted, confused search for identity. He wants, like Vittorio before him, to know who he is and what he is, even if this is impossible. It is the only logical endpoint of his existential angst, observed with such individualism by the four narrators. It is not surprising, then, that their stories cannot be told as one thread of truth. Their narratives have to conflict because the chronological truth of Jesus' life is not what is important, either to Nino Ricci or to history. What is important is an internal sense of the man, a feeling about him. This internal sense is presented by Yihuda when he talks about Jesus' method of teaching:

> Yeshua's usual practice when he arrived in a town was
> to go to the house of one of his disciples and share a

bit of food or wine there while word of his presence
was sent around to any other followers he might have
in the place. When people began to gather he would
tend first to any sick who had come, then settle in his
host's courtyard to do his teaching or perhaps repair
to some field outside of town. His methods were very
informal — usually he simply sat in amongst his dis-
ciples and answered the queries they put to him, often
turning the question back onto the questioner in the
manner of the ancient Greek philosophers. Much of
what he conveyed in this way was no more than what
one heard in the assembly houses: follow the com-
mandments; give alms to the poor; believe in the one
true God. But he had a way of making these notions
seem new again, and vital, while most teachers in-
toned them as if they were the remotest arcana of a
forgotten era.

What struck me in these sessions, however, was
how he did not condescend to his pupils, or consider
anything above their understanding; and this amazed
me, for when it came to the core of his teaching, and
to those notions that were distinctive to him like that
of the kingdom, it often seemed to me that not Hillel
himself could have followed the nuance of his thought.
(48-49)

This idea about Jesus, if it is introduced by the structure
and the motives of the characters who operate within
that structure, is sealed by Ricci's use of language, the
words of the narrators as well as those of Jesus. It is, for
the most part, Biblical in nature and in some ways the
utter charm of the book can be traced to this convention.
With the exception of Yihuda of Qiryat's portion, which
is curiously modern and forthright, almost militaristic

in style, but fitting because he is, after all, a rebel, a soldier of sorts battling against the occupation of his home, the text is punctuated with nuances of the Bible:

> Tsef had always been much looked to for wisdom ... (138).
> Then it happened once when we were in Arbela ... (143).
> I had never seen such wonders nor heard their like spoken of ... (146).
> As it fell out ... (234).
> Then, when he had been with Zekaryah for a year, he came to me and said ... (241).
> As the sabbath was coming on ... (289)

The examples are endless, but perhaps the most telling aspect of this form is the convolution of the sentences. To a modern ear, they sound just a little odd. Sentences are longer than they need be, there are more words included in any explanation than might seem prudent, and there is an elevated tone to the choice of language that suggests the import of what is being said is noteworthy. This is, after all, the tale of tales. It deserves such attention in its retelling. The particular use of language is evident, for example, in the following paragraph from Miryam's, his mother's, section of the text:

> As the sabbath was coming on, I had to make haste to reach Ammanthus before dusk. So I departed from Kefar Nahum without any sight of my son and with no comprehension of his plight. From Ammanthus, when the sabbath had passed, I immediately returned to my home so that Yaqob and I might confer, for of my children he was the only one with some understanding of his brother. (289)

What is she saying? Simply this: she had to get home from Ammanthus to talk to her son Yaqob about his brother because he was the only one in the family who understood him. That's all. But the language is mellifluous and soft. There are twists and turns, grammatical departures from simple sentence structure — a coordinate conjunction beginning a sentence, a sentence begun with a prepositional phrase immediately followed by an adverbial clause, another begun with an adverbial clause, and some very interesting verbs: "coming on," "had passed," and "might confer." All these devices are in the interests of rendering the reader slightly disarmed, slightly out-of-sorts in terms of grasping at first blush the essential meaning of what is said. In its very unusualness, the language both distracts the reader's attention and grabs the attention, and this is a marvellous stroke on Ricci's part. The reader is fairly mesmerized as the story builds, by not only the narrative structure, by not only the conflicting perspectives of the characters, but by this odd use of vocabulary and sentence structure, which is nearly brilliant.

In order to capture the essence of the story, the reader needs to constantly compare the original Gospels and their message with this new version of the Gospels. What better method of assuring that this is attended to than replicating to some degree the method of telling the story?

The most striking use of language is reserved for Jesus himself. The tone of his speeches to his followers, particularly when he launches into a parable, recognizable or not as comparable to something from the original Gospels, is masterful. The unbalancing of the reader, as to whether he is God or a man, is absolutely sustained at these moments. For example, this is what Jesus says when Miryam of Migdal and others question him after he has turned his mother away from his door:

> When we questioned Yeshua about the incident, he grew angry with us. Why do you trouble me over this, he said. It was the first time we had seen him this way, and many of us were frightened.
>
> Yaqob said, But the law tells us to honour our mother and father.
>
> The law also tells us that a man leaves his mother and father, Yeshua said.
>
> But that is to marry.
>
> And so I've married you, Yeshua said. Now my followers are my family. (133)

Or it is when one of Herod's spies attempts to trap Yeshua by asking him about the kingdom he speaks of and in so doing reveal him for the rebel and threat to the established order he is thought to be:

> He was quick to ask about the kingdom saying he had heard others speak of it and wondered if it was a place of the heavens or of the earth.
>
> But Yeshua knowing his intentions, said, What do those you speak to tell you.
>
> Truly I don't think they've understood you, Chizkijah said, because some say it's in heaven, some on earth, and the rest somewhere in between, at which many in the crowd laughed, for though people despised him, he was clever enough to amuse them.
>
> Yeshua said, Then they've answered rightly, since it's all these things.
>
> But how can it be on the earth, Chizkijah said, when the Galilee belongs to Herod and Judea to Rome.

Tell me this, who does the wind belong to, Yeshua asked him.

How can the wind belong to anyone.

Then the kingdom is like the wind, Yeshua said, which is in heaven and on earth and in between, and belongs to no one. (191-192)

He gives the impression of being a latter day Socrates, full of the wisdom of knowing what he does not know and being able to accept it, unlike his enemies.

The use of language in this way works well for Ricci, for it allows him to present his Jesus at one moment as a thorn in the side of authority and at another as a father-protector of those who would follow in his wake. It makes him human, like all the others around him. In his humanity, he is acceptable as the icon he is purported to be.

Testament, then, is a book that functions within the parameters that it sets out for itself. Nino Ricci is not attempting to present a man who is in any way, shape, or form to be perceived as all things to all people. He is simply a man who saw things differently as more than one of the narrators is at pain to say. It is because of the difference in his thought that they are attracted to him. It is in the quality of the difference, then, between this fictionalized gospel and the other Gospels that readers, too, will be attracted to this book and find worth in it.

Notes

1.   Joseph Heller, *God Knows* (New York: Alfred A. Knopf, 1984)) 157.

2.   Nino Ricci, *Testament* (Toronto: Doubleday Canada, 2002), 227 [Page numbers for all other quotations from

this novel are in parentheses after the quotation.]

3. Nino Ricci, *Where She Has Gone* (Toronto: McClelland & Stewart, 1997), 321.

4. "Gospel of St. John," *The Holy Bible: King James Version* (Cleveland: The World Publishing Company), 11:25, 26, 27, 41-44.

Marino Tuzi

Science, Human Suffering, and Revelation in Nino Ricci's *The Origin of Species*: A Literary and Thematic Study

FILTERED THROUGH THE consciousness of the central character, Alex Fratarcangeli, the novel, *The Origin of Species*, presents the behaviour and attitudes of individuals, the unfolding of events in particular time frames, and the various social and cultural environments in which people live and the events occur. Yet, the unreliability of this subjective narration constantly reminds the reader that he or she might be getting not only a biased view of the situation, but that any given observation on Alex's part is partial, omitting a full picture of what is taking place. The unreliability of Alex's perceptions of what is happening before him is partly the result of his contradictory emotional state. He holds two opposing emotions — affection and resentment — towards particular situations and individuals. The unreliability of his observations is also the result of his inability to stand back objectively from what is taking place.

Alex appears locked inside himself, unable to put aside his preoccupation with who he is and how he should be in the world. During a psychotherapy session with his psychiatrist, Dr. Klein, Alex admits to himself that "for most of his life he had striven to hide from the world, namely, the dark den of banality and self-absorption that his mind truly was" (23). (*The Origin of Species*, Nino Ricci. Anchor Canada, Random House, 2009. All other quotations are from this text.) This self-absorption at times slips into a kind of extreme form of self-consciousness: he sees himself involved in a particular behaviour and observes his emotional response. This acute self-consciousness, in which he is both the viewer and the actor in his own life, is intensified by the use of a third person narration. The removal of the "I" in the narration and its replacement with "he" convey the omniscient narrator's distance from the experiences of the central character while at the same time this anonymous narrator presents the personal side of Alex's experiences. For instance, in his relationship with Ingrid in Sweden, we are given the following passage: "At night, making love with Ingrid, he could taste the sea on her. It crossed his mind that it could actually come to pass, his remaining here. The oddest sensation went through him at the thought, not unpleasant but hard to place, like an unfamiliar smell" (65). In another example, when he is in the Galapagos, assisting the naturalist, Desmond, in his work, the reader is told: "Alex didn't like to admit it but he was starting to feel a sort of grudging respect for the universality of Desmond's disdain. Probably his tooth-and-claw routine was just a way of justifying what a bastard he was. . . If Alex wasn't careful out here ... he was going to start thinking like the man." 260 - 261). Distance and intimacy, observation and emotion, constantly work against the maintenance of a pure emotional rendering of the central character's story. Unlike conventional third person narration in the realist novel, wherein the omniscient narrator moves in and out of the consciousness of various important characters or provides contrasting points of view unmediated by the consciousness of the central character, in *The Origin of Species*, the omniscient narrator concentrates solely on the consciousness of the central character: on what he sees, feels, and thinks. The behaviour of individuals and the presence of a specific physical environment are presented through the consciousness of Alex Fratarcangeli. What the third person voice tends to do is to duplicate the nature of Alex's existence, in which being in the world and an awareness of being in the world frequently converge. The inner turmoil of Alex's life promotes his contradictory and unstable emotional state and it also sustains his unrelenting self-consciousness, leading him both to observe the world as it is and to distort it because of his emotional instability.

The first person voice enters the narrative only in the short passages when Alex conducts his imaginary conversation with Peter Gzowski, the popular CBC television and radio show host. But the imagined conversation is a construct for the actual conversation that Alex is having with himself. This conversation allows Alex to have a dialogue with himself, acting as questioner and respondent, in which he can probe the motivations behind his behaviour and attitude. Self-conscious about what to tell his psychiatrist, Dr. Klein, in a psychotherapy session, Alex engages in an imaginary conversation with Peter Gzowski:

> *Well Peter, I suppose what stopped me from bringing things up with him was a kind of superstition, really, the fear I'd wreck this precarious balance I'd set up.*
>
> *Isn't it interesting. So you thought that by not talking about things you'd somehow keep them in check.*
>
> *Something like that. (23)*

This literary device of the imaginary dialogue repeats the idea that Alex is both engrossed in the immediacy of his given experience and he is standing back watching it impassively as it unfolds before him. In effect, Alex's imagined dialogue with Peter Gzowski mirrors the third person narration in the novel: the omniscient narrator describes Alex's behaviour and tells us what is transpiring in Alex's mind.

So in the novel, Alex's acute self-absorption, as he constantly analyzes what he sees and feels and thinks, obsessed with himself because of his sense of inadequacy, co-exists with the narration's sheer objectivity, in which the physical environment is presented to us in tenacious detail. For instance, walking through Montreal at night he notes: "He had reached McGill. Around the residences great heaps of belongings had been piled up along the curbs, bean bag chairs, stereos, green garbage bags full of clothes, while squealy girls in tennis gear or sloppy sweats hugged each other and cried and made fusses and their fathers stared off into the middle distance or loaded things into their cars" (441). Attention to detail is also evident in this passage from the Galapagos story: "The weather continued as before, with the same haze clouding the sky, the same hot wind, the bouts of drizzle when the wind died and the rain came down straight as falling pins" (275). While there is an association with the atmosphere of a particular situation and Alex's immediate mood, which most often is solemn, the description of the external world is not noticeably distorted by Alex's consciousness. The acuity of detail indicates an external reality that is separate from Alex's mental state. Along with this fine description, there is Alex's recurrent intellectualization, which typifies a habit of mind, on various topics, spanning from politics to science, religion, philosophy, and literature. These narrative elements present us with a story in which the central character is both absorbed with himself emotionally and is still connected to the social reality that shapes his existence.

In terms of the style of language, the omniscient narrator weaves ordinary words with poetic and abstract diction to give the reader an impression of how Alex's mind works and to suggest the cultural and social influences that have shaped Alex as a person. Instead of using only simple and straightforward language or making use of sophisticated allusions and complex diction, the omniscient narrator constantly merges the two levels of language to develop the consciousness of the central character. For instance, in describing the content of the letter that he had received from Ingrid, his past girl-friend, who lives in Sweden, Alex tells the reader: "She gave an account of her life, harrowing in its concision, from when he'd left her at the Copenhagen pier. Her discovering that she was pregnant and then the series of Hardian misunderstandings between them, the letter she'd sent, the dismissive one he'd sent back" (228). When he describes his ambivalence towards Desmond during his trip in the Galapagos with him, he notes in puzzlement: "Somehow, the more time he spent with Desmond and the more reasons he amassed to detest him, the more he felt in his thrall. He wasn't sure what sort of pathology might be behind this, if he was drawn to him because he thought them so different or because he thought them the same." (269) Reflecting on his failed relationship with Liz, he tries to figure out what went wrong:

> He might turn it over and over in his head and never see it right, whether he should have done this or that, what Liz would have done in turn. Who had been dishonest

> or disingenuous or manipulative, or whether, if he had
> just bitten the bullet and said yes, Liz, out of sheer
> contrariness wouldn't have had the abortion anyway.
> He thought of Liz the way Freud had thought of
> dreams, that there was a point where matters re-
> treated into the unfathomable like the umbilical cord
> into the womb. (100)

The use of this kind of mixed prose suggests a kind of
literary sensibility that reflects the essence of contemporary culture. The ordinary and the practical coincide
with the high plane of intellectual life. Intrinsic to this
situation is the breaking down of class boundaries.
Working class life has affected the nature of middle class
or bourgeois culture. Alex Fratarcangeli is not only emblematic of this uneasy coexistence. His personality and
cultural orientation have been forged by his working
class and ethnic family background and by his middle
class, urban lifestyle and by his elite university education.

The literary style of the novel then is a reflection of
the worlds in which Alex moves both psychologically
and intellectually. This bringing together of two forms
of linguistic expression, the ordinary, and the abstract,
is a constant feature of the way the novel constructs the
narrative voice of the central character that is invoked
by the omniscient narrator. The omniscient narrator
does not directly intervene in the storytelling by presenting any kind of judgment, observation, or criticism.
Rather, it is only through the consciousness of the central character, a person who is marked by contradictions
and self-criticism, that the reader gains a sense of his
failings and virtues as an individual. Part of the chronic
ambivalence of Alex Fratarcangeli, which many times
leads to impassivity or detachment, is an inability to find

a balance between his rural, familial and ethnic upbringing and his urban, and individualistic lifestyle. Whole sections of the novel are devoted to the rituals of daily life in mostly urban and rural settings, in parts of Canada and in several foreign countries. These rituals involve activities and relationships that for the most part are quite commonplace. The use of simple and straightforward language, in dialogue, description, and narration to advance the story and to show the character development, dominates much of the novel. Yet, added to this use of ordinary language and conventional storytelling are whole passages which are purely literary, whether they are pieces of analysis from Alex's dissertation, or his presentation of various discourses connected to his studies or his intellectual interests or even his reflections on the lives of politicians, such as P.E. Trudeau, and thinkers such as Charles Darwin, whose seminal book on human evolution sets up an important theme in the novel and gives the novel its title. Referring to Charles Darwin's drive to achieve fame in his field of study, Alex tells the reader: "He had acted at every turn for his own preservation, had marshaled his forces and then, when the moment had come to move forward, had done so with brutal resolve" (465).

In constructing the consciousness of Alex Fratarcangeli, the various narrative and literary techniques create a sense of how Alex's mind works, profiling his complicated emotional life, in which his need to connect emotionally to others is constantly subverted by his insecurity and low self-esteem. Most often, there is a convergence of emotion and intellect. The emotional state shapes his intellectual understanding. The reverse also occurs. His intellectualization leads him to behave in ways that he knows are not natural to him. So in the novel, there is no clear boundary between Alex's personal life and his public role. For instance, his sense of marginality, of not feeling comfortable in a given social context, allows him to have sympathy for individuals who feel that they have been treated unfairly by other people. During his expedition in the Galapagos, although he finds Desmond arrogant and utterly selfish, often threatening Alex's physical security, Alex feels compassion towards him: "It was almost heartbreaking to see Desmond's vindictiveness, his sense of injury, exposed so badly ... Perhaps there was a sort of dignity in that, in hard-won bitterness. Alex had his own share of it" (301).

Alex's emotional connection with Desmond influences his thinking not just about human evolution, but also about the meaning of human existence. It is Desmond who exposes Alex to the ideas of Charles Darwin through a copy of Darwin's book, *Origin of Species*. Desmond's hypothesis is that the process through which rudimentary plants adapt and evolve is prone to unpredictable factors, which are sometimes the result of mere chance. This contention affects Alex's interpretation of Darwin's theory about how a species is created and it leads him to a general philosophical view about the basis of human existence: "There was no telling, really, that was the thing: there was no Plan. Things went on and on, this happened, then that, and it was all the merest chance" (297). The feeling that his life has been shaped by a series of unplanned, random events, since he has been unable to find emotional stability in his life, is projected unto Desmond's sense of betrayal, of being let down by the people he depended on, in this case his thesis advisor who forced him out of his doctoral studies on plant life in England. Moreover, Alex's emotional displacement finds its explanation in his almost existential interpretation of Charles Darwin's theory of environmental adaptation. Alex's existential

Darwinist view is supported by Desmond's unorthodox plant experimentation on the islands of the Galapagos. This is the very place where Darwin's investigation of the local ecosystem began his thinking about natural selection and adaptation and the basis for the creation of new species in nature. This kind of psychological projection of Alex's emotional and social displacement is reiterated in his attitude towards literature, the study of which continues through his dissertation in the present in Montreal: "Back in his undergraduate days he had thought of literature as a kind of religion, as the straight road to whatever truth might exist out there in the ether, but nowadays he couldn't pick up a novel without a great feeling of irrelevance coming over him" (194).

Alex's ability to intellectualize, which is a product of the years he has been a university student, culminating in his doctoral studies, becomes a strategy to protect himself emotionally when he feels incapable of facing a challenging moment in his life. Alex admits that in most of the sessions with his psychiatrist he did not disclose his true problems. Even when he tried to talk about an immediate emotional concern, he resorted to embellishment and invention to minimize its impact on him:

> Alex had to wonder if there was any difference, really, between his little chats with Peter and these sessions with Dr. Klein. In both cases he seemed to be making things up as he went along, whatever sounded good, whatever he could twist into a version of himself he could live with ... He was starting to think that consciousness wasn't some lighthouse of self-knowing but merely a little cave where you made up stories about yourself, whatever it took to hide the shit and the slime. (383)

Alex is fully aware that he tends to use his intellect to avoid addressing his emotional problems, which can be self-defeating, especially when he has voluntarily chosen to undertake psychotherapy to cope with his borderline depression. However, Alex applies the knowledge that he obtains through his academic research to support his feelings towards a given situation. Referring to cultural nationalism, using Quebecois nationalism as an example, he notes that a person's culture is not based on biology or even inheritance, but on the flow of social and cultural influences:

> Like Alex's claim to the [ancient] Samnites — all bunk he'd discovered ... He ... had found out that the Romans ... had scattered [the Samnites] to the winds, replacing them with Albanians, Macedonians, Turks, whatever slave race they could put their hands on. It turned out Alex was a mongrel through and through." (396)

This idea about constant cultural transformation becomes attached to his own rationale about his relationship to his Swedish son, Per, who has grown up without his presence: "He had been blond as a child, well into his teens ... As blond as his son ... It was a link" (397). By showing the interplay between Alex's emotional makeup and intellectual ability and by presenting his deployment of simple and complex language, the novel indicates how Alex makes sense of what happens to him and how he expresses this understanding to himself and to other people who are close to him. Yet, as the novel suggests, the personality of the central character has been shaped primarily by two social contexts, whose standards of behaviour and cultural values are not often compatible with each other. This incompatibility results in a sort of reflex detachment, which is especially noticeable when he is in a situation that requires him to behave in a conventional manner. A dramatic example of this emotional detachment, which compounds and complicates his borderline emotional state, occurs when he discovers that Liz, his girlfriend, with whom he has made a commitment to a long-term relationship, the first time that he has done so with a woman, is pregnant with their child. Instead of responding with approval to her pregnancy, since becoming parents would be a natural part of the commitment that they have made to each other, Alex does not clearly state how he feels about becoming a father. Almost immediately he shifts the responsibility for having the child to Liz by making the following statement to her: "'Just tell me what you want to do'" (107). Even as Liz is at the brink of getting an abortion, Alex maintains his feigned neutrality, as if the pregnancy does not involve him, as if suddenly he is standing outside of his relationship with Liz. As such, his words of reassurance are essentially empty of conviction. As he tells her: "'We could make it work,' he said, not meaning it. 'I could get my teaching certificate'" (107). Alex's ostensible neutrality and tepid encouragement convey to Liz that he does not want to be a father and he reinforces Liz's decision to have an abortion, since she does not have the wherewithal at this point in her young life to take on such responsibility on her own. As the novel shows, the abortion results in an ongoing sense of distrust and resentment that will eventually destroy the relationship. Alex's incapacity to engage in normative behaviour, assuming shared responsibility for the pregnancy, appears to be the result of a mixture of situational and emotional factors. As a young man, wanting to

develop an academic career, his professional priorities
take precedence over the conventional role of fatherhood. He does not feel emotionally prepared to deal with
the demands of fatherhood, given especially his own difficult family past. While he cares for Liz, he does not feel
passionate towards her, since the relationship developed
circumstantially out of a high school friendship. Alex's
response indicates that he has his own priority for what
is important in his life. It is a priority that is built on the
main premise that meeting his needs is more important
than anything else.

Driven by the view that social attitudes and inter-
personal behaviour are not determined by fixed social
norms, this individualistic mindset is reflective of an
urban social system, in which group relationships are
not critical to a person's survival. Instead, urban living,
with its access to social services and a spectrum of economic opportunities, allows individuals to make decisions that support their goals and not those of the group.
What the incident involving Liz's pregnancy reveals is
that Alex is the product of two distinct social and cultural milieus. Alex's upbringing in rural Ontario was
community and family-based. People had a set of social
obligations to each other that they could not easily disregard without facing social censure. In contrast to this
rural way of life, Alex's lifestyle in a large city, a diverse
urban, social environment, whether it is Toronto or Montreal, is individualistic and for the most part relationships
are voluntary and inspired by a host of priorities. It is
when Alex breaks away consciously from what he knows
his upbringing has told him is the correct action he must
take in any given situation that the reader sees that Alex
is in a state of social reaction to anything that invokes
his background. Reflecting on what he knows about the

background of his psychiatrist, Dr. Klein (which is information that he has gleaned as a result of his own initia-
tive to find out about Dr. Klein's personal life), Alex projects a part of himself into Dr. Klein's past behaviour,
admitting the effect that his small town upbringing had
on him: "All this seemed so familiar to Alex that he felt
as if he had lived it. In fact, he had. Duddy Klein was
himself: problems with authority, averse to criticism"
(382). In this state of reaction, Alex often finds himself
unable to commit to any kind of action that is motivated
by a particular belief system or ideology. Referring to the
El Salvadorian political refugee group in Montreal that
he has become associated with in order to pursue Maria,
a member of the group, whom he wants to be his girl-
friend, Alex states: "The world was divided neatly into
peasants and imperialists, the vocabulary so familiar by
now he didn't need a translation" (360). This understanding that he has about his own limits does not prevent
him from being continually confused and even bewil-
dered in responding to a particular challenge.

However, when he decides to do what he thinks is
best for himself, he is unable to find any kind of equilibrium in his life. During a psychotherapeutic session with
Dr. Klein, Alex, in his mind, tries to find the real motivation for his behaviour towards Liz's pregnancy. Instead
of obtaining a better sense of the emotions that triggered
his behaviour, which he seeks in order to quell his relent-
less sense of inadequacy and shame, for by this time he
has convinced himself that he acted almost monstrous-
ly towards her, he realizes that he had been emotionally
uncommitted to the relationship. As he tells Dr. Klein:
"The thing with Liz ... was that nothing was ever clear.
We were both these smart people, but it seemed like we
never had the least idea why we did things. Why we were

even together." Even as he said this, Alex understood that this was exactly why they had been together, because things were unclear, because there was safety in that (371). Yet, this is not really a revelation, because he concedes, in his reflections about the relationship, that circumstance and routine had led him to become intimate with Liz. Except for the friendship they had shared in high school, he had not felt any passion towards her. In his state of reaction, in which he cannot naturally commit himself to something that is beyond his immediate needs, Alex finds, through his own admission, that he was both an observer and a participant in his relationship with Liz. Equally important, the absence of an emotional bond between Alex and Liz reinforced his view that his relationship with Liz would not cure him of his endemic anxiety and despondency.

Underlying his harsh self-criticism, there is the belief that he is bereft of real emotions because he can never fully feel a particular way towards himself without thinking a contrary thought or reflexively going through the opposite emotion. Contemplating on his role in his failed relationship with Liz, he states: "He didn't know what he was crying about — that he was a heartless ass, he supposed, that Liz deserved better than him, though it was hard to make out if he was feeling a twisted sort of self-pity or if some alter ego in him was truly coming to terms with his emotional bankruptcy" (372). The novel frequently gives the reader examples of Alex's habit of responding to a situation by holding several contradictory feelings not only towards himself but also towards a specific person that is close to him. For instance, when he is with Felix, a well-placed Quebec businessman, whom Alex is tutoring in the English language, Alex "[feels] the flush of conflicted emotion rise up in him that Felix always stirred, a strange mix of attraction and its denial" (39). Also, after inviting his thesis advisor, Jiri, to stay with him at his apartment, Alex gets so aggravated with Jiri's selfishness that he tells him to leave. Yet, Alex's anger towards Jiri subsides later on in the story when he hears of Jiri's troubled family life: "It didn't make him pity him exactly ... but it dirtied things in some hopeless way" (408). In another scene, which explores Alex's contradictory and impulsive emotional state, Alex spends time in a nearby park with his friend Stephen and Stephen's son, Ariel. The presence of Ariel reassures him about his decision to acknowledge his own son, Per, who lives in Sweden with his mother. He tells us: "Corn-child as he was, Ariel was still a link for Alex, a kind of expiation" (341). But when Ariel viciously shoves a local boy to the ground because the other boy intrudes in his space while he is playing, Alex soon afterwards has a marked change in his attitude towards Stephen's son. He sees a violent, unpredictable streak in Ariel and the other boy and he doubts his own ability to be a father to his own son: "They'd been nothing but animals then, bundles of instinct. The most dangerous creatures on earth ... He wondered how he could ever be trusted with that, how he'd ever be up to it" (347).

The central character's emotional volatility and his self-absorption indicate that his reaction to his upbringing has been greatly responsible for his behaviour after he left his family and rural community. Until he went to university in Toronto, Alex was a part of a rural, working class community. The mundane quality of small-town, agrarian life was intensified by his Italian immigrant family, for whom practicality and loyalty were paramount. The family's immigrant heritage appeared to be in tune with the rural world in which the family members found themselves. Hard-work, modesty, and dedication to the group, respectively the family and the community, were the traits that were valued by the community and his family. This way of life affirmed a set of values and shaped the identity of the individual. Given his emotional sensitivity and his tendency to be imaginative and inquisitive, Alex had a very difficult time in becoming part of the community. The insularity of the community, whose effect was compounded by the traditionalism of his family, seemed a barrier to his self-actualization and motivated Alex to leave home, after completing his high school diploma, to go to university in Toronto.

His decision to attend university gave Alex the freedom to choose what he wanted to do, permitting him to study literature, which cultivated his imaginative and inquisitive abilities. As the story insinuates, this intellectual activity involved exposure to ideas and to thinking about the possibilities that comprise human existence. From Alex's perspective, this intellectual orientation was in sharp contrast to the utilitarian culture of the rural community from which he had originated. Alex discovered that urban life was based on personal ambition, since individuals were free from the need to be part of a family in order to secure economic and social status. This individualism was not directly tied to a particular group, and therefore the kind of identity that one developed was much more open-ended and flexible.

It is two seemingly very different cultural and social environments, respectively rural and urban, that have shaped Alex's identity. As the novel implies, it is these two sides to his socialization that continue to generate the emotional and cultural contradictions in his life. His deeply rooted reaction to his past and the inherent openness of city life maintain Alex's state of indecision, in which he continually wavers between opposed points of view. It is a vacillation that is especially acute when he is confronted by a pressing issue which he has to deal with.

In the novel, the critical periods of Alex's adult life take place outside of the community and family that he has distanced himself from. What Alex realizes is that he cannot rid himself of the internal conflict between what he needs to establish his identity and what he has to do to meet the expectations of the existing social milieu. This situation implies that it not just his upbringing that is responsible for the crises that he has to cope with. In spite of the opportunities for self-actualization offered by modernity, contemporary urban society appears to be equally imperfect as the rural community because its values are not fixed but in continuous flux. The pervasive image of a world in a state of transition is conveyed by the persistent references to current social and political realities, ranging from the Chernobyl nuclear disaster, with its global environmental ramifications, to developing countries in strife, reflected through the El Salvadorian political refugee community in Montreal, and to the ongoing political tensions in Quebec over cultural nationalism, which affect Alex's position as an Anglophone. In this type of unstable social setting, it is necessary for individuals to have a strong sense of what is important to them or they turn to a particular ideology to guide their behaviour and give meaning to their lives. Most of the individuals Alex encounters have attached themselves to some cause or plan that defines who they are. This emotional attachment can be self-destructive, as evidenced by Desmond in his obsession to present a radical theory on plant life on the planet. Or such fervour can bring one to the brink of delusion. For Alex, this psychological condition is exemplified by Esther, who

clings to the hope that there is a cure for multiple sclerosis despite the progressively degenerative nature of the
disease.

In the consciousness of Alex, there is the coming
together of two distinct social worlds, with their own set
of values and lifestyles, which are expressed by two different levels of language and which produce a personality whose contradictions, volatility, and self-absorption
make him an unreliable commentator on his own behaviour and views and on the actions and attitudes of other
people. Yet, it is through the consciousness of this visibly
flawed person that near the end of the novel the narrative arrives at a philosophical view of life. Alex realizes
that, despite the arbitrary way people engage their lives
and the accidental nature of events, this instability does
not negate being in the world but it reaffirms that wonder that permeates all forms of existence.

While undergoing his doctoral studies at Concordia
University in Montreal, Alex tries to see the connections
between the crucial situations in his past and the sort of
life he now has in the present. At this point in Alex's intellectual life, the work of Charles Darwin, comprised of
his scientific ideas about evolution and his accounts of
his scientific explorations, has become a major influence
on Alex's way of thinking about modern society. He turns
to evolutionary theory to help him understand the purpose of being alive. But Alex cannot see any solid foundation to his own existence. He perceives himself to be
another example of a biological anomaly among a host
of organic mutations:

> He seemed such an unlikely hash in that instant, as
> unpredictable and strange in his lineaments as the
> arthropods of the Burgess Shale, with their insufficient

> tentacles and extrusions and frills ... It beggared the
> mind to think of all the billion little evolutionary
> mutations and mistakes that had led him here, to this
> freakish amalgam. (82)

For Alex, Darwin's explanation of the pattern of human
evolution does not provide a stable and positive picture
of the nature of human life. Instead Alex infers another
meaning behind the theory of natural selection and human evolution: "[Darwin] wouldn't say it, he spent the
whole of his book finding ways not to see it, and yet there
it was, the unacknowledged elephant: the chance, the
possibility, that all of creation made no sense" (297).

Alex admits that, without God or some higher spiritual power, existence appears meaningless: "There was
no artist, really, that was the problem. *No plan.* This happened, then that; something worked, then it didn't" (464).
Nevertheless, he contends that everything seems to be
related to each other. Chaos and creation are equally
evident in any given time and place. Thinking about Esther, who is dying from multiple sclerosis, Alex notes: "It
was all connected. So little went wrong, but then it took
so little: one microbe amiss, one link, and the whole system ran amok" (465). Nature is conceived as the interplay of opposite forces. Accident and destruction are
interposed with stability and evolution. The operation of
this extraordinary power in the universe, in which chaos
and order are part of the same natural process, is made
known to us not simply through intellect or emotion
alone, but through physical sensation and intuition. Alex
describes the presence of this extraordinary power as
"the thingness of things, their funniness" (471). The
power that governs the universe is both tangible and in-
tangible at the same time. Thus, what encircles people is

both rational and non-rational. It is within our grasp but also inaccessible. "How could [things] fill the mind and yet be so small? There might be gods beyond them, and gods of gods, and, beyond these, things unimaginable, that the human mind could not name or give shape to and yet it could think they were there" (471).

The world that we sense and that appears to us takes shape in that space where the mind meets external reality. From Alex's perspective, in terms of understanding the essence of the human condition, consciousness is not possible without the existence of external reality. A person knows that he or she has a consciousness by being aware of something that is separate from his or her mind. Of course, the attempt to identify the elements of external reality and then figure out how they work provides individuals with great difficulty. Despite the process of conceptualization and the use of empirical methods, the basis of what we see or sense often escapes our consciousness. But, when the mind cannot be sure of the true essence of something in material reality, the mind responds to this absence of knowing by imagining what could be there beyond its comprehension. Given that science is a complex theoretical system that has been developed to explain natural phenomena, the notion, presented by Alex Fratarcangeli, of the way a person employs his or her mind to ascertain any type of truth, implies that the use of science is as provisional as our consciousness and as much a product of the imagination as any other human endeavour, such as literature, psychology, and politics. This almost metaphysical interpretation of human reality and nature permeates the entire movement of the novel, in which scientism, as a kind of belief system, is brought up against the fundamental mystery of existence.

In arriving at his own form of mysticism, Alex tries to give meaning to what he is doing now after so many years of discontentment. The events and experiences that have transpired in his life have been caused by various, overlapping factors: his rigid familial background and the change in social status, his almost idiosyncratic predilections, the choices he often made impulsively, and equally important the unforeseen adverse developments and the unsatisfactory outcomes that resulted from situations which had initially appeared supportive of his interests. Yet, even the choices that he made wilfully have been constantly undermined by the emotional swings associated with borderline depression and by conditions beyond his control. Alex wants to find the real source of his inability to communicate with people and his habitual repression of his emotions. These two problems are tied to his pervasive sense of failure and the shame that comes with it. Wanting to get to the origin of his borderline emotional state, Alex reflects on his relationship with his father. Alex perceived his father to be detached and domineering. Perhaps his father's behaviour was the reason why he left home after high school and why he tried to minimize his contact with his father and his mother and his adult siblings. In recalling an incident, in which the two of them were in a car together, stuck in traffic, his father appears to him emotionally distant and judgmental of people. But Alex realizes that it could not have been simply his poor relationship with his father that had affected his general attitude to life and his behaviour with people:

> Afterwards that line of cars had become a sort of koan for him of the strange ambivalence that surrounded anything associated with his father. What had he

> meant exactly? ... The real battle of course, was the
> one within: his own private suspicion, amounting
> sometimes to a dastardly hope, that his father was
> right, that humans were rotten to the core. (469)

Searching for the root cause of what has turned him into
the person that he is, Alex acknowledges that his father
was not the decisive negative force in his life. Although
he might reluctantly find some wisdom in his father's
pessimistic view of human nature, much of what Alex
has become is the result of factors that cannot be solely
attributed to his father's treatment of him when he was
young.

This revelation about his relationship with his father exemplifies a recurrent view in the novel that the
past does not wholly govern a person's situation in the
present. By not accepting a direct link between one's
past experiences and one's condition in the present, the
novel, through the perspective of the central character,
supports the idea that what marks an individual is the
malleability of his or her consciousness. Consciousness
as an awareness about one's place in the world is affected by material and social forces but it is not totally determined by these forces. Such determinism would erase
the possibility of any kind of free will. It would go against
the basic purpose of the novel, which is to provide a
humanistic portrait of Alex Fratarcangeli, who in his
imperfections, contradictions, and un-heroic qualities,
stands in as a kind of modern everyman caught up in
the flux of contemporary urbanism, where there are no
clear cultural or social road maps to give a person a
sense of direction in life. Consciousness, then, as a person's awareness of external reality, is not a mechanical
act but involves a process of conceptualization that is

influenced by a number of factors: cultural orientation, a particular emotional make up, and personal experience. This viewpoint, which calls attention to a larger philosophical contemplation about human existence, generates a thematic pattern that suffuses the narrative movement of the novel. Through the constant juxtaposition of the present with the past, the novel demonstrates that we understand the nature of consciousness, its essential fluidity, through the accumulation of personal experience, which in this case spans the relatively short but dramatic life of the protagonist, from late childhood to mature adulthood. This life span unfolds through the recollections of the central character, whose memories are invoked by his responses to the pressing demands of the present. Moreover, it is the need to uncover the origins of his emotional tendencies and to bring some kind of resolution to the psychological crises of his past, which continue to affect his behaviour in the present, that provokes his constant return to the past. The novel in its use of the past, mostly in the form of extended flashbacks and through separate narration, is a kind of personal confessional, which has the qualities of a therapeutic investigation.

Deepening the narrative of Alex's constant return to the past is the fact that the entire novel is told in retrospect, because it primarily takes place in the early to mid 1980s. The novel itself was published in 2008, decades after the actual time frame in the novel. Implicit in this contemporary historical fiction is a revisiting of the unique ethos that characterized that specific time frame. The invocation of the particular cultural sensibility of the 1980s contextualizes the beliefs and values of the central character, who is undergoing a process of cultural and personal transition. Thus, Alex is not only searching

back anxiously to his recent past, before his present situation in Montreal, but his current life in Montreal is itself
part of a larger investigation of a modern historical era.
Alex's present-day circumstance in Montreal as a doctoral student in English Literature is interspersed with
critical periods from his very youthful past, which he
meditates on, trying to consciously understand their significance in terms of how they have brought him to
where he is now and how these past experiences will affect his future. Thinking about his relationship with Ingrid in Sweden, almost a decade ago, when he was barely
twenty, Alex explains the motivation for looking back
to his past: "He was slightly older now ... yet he felt less
wise, less grown, than he'd felt then, still awaiting some
beginning to his life that would set it on course" (67).
This observation seems to be applicable to the other crucial periods in his past, which compared to the relative
calm and ordinariness of his present life in Montreal,
forced him to deal with immediate and dramatic situations that he seemed unprepared for both emotionally
and intellectually because of his youth and relative in-
experience.

Fulfilling the conventions of contemporary historical fiction, the novel, *The Origin of Species,* reproduces a
particular era in modern Canadian history, the 1980s, in
a documentary fashion, in which the technical details of
the specific social and physical environment are attached
to the prevailing political and cultural issues of the time.
This literary realism makes the individual characters, in
terms of their views and behaviour, representative of the
time and place that is being reproduced. Although the
actual characters and the events in their lives are fictional, the use of literary realism allows the characters
to appear not just as acts of the writer's imagination but

as reflective of a documented social reality, which has been part of the social process that has led to the attitudes and lifestyles that are evident in the present. For instance, the issues of Quebec political sovereignty and the role of the family and ethnicity in shaping cultural identity in the host country still continue to be issues in the contemporary scene, even though the ways in which these issues are approached have changed and the social conditions might be considerably different from the past. The same can be said about ideas related to the nature of individual experience in a complex, urbanized social system. Also, the discussion about how individuals should exercise their personal freedom, without strict external restraints, such as religion or social institutions, namely the family and the educational system, to give direction and meaning to their lives continues to be pertinent in the present. Added to this situation are ideas about social mobility and cultural transformation, which underlie Alex Fratarcangeli's decision to do his doctoral studies, that persist as major social themes in the present age. Through Alex's story and the stories of the other characters, such as Desmond, Liz, and Stephen, the novel in its own manner depicts the mindset of students obtaining a university education in the arts. The novel also alludes to the challenge that an arts graduate faces in attempting to enter the labour market to secure a stable position and gain social independence. By using the modes of historical fiction, the novel goes back to a point in recent history not simply to reproduce it to meet the requirements of literary realism but to create a social and cultural context from which the reader can understand the nature of the modern world. To emphasize how the past is distinctly linked in certain ways to the present, the novel inserts stories from the past into the chronology of Alex's life in the present as he undertakes his doctoral studies in Montreal. Therefore, the narrative movement of the novel does not unfold in a linear fashion in presenting the story of the central character. The non-linearity of the narrative of *The Origin of Species*, within the genre of literary realism, is the stylistic means through which the strict boundaries between the past and the present are blurred to give a sense of immediacy to the past. This discontinuity in narrative chronology serves to highlight the centrality of characterization as the driving force in the novel, since the use of plot is minimized in setting up the many sides to Alex Fratarcangeli's personality.

While the past events, made important by Alex through his extended recollections, are not depicted chronologically, when they are rearranged chronologically, for the purpose of this literary analysis, these past events do not seem to provide an incremental movement towards personal insight, which eventually culminates in a sense of direction on Alex's part. The chronology of these past events covers roughly seven years, from mid-1979 to early 1986. During 1979, Alex visited Sweden and there he met Ingrid and he got involved with her for a month or so and then left for home again only to return at the end of that year to spend more time with her. After he left Ingrid, for the second time, Alex travelled to the Galapagos Islands, where around January 1980 he met Desmond and joined his naturalist expedition. At the end of this disastrous trip to the Galapagos, Alex returned to Toronto, where a short time later he started a relationship with Liz, which lasted several years. During their relationship, they moved to Montreal, and it is in Montreal that they eventually break up, near the end of 1985. Soon after his separation from Liz, Alex received a letter from Ingrid, informing him that several years earlier, shortly after his second visit to Sweden, Ingrid had given birth to their son, Per. Surprised by this news, Alex visited Ingrid some time later and he stayed with their son, who did not know that Alex was his father. When he returned to Montreal after his visit with Ingrid and Per, neither Ingrid nor Alex told Per that Alex was his father. It is at this point of his return to Montreal, where he resumed his doctoral studies, that the story of Alex's life in the present begins, which starts in the opening chapter of Part One of the novel. The narrative marks the beginning of Part One with the date May 1986. This story of Alex's present life in Montreal ends in Part Three of the novel, which begins with the date April 1987. The overall time frame of the novel, from 1979 to 1987, is made known to the reader mainly through the presentation of events throughout the entire narrative (most of these events are not clearly dated), and through the use of specific calendar dates to mark the major parts of the novel (respectively Part One, May 1986; Part Two, October 1986; Galapagos, January 1980; Part Three, April 1987). The Epilogue is undated, but it follows chronologically from Part Three.

When the events are arranged chronologically, they comprise the time after his graduation from high school to his doctoral studies. Mixed with these events are brief recollections of his childhood with his family in the small town and allusions to the time before his departure for university to Toronto. The lack of chronology emphasizes the associative nature of Alex's recollections, making a link between the immediacy of the present and how this immediacy is provoking a particular issue that is sending Alex mentally back to a point in the past. This lack of chronology also stresses that the true period of maturation on Alex's part, as he sorts out emotionally the dramatic events from the past, is his current life in Montreal, which covers a year from May 1986 to April 1987. It is during this year of his life that the various incidents from the past converge with the present in Montreal, while he is working on his thesis proposal and at the same time attempting to give some direction to his life.

What each story has in common is that Alex gets involved in a particular relationship with another person as a result of circumstance and also because Alex wants to be engaged in the experience that is offered to him by this other person. When he meets Ingrid in Sweden as part of his travels through Europe, at the age of twenty, his romantic involvement with Ingrid is spontaneous. Yet, it is what is demanded of him by Ingrid in the relationship and what he is willing to give in return that overtake the love affair. When he returns to be with Ingrid sometime afterwards, the challenges that the relationship had opened up initially remain unresolved. This irresolution magnifies his sense of insecurity, motivating him to coldly distance himself from Ingrid. In his need to forget the entire affair, he rashly decides to go to the opposite end of the world, winding up in Quito, Ecuador, and from there to the Galapagos Islands, where he finds himself nearly broke, without enough money to return home to Toronto, forcing him to join Desmond and Santos in their ill-fated naturalist expedition on the small islands of the Galapagos. His subsequent romantic relationship with Liz in Toronto, which occurs shortly after he returns home from his ruinous trip to the Galapagos Islands, seems to follow a similar pattern as his failed relationship with Ingrid, in which circumstance combines with the opportunity for personal experience. Just like his relationship with Ingrid, Alex's liaison with Liz, after its newness begins to dissipate emotionally, forces him to deal with a set of expectations, climaxing in Liz's pregnancy, which he is unwilling to fulfill. The final outcome of this break in the relationship is a near deadly sex act, in which the engagement in sadomasochism, with the use of constraining equipment, to keep their sex life alive, results in Alex becoming excessively forceful towards Liz, transforming the activity into a sexual assault. This violent and morbid sex act not only leads to the end of their relationship, but it saddles Alex with a sense of guilt and depression that pushes him to seek psychiatric treatment.

Interposed between the individual narratives of the two romantic relationships is the long, complex narrative of Alex's trip to the Galapagos and the tortuous companionship that he develops with Desmond. At first, Alex finds Desmond appealing because of his adventurous nature and unorthodox scientific views. However, Desmond is also arrogant, callous, and spiteful towards Alex and their navigator, a local Ecuadorian, named Santos. Desmond stimulates extreme emotions in Alex; Alex alternately feels sympathy and hatred towards Desmond. It is a destructive emotional combination that Alex cannot get himself out of, even though he is secretly scheming to abandon Desmond and Santos (who at one point is sexually predatory towards Alex) at the first opportunity. This warped attitude towards Desmond shifts to a deep sense of guilt after Alex is traumatized by Desmond's accidental drowning at sea. Moreover, Alex's terrible relationship with Desmond is almost fatal to him and the navigator, Santos, because soon after Desmond's death the boat runs out of gasoline. Desmond had pushed Santos to continue with the expedition even though he knew that the boat's fuel was almost exhausted. After many days adrift at sea and at the brink of starvation and complete dehydration, Alex and Santos are miraculously saved by a local patrol boat. In a state of shock, at having come so close to death at such a young age, Alex is unceremoniously allowed by the local authorities to leave the country.

It is clear that the three major relationships from his past, which are described above, are different in many aspects. Yet, they seem to be a repetition of the same personal problem: Alex wants to have an emotional bond with another person, but there is a part of him that is unable to create this bond. Through word and action, he constantly shows his incapacity to sustain an intimate connection with another person. What makes the situation very awkward is the fact that each person is unsuited to meet his emotional needs or to provide him with the kind of validation of his selfhood that he longs for in a relationship.

In recalling these three distinct, dramatic stories, Alex divulges the inherent deficiencies of each one of the relationships. The problem arises at the point where his inadequacies meet the insecurities of the particular person, producing an unhealthy codependency. In the case of Ingrid, she is much older than him and what she wants out of life and in a relationship in her mature adulthood is far more complicated than what the inexperienced, youthful Alex can envision for himself. Compounding this problem is the reality that Alex cannot give up his life in Canada to live with her. He is at the beginning of his university studies and of his new life in Toronto, adjusting to his newfound independence from his parents. Equally important, Alex was not passionately in love with Liz. She was an acquaintance from high school and the friendship turns into a romantic relationship after Alex succumbs to Liz's desire to have him as her boyfriend. At the time, Alex was still staggered emotionally from the collapse of his relationship with Ingrid and the disastrous experience with Desmond. Not only is he not passionate about Liz, but his priorities are not marriage and parenting because he wants to focus on his university studies, hoping to pursue an academic career. What intensifies this reluctance to enter parenthood is his unhappy history with his own parents. Liz's abortion is the result of their lack of common goals. The subsequent convoluted sexual activity, bordering on physical violence, is an embodiment of the alienation that has become endemic in their relationship. Alex knows that Desmond is a self-absorbed and deluded person, despite his adventurousness and provocative intellectual approach. It is circumstance that brings them together: Alex is almost broke and in a state of near deprivation at a local hotel where he is staying on one of the islands of the Galapagos. Desmond offers him the opportunity to make some money, by helping him in his expedition, so that Alex can catch an airplane back to Toronto. Alex realizes that each relationship carries a set of obstacles that hinders his ability to achieve an emotional bond. Despite this awareness, Alex still engages each of these individuals.

The three stories establish an emotional pattern in Alex's behaviour that persists in a less severe fashion in the present in Montreal while Alex undertakes his doctoral studies in English Literature. Each story from the past is also juxtaposed to similar relationships in the present. However, these current relationships do not end in a manner that intensifies his anxiety and fears. The accumulation of time and with it experience, within the ten years, after he left his parents, has allowed him to diffuse the potential emotional fall-out.

Thinking about his romantic relationship with Amanda, a fellow student at Concordia, whom he gets involved with after the end of his relationship with Liz, Alex confesses to his own selfishness, in wanting only a sexual relationship with Amanda. But her suicide is the result of a deep depression that preceded her studies in Montreal (as her family tells Alex after her death) and her subsequent brief involvement with Alex. Although Alex for some time feels guilty about his involvement with Amanda and in not being able to help her to prevent her from killing herself, he realizes that ultimately Amanda's suicide was an incident that was outside of his control. In pursuit of Maria, the El Salvadorian political refugee, Alex admits that he is unbearably attracted to her physically and it is this extreme attraction that motivates his persistence to become her lover. Yet, Maria is not attracted to Alex and in her behaviour and words she lets him know how she feels about him. Through her, he believes that it is the power of love that drives people to altruistic acts for she is going back to El Salvador to be with the man she loves, even though this is very dangerous for her since he is part of the resistance movement and he has been involved in his share of cruel violence, being implicated in the murder of a young boy, who was considered by the rebels to be a spy for the military.

While Alex develops a kind of friendship towards Felix, his English language student, who is a successful and well educated businessman, Alex is entirely ambivalent towards Felix, consciously keeping his distance, because he doesn't support Felix's doctrinaire Quebecois nationalism (which Felix presents in a non-confrontational way). Felix is a kind of echo of Desmond, whose obsession with his theory of plant life and plant evolution bordered on a kind of dogmatism. Alex also senses a social gap between himself, who comes from an ethnic, working class background, and Felix, who has transcended his working class origins, to become almost aristocratic in his cultural tastes and material status. Ultimately, it is not Felix's unstated attraction towards Alex, since Felix is a homosexual, which stops Alex from deepening the friendship but the fact that Alex is aware that the disparity in attitude and behaviour between Alex and Felix is not surmountable. After a very uncomfortable dinner meal at Felix's house, where Alex is criticized by Felix's close friend for his lack of Quebecois cultural nationalism, the friendship fades away as Alex decides to focus on what is more important to him, namely his relationship with his son, rather than continuing his awkward association with Felix.

The other side of the Desmond coin is Jiri, who, like Desmond, is haunted by his past. In this case, it is Jiri's traumatic severance from his life in Czechoslovakia because of the Russian invasion. This political and social dislocation has led to his emotional marginalization in Montreal, where he works as a contract teacher at Concordia University, and it has also alienated him from his son, who lives in Toronto. Jiri's social displacement has resulted in a near-alcoholic lifestyle and in him being a poor father figure. In reaction to his absence, Jiri's son engages in antisocial behaviour, joining a skin-head group, which motivates him to savagely assault a helpless bystander. Although Alex is constantly irritated by Jiri's unscrupulous behaviour, he feels connected to him because of his displacement and problem with his son. Also, unlike Desmond, who was intellectually blinkered, incapable of accepting any mild criticism or opposed point of view, Jiri, in the role of Alex's thesis advisor, is open to Alex's approach to his dissertation and encourages him to do his thesis without judgment, providing constructive criticism and positive guidance. The other relationship that proves to be positive in Alex's life is the surprising friendship he develops with Maria's brother, Miguel, who unlike Maria is not driven by passion and politics. Miguel is a simple and straight-forward individual, wanting to enjoy the freedom that the new society offers him, having been fortunate to escape the atrocities of El Salvador.

The outcomes of these relationships in the present are in sharp contrast to Alex's failed romantic relationships, respectively with Ingrid and Liz, and the disastrous friendship with Desmond. The recollection of these three stories from the past also provides a kind of resolution that he can use to affirm his own existence in the present. When he meets Liz many months after their separation, Alex is ready to accept his responsibility for the failure of the relationship. But Liz does not see her past with him in the same way. She is not bitter or angry towards Alex. She has accepted the fact that they were not suited for each other and she has moved on happily in her life. More than anyone else, Liz helps Alex to purge him of his sense of guilt. Alex has a tendency to feel guilty for what he believes are the failures of his past. The relationship with Ingrid may not have been appropriate for Alex, but it produced a son, which now allows him a chance to redeem himself and to start on a new path in his life. Furthermore, there is a positive side to Alex's encounter with Desmond, despite Desmond's tragic death. From Alex's perspective, Desmond's scientific obsession with trying to get to the truth about plant life and natural selection raised questions about the basis of human evolution. Through Desmond, Alex was exposed to the Darwinian notion of adaptation and individuation. As Alex admits, Darwin's concepts about natural selection gave direction to his intellectual life and instilled in him a metaphysical sensibility about human existence. So in recollecting the tragic story of Desmond, Alex traces the origins of his own worldview, acknowledging that ironically his friendship with Desmond made him aware of the essential nature of human existence. Alex attains for himself an understanding about the universality of human experience that he had not thought about until he met Desmond. For Alex, Desmond then becomes a kind of link to Esther, in terms of giving meaning to Esther's disease and in making sense of Esther's impossible positivism in the face of her terrible destiny.

The novel infers that the worldview that Alex develops from his exposure to Charles Darwin's ideas about natural evolution and adaptation is not just an intellectual abstraction without application to lived experience. Instead, this worldview guides Alex towards a fascinating appreciation of the essence of modern existence. Yet, he finally comes to a comprehensive explanation about the purpose of human life through his relationship with Esther. He had initially thought that she was imposing herself on him. He eventually feels compassion for her as he observes her slow physical decline because of her terrible illness. In time, she turns into a cherished friend, who provides a kind of illumination about human suffering for him during his struggles to deal with his sense of guilt and failure. As her companion, helping her to get to places when her strength and mobility begin to fail and watching over her in the hospital when her physical condition worsens, he is accepted by Esther's parents and her brother almost like a member of the family. His loyalty to her during her final days in the hospital allows him to be part of her intimate interaction with her family. Alex forms a friendship with her brother, who depicts for Alex, during their conversation, a poignant portrait of Esther's role in the family. This bond that he develops with Esther's family through Esther brings him to witness in Esther's hospital room the reconciliation between the wayward other daughter and her family, including Esther, who by this time has lost consciousness. This other daughter had turned her back on her family because she felt she had lived in the shadow of Esther, the favoured daughter. The gentle reconciliation in Esther's family prompts Alex to rekindle his relationship with his family. When he goes back home to visit them, he tells his sister and his mother that he has a son. Both of them act as if he has never been distant towards them and critical of their attitudes and behaviour. They not only accept Alex's son as a member of the family, but they also encourage Alex to be with his son. As a result of the unlikely bond that he has made with Esther, Alex not only resumes willingly his relationship with his family members, but the approval that he receives from his sister and mother for being a father makes him feel that it is natural for him to assume his paternal responsibility and leave Canada to live with his son in Sweden.

Unlike Desmond, who recklessly brought about his own death because of his egotistical fixation with trying to change the conventional discourse on plant life, revising established theories on the evolution of all life on the planet, Esther succumbs to an illness that she cannot overcome, despite all her efforts to continue her studies and to counter with physical activity the deleterious effects of the multiple sclerosis, especially by maintaining her swimming regime. Through Esther, Alex believes that he is seeing the working out of a negative biological process. The slow inevitable deterioration of her body is leading to what he calls "[e]ntropy" "[t]he second law of thermodynamics" (435). It is a kind of static physical state in which "no one thing mattered more than any other ... [and] that a sense of meaning was itself another adaptation" (455). Still he knows that in projecting a theoretical explanation onto what is happening physically to Esther, as she is no longer conscious of the world around her, he is attempting to compensate for his own lack of understanding of what mentally transpires when a person is in such a condition: "He didn't know — who did? — how the mind worked in the end" (468). If there is no reliable scientific knowledge of why biological aberrations occur among a specific species, such as Esther's tragic illness, except that such biological abnormalities are the result of accident and/or circumstance, two factors which are crucial to the Darwinian conception of human evolution, then Alex has to look elsewhere to make sense of human misery.

Alex is acutely aware that he cannot transcend his anguish through the use of scientific theories because they are not absolutely provable and because they tend to be schematic to the point of being indifferent to human suffering. He also knows that in embracing a type of rationalism, albeit scientific, he is trying to discover how he can adapt to a life without emotional depth, which appears to be the crux of his ongoing personal crisis. It is through real positive emotional experience that he can resolve his grave predicament, which is simultaneously philosophical and psychological. His bond with Esther initiates a process through which he can find a way out of his anguish, inspiring him to bring back into his life, in a new form, what he has rejected up to now, which is the presence of family. His affection for Esther and the affection that he sees that her family has for Esther invoke in him the need to be with his own family, whom he visits while Esther's condition gets worse. The act of telling his sister and mother that he has a son gives him the courage to accept his responsibility as a father. Alex realizes that it is by creating his own family, with his son, Per, that he can ultimately lift himself out of his entrenched despair, epitomized by ceaseless guilt and shame.

In the narrative of Alex Fratarcangeli, the idea of the centrality of family is reiterated through the theme of the father-son relationship, embodied in Stephen's relationship with his son Ariel, Jiri's relationship with his troubled son, Alex's relationship with his father, and ultimately Alex's relationship with his own son, Per. This leitmotif of the father-son relationship which focuses on how the father shapes the life of his son is extended to Alex's study of Charles Darwin's life and that of his scientific collaborator and eventual rival for scientific primacy, Alfred Russel Wallace: "Darwin's father had prospered where Wallace's had failed; and so the die had been cast" (461). As Alex notes, he was trying to find a way to write about fathers and sons because it spoke to him emotionally: "Alex might be able to work up into a clever meta-commentary about fathers and sons" (456). The theme of the relationship between father and son is also inserted in the symbolic relationship between Desmond and his science teacher, who Desmond believed had betrayed him by assisting in Desmond's removal from university.

The depiction of the relationship between father and

son is not only emblematic of the critical element in the development of a man's masculine identity. The presentation of the father and son bond is also the way the novel conceptualizes Alex's experience of family, as being alternately a potentially oppressive and alienating force and a powerful, liberating and humanizing influence in one's life. Furthermore, the novel reverses the trajectory of the power of the father-son relationship by showing that the son can also overwhelm the father. This is exemplified by Ariel's disregard for his father in the presence of his mother and the contempt that Jiri's son demonstrates towards Jiri by joining a reactionary group in Toronto. However, the novel does not draw a deterministic link between the behaviour of the father and the consequent behaviour of the son. Instead, the father is presented as participating, either intentionally or unconsciously, in the process of the son's movement from boyhood to manhood. This is a process that the son negotiates in terms of his own needs and the choices that he makes to meet his needs. What eventually motivates Alex to assume his role as the father of his son is a recognition that the father and son relationship is dynamic and not static. As Alex suggests, the assumption of fatherhood is not simply a conscious act of social responsibility, but it is an act that is necessary for the emotional well-being of the father as a person: "He felt the imperative of this as he said it, of going: it was not a choice" (467).

Thus, the father-son pairing seems to be an intensification of family relations, reinforcing the basic features that constitute the nature of family. As the various family groups in the novel attest to, such as the Fratarcangeli family, Esther's family members, and the relationship between brother and sister, in this case Miguel and Maria, family is more than a cultural and social organization. There is an atavism that lingers in family relations. It is a kind of instinctual bond in which emotion and physicality ensure the survival of this bond. Despite the family's potential to do harm to its members, as alluded to in reference to Alex's uneasy relationship with his father, or that of Stephen and Jiri with their sons, or the family's inability to protect its members from disaster, as in the case of Amanda's suicide or Esther's fatal disease, the family remains a decisive force in the lives of the characters. It is the family that ultimately gives comfort during great suffering, especially in the story of Esther, and it is family that provides the love one requires to give substance to one's life. For Alex, his life cannot be measured by external standards, but by the quality of his bond towards his son: "He would never finish his dissertation. Or he would finish it ... There it was in his breast, he could feel it battering away at his ribcage, like a trapped bird, hope" (470-471).

Within the philosophical perspective of the novel, which transmits a non-religious, spiritual view of the human condition, and which suggests a transcendence that exceeds the limitations of the material, the almost incontestable power of the family lies in the fact that it is the locus of one's biological entry into the world. In this sense, the family is more than about cultural and linguistic origins. The family comes out of the same natural process that involves all life on earth. The persistence of the family is part of the maintenance of the natural world, and as a form of biological reproduction the family is affected by complex and mutable forces. The conclusion of the novel offers an eloquent appeal to the mighty presence of the family, evoked through a father's expression of his love for his child. The novel moves towards its conclusion by interposing the idea of biological genesis, presented through the story of how Charles Darwin finally published his seminal work on natural selection, *Origin of Species*, with the mysterious power of parental love, reflected in Alex's decision to go to Sweden to be with his son, Per.

The literary convergence of scientific history, of how Darwin makes use of and then bypasses Wallace to produce his masterwork, and fictional biography, in which Alex achieves his epiphany by accepting fatherhood, invests the theory of evolution and adaptation with a romantic, almost metaphysical quality. This unique stylistic gesture immediately brings back into full focus the crucial significance of that long, detailed, and astonishing narrative about Alex's trip to the Galapagos with Desmond, where for the first time in his life he experiences the raw violence and pure beauty of nature. During this remarkable expedition, he is exposed by Desmond to the source of Charles Darwin's classic theory of naturalism, which was Darwin's surprising journey to the Galapagos. Desmond carried with him a worn copy of the book, *The Voyage of the Beagle*. This was the book where Darwin described his revelatory discoveries about anomalies among the same primitive species still thriving in the inhospitable landscape of the Galapagos Islands almost an infinity after the appearance of the original species. Desmond asserts that he can manipulate the evolution of plant life by introducing particular plant specimens in places where they were not supposed to survive, thus proving that natural evolution as a process which resulted in individuation, or the creation of a new species, was not gradual and progressive but sudden and revolutionary, in which the new life form broke away from its genetic origins. Although Alex is impressed by the results of Desmond's haphazard experiment with plant life on the disparate, rocky, moon-like terrain, he still believes that the modern natural world, including plant and animal life, and by implication human beings as a distinct species, was the product of an infinite and comprehensive development, whose present day manifestation could not be scientifically reduced to any particular point in time: "Alex didn't think evolution happened like this overnight — it took millennia, eons, while whole continents shifted and mountains rose up and decayed" (310).

However, without an overarching explanatory ideology, such as the belief in the supernatural and God, or without an adherence to a kind of idealistic scientism, to make sense of all creation, Alex sees that the underlying implication of the scientific naturalism proposed by Charles Darwin, of the constant adaptation of living organisms to the contingencies of the moment, was that whatever nature produced was essentially provisional and accidental, not the outcome of any logical design or divine intent: "There was no end point, in [Darwin's] version of existence; there was an order, but it was a sort of order without Order, that carried on blind" (297). For Alex, rooted in the experience of the present is an awareness of the origins of all creation. Looking out into the open plain from the mountain-top, above the city of Montreal, Alex states: "In its truly virgin days the mountain had been a volcano and everything around it barren waste. That was a bit harder to get his mind around, that this landscape had once been Galapagan in is newness" (445). At the end of the novel, when Alex revisits intellectually the notion of an endlessly random natural transformation, he looks at the unpredictability of nature not as a personification of the essential hopelessness of the human condition, in which human existence is a kind of aimless, prolonged period of waiting for the inevitability of death. Thus, instead of existence being reduced to a nihilistic existentialism in an irremediable malevolent universe, in Alex's epiphanous state, in the epilogue of the novel, the volatility of the natural environment is a testament to the profoundly miraculous nature of life: "Somehow through the chance of events, the slow building of things with No Plan, the mind had become fitted for such thoughts, for such moments of wonderment" (471). In acknowledging this constant process of mutation, which is the basis of all existence, Alex concedes that "[e]everything had followed from a simple insight that all life was connected, that no difference was absolute" (397). What the idea of a species, of biological individuation, led to for Darwin, and which Alex embraces as a kind of philosophical viewpoint, was that "[a]ll forms were fluid, each contained part of the last and the next" (397).

Hence, in the epilogue, evolutionary theory is seemingly interwoven with phenomenology. In doing so, the novel ironically harkens back to Alex's scepticism about Desmond's uncritical interpretation of Charles Darwin's theory as the greatest explanation of the nature of all creation: "[Alex] had always seen Darwinism as just another of the grand schemes for making sense of the world — like Marxism, say, or Freudianism, or New Criticism — that proved all was right with it" (297). But Alex's epiphany does not lead to another type of dogmatism, in which postmodern ideas about the cultural construction of social reality are applied to science, thus concluding that subjectivity is the basis for all human endeavours, whether it involves the study of literature, science, or philosophy. Instead, as Alex's view on culture throughout the narrative points to, there is no absolute and pure truth that can guide existence. Material and symbolic culture, the modes of production and the conceptualiza- tion of social reality, is circumstantial and constantly modified by the intersection of different, complement- ary, and opposed cultures. This dynamic approach to culture mirrors the Darwinian view of constant biologic- al change, in which one life form emerges from another, carrying with it similarity and difference. Alex's dislike of cultural nationalism in Quebec is not simply about the politics of the dominant linguistic group restricting the cultural and linguistic practices of the various minor- ities, including the Anglophone minority, in Montreal. Just like his attempt to fight the exploitation that he ex- periences as a renter by his landlord leads to failure, be- cause the municipal bureaucracy and his fellow tenants respond to the situation based on their own self inter- ests, politics in general, whether it is in Montreal or in El Salvador, is by its very nature about self-aggrandizement and it shuts down opposing points of view that are critic- al to the way culture actually works. Alex's reluctance to perceive himself in terms of a static ethnic identity, whether it is in relation to his immigrant family back- ground or to the members of the Italian community that he interacts with in Montreal, is based on his conviction that culture cannot be reduced to a set of simple ideas and beliefs.

This view that culture is fluid in any given time or place, such as the ancient culture in Central Italy, where Alex's parents come from, or the Calvinist-Scottish com- munity in turn-of-the-century Montreal, or the Latin American political refugee community in Montreal, per- vades the way that Alex situates himself in his social environment. Even his dissertation is affected by his desire to avoid statism, refusing to adhere to established intellectual doctrines and refusing to accept the separation of intellectual authorities. Alex wants to find in literary criticism, scientific theory, and cultural studies a space in which they can converge. It is in this space that he wants to sculpt a thesis that is immediate to his own experience of the world. His resistance to any position that advocates a static cultural identity is a reaction to the limitations he experienced as the son of immigrant parents and a validation of his liberal education and liberal lifestyle. The embodiment of this type of liberalism is Pierre Elliot Trudeau, for whom Alex feels a kind of reverence, to the point that he imagines meeting him as he makes his way to the top of the mountain in Montreal. Alluding to Trudeau's view on cultural nationalism, Alex notes that the notion of a pure culture based on ancestry did not belong to the modern world: "Trudeau had been right about that at least: there was no building a nation on bloodlines" (396). While people inherit their culture, this culture is the product of diverse elements that have been absorbed over time, and it continues to be modified as it adapts to changing circumstances and as it is exposed to other cultural influences. Just like nature, which is involved in a process of constant transformation, culture is not static but impermanent and mutable.

As the novel, *The Origin of Species*, poignantly affirms, through its multi-layered representation of the complex story of Alex Fratarcangeli, there is an unavoidable instability that underlies all facets of existence, in which tragic events are strangely interwoven with an inescapable, ethereal beauty. As Peter Gzowski, his alter ego, tells him:

> *But look at your life. It's just one damned thing after*
> *another — the Galapagos, Liz, Amanda, then this amaz-*
> *ing woman ... who's dying in front of your eyes and this*
> *whole other woman [Maria] who suddenly picks up and*
> *heads home though she's got a death warrant on her.*
> *And then at the end of it: hope. This little child. This*
> *gift.* (368)

At the conclusion of the novel, this personal insight about the unpredictability of being in the world, which is tinged in a joyful irony, finally lifts Alex out of his gloom and he sees who he is regardless of his imperfections and he considers the possibilities that surround him, in doing so, dispelling his burdensome despair and self-defeating pessimism. In the epilogue of the book, as he quietly acknowledges, with a strong feeling of relief, it is only through some form of idealism, which for Alex has been inspired by the presence of his son, Per, that he can find the courage to allow himself to be guided in his long, difficult trek towards a newfound destiny.

Work Cited

The Origin of Species. Canada: Anchor Canada, Random House, 2009.

Brian L. Flack

Sleep ... Without Reason Breeds Monsters[1]: An Analysis of Ricci's Novel

THERE IS A very healthy literature populated by self-destructive individuals. Some of the more memorable among them are Wilde's Dorian Gray[2], Plath's Esther Greenwood, Fitzgerald's Jay Gatsby, Brontë's Heathcliffe, Tolstoy's Anna Karenina, Dreiser's Clyde Griffiths, Banks' Wade Whitehouse, O'Connor's Hazel Motes, Dostoevsky's Raskolnikov, Wharton's Ethan Frome, Melville's Captain Ahab, Lowry's Geoffrey Firmin, and almost any character in Hubert Selby Jr.'s *Last Exit To Brooklyn* or in the collective novels of Thomas Hardy.

Professor David Pace, the principal character in Nino Ricci's novel *Sleep*, can now be added to this list. There is no question that Pace holds his own with the individuals enumerated above, and a host of others down through the ages.

From the novel's first paragraph, it is clear that something is very wrong with this man:

> A wash of chemicals floods David's brain and at once the urge is there, irresistible. What is the trigger, what switch opens the floodgate? If he could find it, he could control it. But even to think of the urge is to bring it on. (3)[3]

227

Like a corkscrew twisting ever deeper into a wine bottle's cork, Pace, beset by a rare form of narcolepsy, spirals into an existence wherein no opportunity to degrade, to offend, to belittle, to harass—both others and himself—is lost. One wonders, when the end is reached, how the man managed to survive as long as he did. But that —to wonder how he lived as long as he did—is getting a shade ahead of what makes *Sleep* interesting. The book's excellence lies not so much in the 'way' Pace lives, but in 'how' Ricci tells his tale. The 'how' is what allows *Sleep* to burrow beneath one's skin. The 'way' is what makes David Pace's existence tragic.

***

The book is divided into two parts, innocuously labelled Part One and Part Two. That, however, is where all that is innocuous with this narrative begins and finishes.

Part One is divided into three chapters: "Methylphenidate," "Fluoxetine," and "Sodium Oxybate" ... and not for nothing. They are the prescription drugs Pace repeatedly uses to treat the worst effects of his sleep disorder. They are not uncommon drugs. They are widely prescribed, harmful when used in abundance, and addictive in combination. They are the drugs that conspire to do the man in.

Methylphenidate is a synthetic drug that stimulates the sympathetic and central nervous systems. It is used to improve the symptoms of attention deficit hyperactivity disorder, depression, and narcolepsy. It is most well-known under the trade name Ritalin. It has been around for over 50 years. Since the use of it began in 1960, the drug has been slowly, but increasingly, prescribed. Then, in the 1990s, the number of prescriptions written mushroomed. A panacea for the worst of modernity, it increases or maintains alertness, combats fatigue, and improves attention. In the narcoleptic, methylphenidate is a godsend because it increases wakefulness, vigilance, and performance. It is in the area of adverse effects, though, that methylphenidate would have been of interest to Ricci because those ill-effects include, among many other things, increased insomnia, restlessness, irritability, and lethargy ... the bases of David Pace's character flaws.

Methylphenidate can also worsen psychosis in psychotic patients. In some cases it even exacerbates the emergence of new psychotic symptoms. It is in this that it might have been of even greater interest to Ricci in his creation of Pace because, as some literature suggests, it should be used with extreme caution in people with bipolar disorder. In them, it can induce mania or hypomania. In effect, for Ricci to achieve the ends he obviously wanted, it was the perfect drug to feed the possibly bipolar Pace. Methylphenidate's stimulant effects also make it rather addictive, especially when used recreationally. When used above the medical dose range, it can promote stimulant psychosis and, by any reckoning, David Pace's use of it far exceeds a normal dosage.

Fluoxetine (Prozac) is also a synthetic compound that inhibits the uptake of serotonin in the brain and is taken to treat depression or obsessive-compulsive disorder, arguably the sort of conditions prompted by an overindulgence in methylphenidate. Sodium oxybate (GHB, the date rape drug) is used for the treatment of excessive daytime sleepiness associated with narcolepsy. By all accounts, it induces sleeplessness.

Taken independently, each of these drugs has the ability to ameliorate any number of conditions, but when taken collectively and in doses that far exceed what is recommended, they reduce Pace to a shell of a man, hardly capable of recognizing his humanity, much less a person capable of functioning normally in society.

***

Part Two of the novel is divided into two chapters, each named for a firearm.

The first is "SIG Sauer P250." This is a modular format, hammer-fired, and mighty powerful handgun. That it is modular means it can be fine-tuned with options to fit the discerning needs of a variety of shooters. The bottom line is that this is a serious killing machine and, depending on its configuration, can hold up to 17 rounds. It's a bit like Pace himself, a character who may be one thing on Monday and another on Tuesday, but who, in the end is always the same thing: a menace, to himself and to everyone around him. He is a man who creates mayhem by simply being there, and when he metaphorically 'fires'—the more often he 'fires,' the mayhem escalates.

The final chapter is "Beretta M9," another serious killing instrument with a chequered past, again, much like Pace himself. Used for years by both law enforcement and military personnel, it seems that while it remains in favour with the former it has fallen out of favour with many among the latter, due to malfunctions of one sort or another. Still, it does the job, most times, for which it was created: to kill. Given its history, it seems somehow appropriate that it's the weapon associated with Pace's final moments.

***

The story begins in a car. Pace and his five-year-old son, Marcus, are heading home from a day at the zoo. They are late, wending their way without having made a call to Marcus' mother, Julia, who is impatiently waiting for them. At once, tension is introduced. All is not well in the adult Pace world. As they make their way down the "valley parkway" (6), Pace falls asleep at the wheel, only to be abruptly awakened by the shouts of his son from the back seat. They are drifting off the roadway onto the side shoulder where a stalled car lies in wait. At the last second, Pace makes an adjustment and steers his vehicle back onto the roadway. The adrenaline rush he experiences causes something akin to having his life flash before his eyes. When he recovers himself, he makes light of the near death moment for his son's benefit. As stoned as he already is, he takes more pills.

He digs his little pill container out of his pant pocket and dumps the pills onto the passenger seat, then grabs two by feel and crunches down on them. Do not chew. They are bitter like cyanide, like hemlock (4).

At that moment, the reader knows full well where this novel is going. Two death-inducing drugs have been introduced on page four. However, that 'where' it is going is clear is almost beside the point. As noted earlier, the real story is 'how' Ricci gets Pace there and, for the most part, the 'how' of it is masterful.

Pace and Marcus eventually arrive home — safely, but not before he calls his wife. She berates him for calling from the car, loudly and profanely, not thinking of the fact their small son is sitting behind Pace listening to every word she says. He uses the call to excuse-make for his tardiness. "We're stuck on the parkway," (7) he says. But when the call ends Pace is furious and only manages to quell his anger by assigning blame for his troubles to her. He has made it clear that she should not call to check up on him, but when he calls her, she reams him out. In his view, this is the behaviour of a "she-wolf" (7), a woman who has emasculated him, leaving him in the state he is in.

The incident propels him into a brief reminiscence of his own childhood. He recalls visiting the neighbourhood in which he now lives and how distressed he is by the way it has changed, "all burnished and bevelled and bleached for maximum value added" (10). This is followed by another that rifles bitterly through how he and Julia came to be living in and renovating the house he is driving to. These are the first in a series of references to the past: his youth; his early academic life; his courting of Julia; their life together; his problems in academia, first in Montreal and then in Toronto; his interactions with other women; and his history of progressive drug taking and the terrible toll it has exacted on both his personal relationships and those in his working life.

So, just a few pages into the narrative, the winding down has begun, in earnest. From there, it is simply a matter of piling incident upon incident, drug ingestion upon drug ingestion, until he runs out of options.

***

Pace's fall begins innocently enough when he is still in the early stages of his academic career. It is a case of bad judgement exercised, induced by a motivation he cannot get to the bottom of. It is a behavioural glitch. In Montreal, he has plagiarized a student and used the words lifted in a newspaper article ... then assigned the student a B minus for his work, a grade appealed on the boy's behalf by his mother. Pace's status as the author of a best-selling academic book, *Masculine History*, is unable to save him from the fallout of this transgression. He has to leave town. He does, however, manage to make fleeing look good:

> David had been proud then of how well he had arranged things, had thought himself bold, the master of his fate. He had managed to talk Julia into the move through a blend of seduction and coercion, taking her out to a resort in the Townships for a weekend getaway with a big diamond ring in tow and making her promises and telling her lies, framing the move as a matter of getting better terms for the both of them, of catching the tide ... all to the greater good of their relationship. (51)

He and Julia relocate to Toronto, to dual academic appointments. To another university populated by petty, narrow-minded people concerned only with their own welfare. In no way a change from the academic world they left behind in Montreal. The administrators in both settings reap the greatest scorn. Almost to the last one, they are uninspiring functionaries, seemingly without the ability to actually be academics. They are paper pushers and people manipulators at best. But Pace, sadly, is just one more in the crowd. Once there, as it would be anywhere he was, he cannot help being himself. What follows is a careful detailing of the poison that he injects into (and a measure of the poison he receives from) all his relationships: both at work and at home.

He does try, though, to get to the bottom of his "deep brain disorder" (22), going so far as to visit a clinic for sleep problems, for two days and two nights. Interestingly, in

this clinic, each of the sleep rooms is named after a paint-
er, with a print of an appropriate painting by the artist
hanging on the door. One is Dali's "The Persistence of
Memory," with its melting clocks. Another is Goya's "The
Sleep of Reason Breeds Monsters," with its sleeping man,
fearsome bats and owls, and a wide-eyed lynx. Pace's
room is named after Henri Rousseau's "The Dream," with
its reclining nude, exotic animals, and mysterious flute
player buried in a lush jungle. The point being, of course,
that the realm of sleep can be a dangerous place and the
clinic is there to ease the sufferer's pain.

Here, he is hooked up to machines that could, with
luck, sort him out. But the "moral ambiguity" (23) of the
place, overseen by "surly technicians from ... war torn
countries" (23), only pushes him into the waiting hands
of Becker, the doctor who never visits his clinic. Becker,
whom Pace suspects might have been "some sort of
Mengele in his former life" (23), introduces him to the
drugs: Ritalin at the outset with the others to follow. Over
the next half year, the dosages increase, but sleep is still
an issue. For his periods of loss of control, there are more
drugs. In this way, the cycle begins.

Eventually, his marriage crumbles. Then he takes lib-
erties — a long, drug addled part of the narrative — with an
aboriginal colleague, a debauched evening in his apartment. The after-effects, which he cannot understand, are
cataclysmic. All he can think, once the details of their
evening have come to light and the woman is seeking to
be released from her contract, is that something is being
made out of nothing: "She is over-reacting, clearly, is be-
having like a child. All they did was *fuck*, for Christ's sake"
(131).

In effect, this indiscretion welds the academic doors,
doors that have been so open to him, virtually shut. Every

which way he has turned, he has alienated: the Academy, his wife and child, his colleagues. And he has lost any opportunity he might have had to make amends. He is even courting trouble with the law: drug infractions. He has been working the "double dip" (122), visiting multiple drug stores to acquire additional quantities of what has become his lifeline: the uppers and downers and related chemicals that move him sideways ... the friends he cannot live without.

He has been reduced to functioning like a quasi-criminal lab rat. He spends far too much of his time "scrambling for some sort of handhold," one that never comes, spurred instead by "the panic, the horror, at this oblivion that trails him, that continues to steal up ever closer at his back like his own death" (134). He feels like a sleepwalker. He feels like the gentle man who drove across a city to murder the in-laws who loved him or the Mormon who stabbed his wife of twenty years and against whom he had never so much as raised his voice. He knows there is always a reason why he and those like him, do what they do, even if it is hidden. It is the reason that gives permission. He feels like a "guinea-pig" (134), one of those "epileptics" (134) whose brains have literally been cut in two and led researchers to an interesting discovery, one that becomes his justification for his behaviour:

> ... the brain houses within its separate hemispheres actual warring consciousnesses, each so distinct from the other, down to the level of political affiliations, of food preferences, of religious beliefs, as to seem those of entirely different people. In the normal course of things one side dominates and the other gets suppressed, though what this means is that everyone carries within

> them a shadow self that dogs the dominant one like
> a stalker, always at odds, always seeking an outlet,
> awaiting its chance under cover of dark. (134-5)

Finally, he reaches a point of near destitution. He loses the condo he got in a deal brokered among him, his father, and his brother when he exited the family business. He turns his sympathetic brother against him. His wife has gone. He is about to lose his job. To make matters worse, he is "blocked." He cannot finish his new book, the one he has been working on for years. It is the book that was supposed to salvage his dwindling reputation. The one built on his best seller: *Masculine History*, the book that feminists hated, as one woman (at least) has pointed out to him. But a book that has bought him a lot of time and patience he would never have warranted had he not written it.

Reeling, broke and drug-sick, he plays the disability card at his university, hoping that it will save him the ignominy of outright academic dismissal. But, ultimately, this fails. Too many conditions are placed on him and his spiral to dissolution picks up speed. Once again, with help from an unlikely source, an old colleague, a man whose work he had ripped off in graduate school (a sin which, in good time, will be discovered), he leaves the country, exhausted, drug dependent, and almost, but not quite, broken. What is seemingly his last chance staring him squarely in the face.

***

He lands in America's Rust Belt, on a year-long visitor's chair at the kind of prestigious American school he "never got to" (141). It is there that the final nail will be driven into the life he had hoped to have and he is finally set up for the life he is going to have. That nail is Sophie, the wife of Greg Borovic, the man who has secured the appointment for him. Under her spell, he becomes a near-helpless bystander in the last chapters of his ruin. For a passing moment in this new setting, however, he starts to feel something different stirring in himself: "Since his arrival here he feels he has finally turned the corner on his doomsday book, his head cleared of all the static that filled it back home and the ideas starting to flow again" (155).

He begins working harder, concentrating. He rises at dawn to run in the woods, hoping to get back into some kind of physical shape so that he might save himself. Then, in a conversation with Borovic and the university provost at a faculty mixer, he says of a student: "To be honest, there's an African-American girl in my class I'm already having a hard time keeping my hands off" (151). Granted, at the time he had downed three quick vodka and tonics chased by a tab of methylphenidate. Still, the remark is not taken well. The provost replies: "Dave, I don't know how you do things back home, but down here we don't joke about these matters" (151).

Even without realizing what he has done, he has stepped squarely back into the maelstrom. But the moment does not cow him. He remains dedicated to the fact his "guard" (152) will not be let down.

Not long after this gaffe, he makes an off-handed remark about slavery in class, snapping to attention the very same black girl whose person he had, in his first days in his new home, insulted. He co-relates slavery in ancient Rome — "it was what you did, not what you were" (157) — with America in the present, noting that "we still can't look at someone like Abby without thinking she came from slaves" (157). The young woman looks at him and her "eyes go to stone" (157). To his surprise, she agrees with him. "The point is it's true" (157), she says, starting a long and fruitful discussion with the class that makes Pace think some corner in his academic life has been turned, like the thrill is back.

He relaxes but remains wary. He spends the next few days waiting for a call from Borovic, followed by whatever will pass in that setting for a pink slip. But neither materializes, not right away at any rate. When the hammer does fall, when Borovic does mention what happened in that class, Pace thinks the worst. But it is not to be. Abby has indeed been to visit the provost but not to complain about his "slave" remarks. Rather she has come to praise him, not bury him. She has told the provost that he is the first teacher who has ever been honest with her. He and Borovic joke about how disappointed the provost must have been that it took an "outsider" (162) to provoke such a comment from a student. But the exchange puts Pace back on high alert. Perhaps, he thinks, there are knives being sharpened for him.

This conversation takes place at Borovic's home, during a dinner. The news about Abby is buoying and gives Pace some breathing room, but it is on the same night that, ever the tragic figure, the next step in his descent is unveiled before him in the person of Sophie, Borovic's wife. All that Pace remembers when he is driving home is his last moment with her:

> Somehow the evening has ended in exactly the absolution David has dreamed of. Yet now that he has it, it only feels like a burden, something to get free of. Now that he has it, all that he can think of on the drive home is Sophie's heat against his palm as he bent to kiss her. (162)

But she has been revealed and, for him, there is no going back from her. Sophie is something of an enigma wrapped in a conundrum. Quiet and retiring, she seems like the perfect faculty wife. She cares for her child, keeps herself in shape and, given that she has not obtained her doctorate, that she is ABD, she takes a back seat to her husband in the academic world. But to suggest that Pace is obsessed with her is to understate the situation. He remembers encountering her on one of his runs, so he begins to watch for her. Eventually, after a cat and mouse game that lasts several days, he meets her on one of the forest running trails. They talk, small talk, but Pace's infatuation grows:

> He stays with her for the rest of her run. He can feel his blood thrill at being this close to her again. For many days now the images of her have crowded his head, the thoughts of what he might do to her. It is madness, of course, would put everything at risk again, yet the more he tells himself this, the more the thoughts fill him. (164)

Therein lies the crux of Pace's lifelong problem. He is more than marginally self-aware. He knows what he is doing. He understands the consequences of his actions, whatever they may be. But, self-confessed "badass" (163) that he is, he simply cannot help himself. He cannot help being a son who finds his parents a burden, or a brother who will not accept the good will and love of his sibling and his family. He cannot help being a reluctant father who seems to wish that his son were someone else. He cannot help being a husband who lives to pull the chain his wife so compellingly leaves dangling about her person. He cannot help ripping off a good idea someone else has and then running with it. He cannot help indulging in his sexual proclivities. He cannot help ingesting a witch's brew of harmful drugs. In each instance, he knows both the upside to refraining from caving to his baser instincts and the downside to indulging. Yet every time he opts for the latter course. It is no wonder that the trajectory of his life has been a perfectly straight line downwards. Something in him, however, hopes that Sophie is an exception.

Not many more days pass before he meets her once again ... on the running trail. This time they do not run and then separate. They end up back at Pace's house. He offers to make her a coffee. At first she rejects the idea. "Another time, then," she says, but "[i]n the end she is the one who starts toward his house, without so much as a glance at him, only a furtive look over her shoulder as if they were fugitives in a police state, making their escape" (168). He knows what's at stake, beyond a shadow of a doubt: "Any minute the alarm will sound, the shots will ring out" (168), but he follows her and "[h]e is on her the second they are inside" (169).

From this moment, what was a gradual spiral into the dirty morass of a wasted life accelerates. He becomes testy in class, insulting his students, hating their "creeping nihilism" (169), his own "falseness" (169). After going for a run, where Sophie has failed to appear, he panics, thinking she might have "slit her wrists" or "confessed everything ... in the dead of night" (170). In the midst of his semi-panic, Julia calls. They butt heads and he becomes unglued. She follows his lead and they fight. The subject is an imminent visit from Marcus. He tries to back out, calls the fact of it "bad timing" (170) but Julia does not give in, challenges the meaning of his paternity and that is too much for him. He reluctantly agrees to follow through with their plans, with no idea how he is going to manage.

It is at this point in the narrative that guns, which have been an undercurrent from the outset, move to centre stage. A gun entered the tale when he came to possess, in a roundabout way, his father's pistol: a Beretta M1935, a Nazi pistol manufactured during the war by the Italians. His mother had unthinkingly given it to Marcus. She had waved off her indiscretion by saying, "I just wanted him to have a keepsake, that's all. Something of his grandfather's" (92). Complicating the fact of the 'gift,' though, is the fact that she has given it to Marcus without ever checking to see if it is loaded. But it is loaded, compounding Pace's horror. So, he confiscates it.

At first Pace is mystified by its existence, how his father came to have it. But now that he has it, he wonders what to do with it. Wondering, though, does not last long. His curiosity leads to handling it; then researching its provenance; then firing it at a gun club; then, once Pace is in America, where obtaining a firearm is akin to buying a Big Mac, to the purchase of further firearms. And it is through guns that, during his son's visit, he manages to connect with the boy in a way he has never done before. It is a clear moment of potential salvation that is ultimately squandered.

After a morning run, he arrives home to find Marcus playing with his loaded SIG Sauer. Inside, he freaks, but controls himself. He blames himself before Marcus: "Nobody's angry at you," he says. "It wasn't your fault. I shouldn't have left it unlocked. I shouldn't have left it loaded" (172). He tells the boy that this isn't the only gun he has. He's got a Colt, too. Of course, this is the gun once owned by his father, Marcus' grandfather. The boy is intrigued and soon they find themselves at a gun range blasting away. Pace's only proviso: "Don't tell mom" (172).

As it turns out, Marcus is a natural. He loves the shooting. The rest of their visit passes on a high neither of them has ever experienced. When he hands Marcus back to Julia at the airport at the end of the visit, he seems a changed man. Their connection has led him to make some resolutions: He will drive six or seven hours on weekends to spend time with the boy. He will sign him up for shooting lessons. He will break things off with Sophie. But the next morning Sophie knocks on his door and "every resolution gives way" (175). He knows, once again, what he is doing. He knows the consequences. But he dives in anyway. At the crest of this wave of self-knowledge, what might be a suitable catch phrase for his existence becomes apparent: nothing lasts.

In due course, he discovers troubling things about Sophie: "She likes him to hurt her" (176). He soon realizes that he likes to hurt her. So, the affair carries on, as though they are "blind things" (177), which they are. They become so immersed in the immediacy of their sexual gratification, their addiction, that they cannot stop. All that happens in the rest of their lives becomes mundane. All that exists for them is that "shadowy country they defect to together" (177). But, like everything else, it is momentary bliss.

There is something of a reversal at work in this total immersion. Always, to this point, Pace has been the leader in his own devolution. He has always taken the lead with his family — father, mother, brother, wife, son; with his lovers; in his academic life; in his drug-taking. But with Sophie, he becomes the follower. He discovers, when he asks her what her domestic sex life is like, that all she is doing is recreating, with him, a reality-based approximation of the cyber sex world her husband, Borovic, inhabits. At first, he mistakes what she is confiding. He thinks that Borovic is addicted to weird internet porn. However, he is shocked to find that it's not that he visits porn sites but that he "builds them" (178). With that knowledge in hand, Pace's life ratchets down another notch. From that moment, he knows that Borovic will be in his head, a man possessed of a strangeness that is "not so different from his own" (178). That what is really at stake in this affair is his relationship with Sophie's husband. She is "merely collateral damage" (178).

Not long after, he gets into a fight with Borovic. It escalates when Sophie shows up at his house and won't stay, cryptically mentioning how much her husband was looking forward to Pace coming to his school. He never sees her again. As a consolation, and using Sophie's avatar, he visits Borovic's site, the one he built, the one she had showed him. In his mania to discover, he gets sloppy and fails to cover his cyber tracks. Sophie calls him in a panic. His using her to spy has been discovered.

Almost as a make-up gift to himself for the loss of her, he buys another gun, a bolt action Weatherby, a hunting gun, and books a visit to a hunting lodge where, after watching a buck and doe couple, he shoots the buck dead. The parallels between this interlude and his own life seem a bit forced, but the image is telling. He cannot even take the meat of the buck home with him. He just packs up and leaves, ruins all about him:

> David feels a blackness ... that he can't seem to shake. Nothing like guilt over the kill yet somehow the kill is the source. The thought of returning to his job, to his friend, to his book, his familiar heap of lies. (184)

The next morning, still stoned from a double dose of sodium oxybate, he hears a key in the door but feels instinctively that it is not Sophie. He is right. It's Borovic. He's sitting in the kitchen when Pace comes downstairs, the Weatherby close at hand. He imagines mayhem: a "[c]rime of passion" (185). But that is not to be. His one-time friend and benefactor is not there to murder him, just to kill him inside. A dressing down ensues, one involving deadlines, grades, and resignation letters. All Pace can think is, "Open your eyes. I put a gun to her head and I fucked her, and she liked it" (185).

Borovic enumerates Pace's misdeeds before leaving. He tells him he is finished at the school and threatens to put a bullet in him if he comes within a hundred yards of Sophie ever again. When he is gone, Pace notices Borovic has left a copy of a newsletter from when the pair of them were students. He knows, even before reading it, what it is: evidence of his plagiarism:

> ... the pillaging is clear, right down to the examples and subheadings he ended up using in *Masculine History* almost verbatim, and that surely would have been enough to sink him had anyone bothered to make the connection. Even more damning, perhaps, is that the eventual backlash against David's revamp seems already prefigured in the satire of the original. (186)

Pace realizes that it is Borovic's "moment of vindication" (186). He knows that he has "proved worthy of every calumny" (186). It all seems so appropriate, his fall, like that of a Roman in the period he focuses on in his writing. At this moment, he is well and truly finished: "He has no last resort, no plan, no hope. It is something at least. Like finally hitting solid ground" (186).

***

Then, without warning, the final chapter, "Beretta M9," begins. So far, the novel has been controlled and interesting. The pieces fit together, from first principles — a man in deep trouble with a sleep problem, a drug problem, and a number of personal relationship problems — to the moment he sees, as it were, the horror of his existence: his life in shambles; his options collapsed.

There is an ethic at work thus far in the narrative. Ricci has undertaken, with startling coherence, a difficult task. He has shown how a life beset by a sleep disorder can crumble, even when the principal is mostly self-aware. The telling has been at once exuberant and controlled. The writing is superb, deeply nuanced and fluid. The characters are sharply drawn. The progression has been slow and calculated, not a beat missed.

But "Beretta M9" provides a marked change in the tone of the novel. Some of the tautness of the preceding narrative vanishes and a surreal quality to the telling emerges. It is in sharp contrast to the beauty that led to it. Suddenly, Pace is in another country and in another time. How much time has passed since the debacle with Sophie and Greg Borovic is uncertain. Perhaps it is a year or more later. How Pace got to this country is unclear. What country it is seems immaterial. That it is war-torn and violent, though, is not.

In the interim, Pace has gone back to Toronto. Julia has sold their home and taken another job in Montreal. She has moved with Marcus. He has found himself in a small rented apartment, his condo long gone, sold to pay debts and give him something to live on. His son has become well and truly alienated from him. The promise of their gun moment has come to nothing. Ricci gives the impression that rock bottom has been reached and, without an academic job and no other means of support, his book in limbo, Pace has turned to journalism. He has even taken a self-defence course in Buffalo to prepare himself for whatever he will encounter in his journalistic travels ... and those travels have brought him to this god-forsaken place, buried him in this godforsaken place.

He is staying in a hotel that has seen better times, interacting with characters who have had no previous roles in the novel: Yusuf, the hotel owner; Said, a young man who drives for Yusuf; and Wali, a clearly subservient individual who also works for Yusuf.

As the chapter opens, he is leaving the hotel, for the first time on his own, and venturing into the city. He is going to a gun market. He appears bored, counting the minutes while he awaits a promised interview with some-one called Malana, "a Western-style do-gooder [he] has been researching with whom Yusuf has promised to get him an interview" (188). However, for whom he is going to write the article based on the interview and what the subject might be remain unknown to the end of the novel.

On the way to the gun market, he stops and buys a Fanta, a drink invented in Nazi Germany during WWII when the ingredients for Coke were not available. He doesn't know about the drink's history, but his buying it does seem a subtle reminder, perhaps, of his father's Beretta M1935 or of the sort of society he has found him-self in. The vendor looks at him and says to him: "Amer-ica? CIA?" But the narrator tells us that:

> Anywhere else the question might be a joke. Here, half the guests at David's hotel seem to be agents of one sort or other, selling arms or buying them, gathering intel, playing factions one against the other or paying off the warlords they have failed to depose to kill off the jihadists they once supported. (190)

Without thinking, Pace answers him, "Not CIA. A journalist" (190). With this admission, it becomes baldly apparent how far he has fallen. He is in this country, under these conditions, for his book, his "doomsday book" (155). The book that, now a decade in the writing, will "remake" his reputation. The book that will introduce to the world his new theory: given the opportunity and the means, human beings will always resort to violence. A time-tested response to hardship that is hard-wired into our make-up. To achieve this end, he has pitched ideas to magazines to help pay for the trip, a trip to "rethink his original concept" (190).

One question — Why the rethink? — comes to mind and it is answered:

> [I]t was getting too bloodless, too invested in his own theorizing. What he needs is something more visceral, exactly what served him so well back in *Masculine History*. That is what brought him here, the hope that this place's reversion, it's constant tottering toward anarchy, might give him a paradigm for the failure of states; the suspicion that what is happening here is not some bizarre aberration but the human default, a microcosm of the brutality and blood lust that have spurred human history ever since *Homo sapiens* pushed Neanderthal off an evolutionary cliff. (190)

With these words, what this book, *Sleep*, is about is finally revealed. The key word is "reversion" — "reversion" to violence: historical reversion, state reversion, psychological reversion, and emotional reversion, and it is, without question, a theme that winds its way through much of Ricci's work.

In his *Lives of the Saints* trilogy, for example, this "reversion" to violence involves movement. Vittorio moves from the psychologically violent dysfunction of his family in the Old World through the immigrant experience (necessary to halt dysfunction) to a harboured emotional life in the New World, where an opportunity for the freedom from violence he could not achieve where he was born, and where he has left, presents itself. In a way, he goes back, or "reverts," to a place he once was but which he now sees differently when he dreams of the "ten thousand" fires "burning away" at the conclusion of *Where She Has Gone*, and he experiences a "coming-together."[4] The whole basis of his need for "reversion" very likely predicated upon his half-sister's false accusation of their father's violence against her in the second volume of the trilogy, *In A Glass House*. The man did not beat her, but she uses the idea to achieve what she wants ... to escape from the life she has and this resonates mightily in Vittorio/Victor. In this, the pair of them are certainly forerunners to Pace. The idea is further reinforced in *Testament*, the four-fold, shifting-perspective retelling of the life of Jesus/Yeshua in the four Gospels of the New Testament. Yeshua, in this novel, is a man, not a god but a god-like man, and, as such, can be victimized by the exercising of routine violence by people on what and whom they do not understand ... again a foretelling of Pace's ultimate fate. Yeshua does nothing throughout *Testament* to warrant his fate, but violence, crucifixion, is nonetheless delivered to him.

Clearly, there is a nihilistic thread running through these four books as well as through *The Origin of Species* in which Alex Fratarcangeli, a poster boy for violent emotional and psychological dysfunction in almost everything he does, is deconstructed before the reader's eyes. But the idea is more pointedly developed in *Sleep* than in any of the other novels. Ricci finally focuses solely on what he has been referring to in his writing for more than two decades. He exiles Pace to a degraded outpost of humanity where he might embrace the "reversion" to violence necessary to achieve the absolution for his sins he requires. He reaches a literal and symbolic "ground zero." He cannot write. He cannot have a relationship with his father, his mother, his brother, his wife, or his son; nor can he have relationships with his colleagues and his lovers. He cannot quit the drugs. He cannot even wean himself away from the drugs. But he has recognized his need to "revert" and he has had to come this far for the opportunity. The question that remains, as he trudges through the chaos to a gun market, is simply stated: Can this be achieved? On the strength of what has come before, one cannot be hopeful. At least Pace has seen the need to try and this is what, for him, trying looks like.

But hope is short lived. In the market, he buys another gun: the Beretta M9. From a particularly astute merchant named, interestingly, Madman. It is he who reduces to its basics a part of Pace's quandary. He places where Pace has found himself in some context:

> "People from your country, they come here, they say factions, they say clan, is a way to say we are not civilized. But we are civilized, my friend, many thousands of years. Before the Romans, before the Greeks. They say guns, they say killing, but where are there more guns, more killing? In your own country." (199)

Pace cannot argue with him. The man makes too much sense. He only notes that "in the long run, such delinquencies hardly matter" (199). In effect, the man has summed up the task Pace has before him: to overturn centuries of conditioning that has brought him to where he is. But he fails the first test: to resist the need to turn to violence. He buys the gun.

Later, back at the hotel, he is introduced to a woman, another journalist, whom he has seen in passing. They have a few drinks and retire to his room where they consume gin, Ritalin, and sodium oxybate. Then they have sex and, in the dubious afterglow, insult each other. She tells him she has lied to him, her claim that she went to Harvard a fabrication. Then she admits she only had sex with him "to get at that pretentious fuckface Eric" (208), another journalist staying in the hotel. She states: "The fact that it got me to your gin was a bonus" (208). He responds by confessing that he really knew it was just the liquor she was after, but that it was he who got the bonus: "I'd have settled for a blow job" (208). She, as a rejoinder, sneeringly refers to his lost academic life and the widespread suggestions of date rape that saw him excommunicated, and says, "I knew all that and still let you fuck me" (208). Not willing to call it a day, she concludes with, "What are you anyway? Forty-five? Fifty?" (208) It is a mild barb but a barb all the same. He asks her if she is trying to sell him life insurance. With the final word, she tells him he should clear out. She suggests he is a dilettante and warns him that "[p]eople die here" (208).

It is yet another of those meaningless interactions that have plagued Pace's life. This is the kind of thing that "will end up seeming a sleep from which people refused to be roused, guarding their small properties and perks ... *Condition White*" (186). Clearly, he also fails the second test. He does not rid himself of his complacency and self-absorption.

He does come close to succeeding with the third test: to jump starting his writing. But close is, after all, only good in horseshoes. After sentencing himself to long days in his hotel room, he starts writing. At first, just attempts at articles he has promised. But this morphs into mining his book files, his notes and outlines and drafts going back more than a decade. He starts over, finds a rhythm, sees pages begin to accumulate. He cuts back on his drug taking, clears his mind a bit. He tries to manage his sleep, napping twenty minutes every two hours, the "rhythm of his disorder" (210). Soon, though, he begins to lose track of time, gets a bit primordial, something he had once accused Julia of being. But it all comes crashing down when he goes in search of paper, paper he never does get his hands on.

Out of his room and down in the lobby, he notes that the hotel seems deserted. He ventures out into the surrounding neighbourhood which is strangely quiet. Then, he walks through a gate and is confronted by a beach and the sea. Children are running about, playing in the surf. This is an unexpected calm in the midst of violence. He has an urge to join them, but does not. He just watches. It is, perhaps, a moment of redemption being offered to him, but he lets it pass. He either does not recognize it for what it is or consciously turns his back on it. The reason remains elusive. Instead, he wanders back to the hotel where he meets Yusuf who tells him that the interview with Malana has finally been arranged. He accepts this, begins to prepare, and never writes again. He fails the third test.

After surviving a near-death experience—having been a bit too close to a bomb being detonated in the city as he is attempting to get to the interview, Pace finds himself back at the hotel where he submerges himself in an Ostia Antica dream, another potentially redemptive memory from boyhood that has returned to him repeatedly:

> The handsome guide is there, walking ahead of David
> with the patrician air of someone who knows he will
> be followed. Past the tombs outside the gates, past the
> warehouses and the baths and the forum, to a con-
> struction site where he is building an apartment block
> amidst the ruins. In one smooth motion he edges a
> brick with mortar and sets it in place. The precision
> of it, the artistry, leaves David breathless. (215-216)

But he is roused from the dream by word that his interview is still on.

So, driven by Said and accompanied by Wali, he sets
out to find Malana. This elusive 'do-gooder' is, of course,
never found. Instead the rest of his experience in this
country becomes a difficult to follow *Lord of the Flies*-
like dream where, after Wali and Said are dispensed with,
Pace's continued existence is delivered into the hands of
a group of marauding boys, perhaps the children of the
beach scene metamorphosed into human animals. As
their captive, Pace seems a Simon to a host of Ralphs,
Piggys and Jacks: they are (as in *Lord of the Flies*) hunters
in a world gone mad. Pace is their game. Wounded and
frantic, drug-starved and afraid, in a landscape he knows
little about, he succumbs to his delusions:

> He can hear the locusts gathering at the base of his
> brain, reassuring almost in their quiet suasion. Some-
> how he has misplaced his pill pod, has left it behind
> in the tattered remains of his blazer or in his pants
> from the morning, so that there is nothing for it but
> to let them swarm. (225)

Once captured, he loses, without knowing it, his gun, his
Beretta M9. One of the boys liberates it and it is not until

some time passes that he becomes aware of its absence.
So, without drugs, without a gun, he is effectively stripped
bare. He becomes something of an elemental being. He
can only, having fallen irretrievably into the boys' hands,
connect them to the one person who, just by thinking
about him, might save him: Marcus. But, like everything
else in his life, this is not enough. It is too little, too late.

The boys taunt him, call him G.I. Joe, torture him,
and watch as he falls deeper and deeper into a sleepy
world where what he is experiencing is divorced from
what he is thinking. He attempts to save himself by trying to convince them he is not a threat, not a G.I. Joe,
just a journalist, but they do not buy his ironically truth-
ful tale. One of them tells him:

> "Lies, my friend! Where is your press card. Where is
> your recorder? Where is your pen? The truth is you
> are a killer, isn't it? The truth is you are a spy, CIA!"
> (233)

To put a fine point on it, he is not CIA. He is not a spy.
But he is a killer. The boys have come closer to the truth
than anyone ever has in his life. He has killed, metaphorically, everyone he has ever known, including himself.
Now he is, perhaps, literally killing himself.

A gun is put to his head and the truth is called for.
All he can do is retreat to a memory, of being in high
school and trying to pick up a few bucks by selling pot
and hashish in another dealer's territory by undercutting
his prices. The dealer seeks him out and threatens him,
not in any wild way, but with a small demonstration. He
puts a gun to Pace's head, calls him a problem and notes
how, "back home" (233) such a trifle would be dealt with.
Pace imagines a "Click" (234), suggestive of a gun firing,

and hears the man telling him this is how the "the problem is solved" (234).

These boys, however, want to "make him pay" (234) and pay he does. Although, in his moment of reckoning, irony abounds: When he feels sure that "he will do the thing that will land a bullet in his brain," he realizes that "[h]e has never felt more awake" (235).

Notes

1. The title exists with heartfelt apologies to Francisco Goya.

2. Dorian Gray (Wilde: *The Picture of Dorian Gray*), Esther Greenwood (Plath: *The Bell Jar*), Jay Gatsby (Fitzgerald: *The Great Gatsby*), Heathcliffe (Brontë: *Wuthering Heights*), Anna Karenina (Tolstoy: *Anna Karenina*), Clyde Griffiths (Dreiser: *An American Tragedy*), Wade Whitehouse (Banks: *Affliction*), Hazel Motes (O'Connor: *Wise Blood*), Raskolnikov (Dostoevsky: *Crime and Punishment*), Ethan Frome (Wharton: *Ethan Frome*), Captain Ahab (Melville: *Moby Dick*), Geoffrey Firmin (Lowry: *Under the Volcano*).

3. Page numbers for all quotations from Ricci's *Sleep* (Toronto: Doubleday Canada, 2015) are in parentheses following the quotation.

4. Ricci, Nino. *Where She Has Gone* (Toronto: McClelland & Stewart, 1997). p. 322.

Marino Tuzi

Interview With Nino Ricci

(This interview with Nino Ricci was completed
before the publication of his latest novel, *Sleep*, 2015.)

Marino Tuzi: What are some of the recurrent themes in
your fiction?

Nino Ricci: It is hard to speak of themes without seeming
reductive. I generally start with characters, not
themes, though certainly recurrent theme-like enti-
ties or motifs have indeed grown out of the characters I've tended to work with. They are the usual
Big Themes, I think: life, death, home, family, what
it means to be human. There are a few subsets within these that are a bit more specific — my obsession
with Catholicism, for instance, which led one critic
to label me as a kind of Canadian Graham Greene,
though I am certainly not Catholic in my life and
really regard Catholicism less as a theme, per se,
than as a particularly tempting corpse to dig my
vulture claws into. I have also been very interested
in the whole issue of displacement, something that
comes out of my immigrant background but that is

really a basic aspect of being human in our time, and one that goes back to many recurring motifs — the journey; the search for home, for a lost paradise — that have been central to the Western tradition.

M.T.: How would you describe your work stylistically and formally? What literary tradition/s are they part of?

N.R.: My formative training in literature was in the English literary tradition — Beowulf to Virginia Woolf, as they say — and that training has stayed with me at a deep level. That tradition is certainly not one to scoff at, and I feel very fortunate to have been exposed to it. At either end of this exposure, however, are a mongrel host of other influences — all the nameless books I read as a child, for instance, and which were really what awakened the force of imagination in me, and then the eclectic assortment of world literature I have come to in one way or another, including through a year I spent studying at the University of Florence. Stylistically and formally — in the architecture of my sentences, for instance, in my use of language, in my reliance on certain conventions of literary realism — I still look back to the English tradition as the important one. But in the matter of tone, I am not so certain. Maybe one of the major influences on tone in my writing was not literature at all but the films of Federico Fellini. There is something in the pathos of Fellini's worldview, in the mix of irony and tragedy, in the willingness to include the whole range of human experience, that is very appealing to me, and that I have also found in writers like Svevo and Calvino. Perhaps this is an area in which my Italian roots have been determining ones.

M.T.: What do you believe are the important contributions of a writer in modern society?

N.R.: I used to make very lofty claims for writers, but now I am more ambivalent. The lofty claims ran something like this: that literature was the true repository of human knowledge, what was most likely to survive over time and what best captured all the nuances and complexities of human experience. We looked to writers, I thought, more than to any other source, to give meaning to our existence. But maybe this was just self-aggrandizement. Most writers are utterly forgotten, and probably don't do much for the furtherment of the race. Then it is an open question whether the race is indeed furthering itself, or if we are on some sort of evolutionary dead end that writers, by giving us a false sense of our importance in the grand scheme of things, have merely helped to obscure from us. Maybe it is true that the important literature, today as in the past, is the literature that reminds us how small we are, and how little we know, and that we will come to dust.

M.T.: How do you compare the *Saints* trilogy to your subsequent work in terms of style and vision?

N.R.: I see quite a bit of continuity between my *Lives of the Saints* trilogy and my subsequent work, namely *Testament* and *The Origin of Species*, which I have just finished. In the end all of these books go back, as I say, to the matter of the big questions. The importance of home and family figures as largely in *Testament*, for instance, as it does in the *Lives* trilogy, as does the issue of faith. My most recent work, *The*

Origin of Species, returns to many of these same questions again, though this time seen through the lens of evolutionary theory. In terms of vision, then, I have been stubbornly single-minded: the same issues that obsessed me when I began writing obsess me still. Stylistically, I have tended to be more wide-ranging, I think, trying on different voices, different tones, though what might seem wide-ranging to me might to an outsider appear predictably homogenous. In my recent book, I have returned, in many ways, to the voice of *Lives of the Saints*, more ironic, more self-effacing, more comic, partly because I feel this voice allows for a more distanced, and perhaps more accurate, view of the human condition.

M.T.: What do you believe makes the novel, as an art form, universal? How does the depiction of a particular time and place fit into this idea of universality?

N.R.: I suppose what makes the novel universal, if it is truly so, is that it is about humans, and we are all humans. From my recent researches into evolutionary theory, I'm tempted to say that even cows and dogs might find the novel universal, if we could find a way to communicate one to them. Given that we are all shaped by the same basic forces, essentially animal forces, anything that speaks to these is going to strike a chord with people. That is what novels primarily do, I think — they speak to our most basic motivations and drives, giving a shape to them that no straightforward analysis or description could ever quite capture.

The question of time and place does seem a bit thorny in this light, but maybe only superficially so. In my own work, time and place are central, I would say, and I think that is the case in the writing I most admire. I suppose we respond to the particular in literature because we live in the particular, and need to feel rooted in some sort of credible world in order for a piece of fiction to work. That world might be quite different from ours; the important thing is that the author makes us believe in it. But part of that belief, I think, has to come from a leap we make at some point, from the gut sense that that different world has become our own, because the author has teased out the merely particular and time-bound and somehow connected these to a larger commonality.

M.T.: Which philosophical influences have shaped your fiction and why have they done so?

N.R.: I have had many philosophical influences in my life, and in the early drafts of a novel I always work very hard to weave them into the text, then spend most of the revision process threading them out. Writers, when they write, have to be bigger, I think, than their own particular philosophical influences; they have to act as if they know nothing for certain, as if all comers have a fair shot at coming out on top. That is the only way to stay true, I think, to what is most important in a novel, the characters them-selves and their particular stories. In the context of fiction, a character's deeply help philosophical be-liefs are much more important than an author's, I think, and they should have every chance to flourish or fail without the author putting his or her two cents in all the time.

M.T.: As an adult, which writers have influenced your work and why?

N.R.: I always cite Shakespeare as a major influence, even though I don't see his plays very often anymore and certainly don't sit down with a copy of *Troilus and Cressida* when I'm looking for some casual reading. And yet still he has a hold on me, from all those university courses where I was forced to read him. The language, the breadth of vision, the breadth of character — all these things. Then as a role model, I find him very appealing. He was not particularly innovative with regard to drama: his general method was to take what was out there and make it much better, the way the Japanese did with cars. In the process, of course, he challenged convention, but always somehow from within convention, which is the sort of subversion I feel most comfortable with as a writer. He was also not averse to playing to the pit, and had the singular talent of having been, despite his literary greatness, very popular and successful.

Among more contemporary writers I would cite Alice Munro, Doris Lessing, Vladimir Nabokov, Virginia Woolf, Thomas Pynchon, among others, for a grab bag of reasons, some for their nuances of language, others for their playfulness and ambition.

What I most look for in a writer is a combination of a kind of catholic view of the human condition combined with the particularity of evoking those nuances of feeling and experience that only literature seems able to get at.

M.T.: How does ethnicity fit into your fiction both in terms of human experience and the nature of the modern world?

N.R.: Ethnicity is one of those words that makes me want to run in the other direction. What does it mean? It almost invariably has a belittling tone. Things are ethnic only by contrast, and the implication is always that ethnic cultures are being contrasted to some realer, truer culture they are merely sideshows to. Alternately, ethnicity is raised up as a banner of specialness, which leads to all sorts of fascistic excesses. I suppose the way in which ethnicity has played into my own work is that I have somehow felt it my job to take apart these notions of ethnicity, and to avoid falling into the trap of them. I am more interested in complexity than ethnicity — the particularities of cultural differences, yes, but only as nuances within a range of other formative and connective forces.

M.T.: When you write, how do you deal with the process of creating fiction and in engaging ideas?

N.R.: This is a rather big question, not entirely answerable. In simplest terms, I start with some sort of idea for a story that has come to me from one source or another — usually it springs from a character or a particular situation or dilemma that seems suggestive — and then I write the story out and hope it works. If the idea is good, more ideas come. As for engaging Ideas in the capital letter sense: I always have lots of those, as I've indicated, and usually I have to throttle them. If the basic idea of the novel is sound — that is, if I have started with strong characters and a strong narrative — then the Idea will grow out of it on its own.

M.T.: What is the role of the novel today, given the massive dominance of visual imagery, especially through television and film?

N.R.: Well, the novel has died many deaths, and still straggles on. In strict percentages, surely a greater proportion of the human race is reading literature today than was ever the case in the past, given how recent widespread literacy is. So there is hope. I think it is also true that people have an insatiable need for narrative, that this is something that is hard-wired into them, and that the novel perhaps remains the primary source for complex narrative. You could certainly make the argument that film, as far as narrative is concerned — and narrative is central to it, as it is to most popular entertainments — tends to be highly derivative and reductive, and that if the novel died, film might go with it.

The novel and indeed most forms of literature have always been more meditative than direct, and it is true that it is hard to compete with the onslaught of much more visceral stimuli. But the brain is a complex place, and will always eventually crave complex enjoyments. So maybe the role of the novel is to be the guardian of the complex, of the view of reality that sees it in its fullness rather than reduces it to its most sensational elements.

Selected Bibliography:
Novels by Nino Ricci

Lives Of The Saints.
Cormorant Books, 1990.

In A Glass House.
McClelland and Stewart, 1993.

Where She Has Gone.
McClelland and Stewart, 1997.

Testament.
Doubleday Canada, 2002.

The Origin Of Species.
Anchor Canada, Random House, 2009.

Sleep.
Doubleday Canada, 2015.

Contributors

William Anselmi has taught courses at several universities on the representation of Italian experience in Canada. This teaching practice is connected to his work as a cultural activist, committed to raising social awareness about the consequences of nationalism and corporate capitalism on ethnic communities in Canada and the USA. He teaches popular culture and Italian Canadian literature in the Modern Languages Department at the University of Alberta in Edmonton.

Howard A. Doughty has written numerous essays for various magazines and journals on a range of social and cultural topics. He has edited and written many books related to an array of social and political subjects, such as the role of the liberal arts in public education, the use of electronic technology in the context of freedom of speech, the particular features of modern corporate capitalism, the analysis of power relations in Canadian and American society. He is a fulltime professor in Liberal Studies t at King Campus, Seneca College.

Brian L. Flack is a retired Professor of English Literature. In addition to teaching, he has written books of poetry and novels that examine the intricacies of contemporary life in urban settings, among them *In Seed Time* and *With A Sudden & Terrible Clarity*. A decade ago, he fled the chaos of Toronto for the peace of Prince Edward County.

Lise Hogan has specialized in modern Italian literature and she has published essays on various aspects of this literature. She is especially interested in how Italian culture is expressed in Italian Canadian writing. She has incorporated her knowledge of literary and cultural theory in her analysis of minority literary texts.

Marino Tuzi is the editor of and contributor to this collection of essays. He has published essays in books and journals on a variety of subjects on literature and culture. His book, *The Power of Allegiances* (published by Guernica Editions), examines the fiction of selected Italian-Canadian writers within the context of the immigrant experience and minority writing in Canada and abroad. Tuzi has also co-edited two books of essays (published by Guernica Editions) related to culture, identity, and society in Canada. He has taught special topics courses in the areas of Canadian Literature and Canadian Studies at Seneca College and York University.

Jim Zucchero has developed a keen interest in Italian experience in Canada, especially in the manner in which it is represented in the literary work of writers of Italian origin. In his published essays, he has incorporated his knowledge of social and cultural history with his analysis of minority literature in Canada.